D0275718

Finding the Key

Alexander Goehr, composer and teacher, and son of the conductor Walter Goehr, was born in 1932. He studied with Richard Hall at the Royal Manchester College of Music – where, together with Harrison Birtwistle, Peter Maxwell Davies and John Ogdon, he formed the New Music Manchester Group – and with Olivier Messiaen and Yvonne Loriod in Paris. In the early sixties he worked for the BBC and formed the Music Theatre Ensemble, the first devoted to what has become an established musical form. From the late sixties onwards he taught at the New England Conservatory in Boston, Yale and Leeds, and was appointed to the chair of the University of Cambridge in 1975. He is an honorary member of the American Academy of Arts and Letters and a former Churchill Fellow, and was the Reith Lecturer in 1987.

His orchestral works include four symphonies and concerti for piano, violin, viola and cello. He has written three operas: *Arden Must Die, Behold the Sun* and, most recently, *Arianna*, a recomposition of Monteverdi's lost opera, which was performed at the Royal Opera House, Covent Garden, in 1995 and subsequently recorded for NMC.

FINDING THE KEY

Selected Writings
of Alexander Goehr

Edited by Derrick Puffett

ff

faber and faber

LONDON · BOSTON

First published in 1998
by Faber and Faber Limited
3 Queen Square London WC1N 3AU

Photoset by Intype London Ltd
Printed in England by Clays Ltd, St Ives plc

All rights reserved

© Alexander Goehr, 1998

Alexander Goehr is hereby identified as author of this
work in accordance with Section 77 of the Copyright,
Designs and Patents Act 1988

The publishers gratefully acknowledge the permission of the following to
reproduce music examples: Exx. 7 and 8, Schott & Co. Ltd (London); Ex. 15,
Universal Edition Ltd; Ex. 17, Arnold Schoenberg Institute; Exx. 18 and 21,
Universal Edition Ltd; Ex. 32 © 1912, 1921 by Hawkes & Son (London) Ltd,
reproduced by permission of Boosey & Hawkes Music Publishers Ltd, 1997; Ex.
33, Universal Edition Ltd; Exx. 38b, 39a, 40 and 41b, Schott & Co. Ltd
(London).

*This book is sold subject to the condition that it shall not, by way of trade or
otherwise, be lent, resold, hired out or otherwise circulated without the
publisher's prior consent in any form of binding or cover other than that in which
it is published and without a similar condition including this condition being
imposed on the subsequent purchaser*

A CIP record for this book
is available from the British Library

ISBN 0-571-19310-2

2 4 6 8 10 9 7 5 3 1

Contents

Preface   vii

Editorial Note   x

1   A Letter to Pierre Boulez   1

2   Manchester Years   27

3   The Messiaen Class   42

4   Poetics of my Music   58

5   Modern Music and its Society   77

6   [With Walter Goehr] Arnold Schoenberg's Development
    towards the Twelve-Tone System   102

7   Schoenberg and Karl Kraus: The Idea behind the Music   124

8   Musical Ideas and Ideas about Music   142

9   Traditional Art and Modern Music   157

10 Brahms's *Aktualität*   175

11 Franz Liszt   189

12 Some Thoughts about Stravinsky   207

13 Music as Communication   214

14 [With Christopher Wintle] The Composer and his Idea
    of Theory: A Dialogue   236

15 Finding the Key   272

    Appendix   305

    Sources   308

    Index   310

Preface

A collection of articles, lectures and off-the-cuff radio talks produced over a period of forty years must inevitably reflect its various
provenances in a certain diversity of level and style. But such a
collection, however discursive in its detail, ought also to be bound
together by a central concern threading its way through its different
parts. Reading back the selection presented here in order to write
the final essay, which also lends its title to the whole, I am per-
suaded that from the beginning, I have continually returned to the
same topics: the same composers, past and present, have preoccupied me and, for all its changes, my music has always been about
the same things.

When in September 1996 Derrick Puffett surprised me by
sending me the manuscript of what, with the exception of the final
piece, he had selected and edited of my writings, he accompanied
it with a letter in which he wrote that he was far from certain that
I would be either pleased to read what he had put together, or
wish to see it published. Why this should be so can be read between
the lines of his Editor's Preface printed as it was written, hereafter.
When talking with him about the work he had done on my behalf,
I firmly refused to allow this preface to see the light of day, proposing that it be replaced by a further piece of my own, to be
entitled 'Reading Composers' Writings', in which I might defend
myself against what seemed to me his kindly meant but for all that
trenchant reservations. In this I would have discussed with him the
writings of Schoenberg, Hindemith, Tippett and Boulez as a separate genre of writing about music that is by its very nature different
from professional critical or scholarly enterprises. Composers, I
wanted to assert, do their real work with notes, and their writings
have a point only insofar as they illuminate the notes.

The idea of making a collection of essays had its origins in the circumstances of the Reith Lectures of 1987. For the first series of these prestigious lectures ever to be devoted to music, the BBC producer Louise Purslow asked me for a subject of general rather than specialised concern. My title, 'The Survival of the Symphony', was not intended to imply an examination of sonata form, but rather a questioning of the nature and likelihood of survival of the public institution through which music in the Western world has been broadcast since at least the time of the Viennese Classics. Its survival, in the face of colossal changes brought about by the mechanical reproduction of music and the emergence of a powerful and influential music industry, at first subservient to, but ultimately by its sheer scale engulfing, the musical profession, would seem to be in doubt. Furthermore the institution of the public concert and the symphony orchestra that performed it were further weakened by the emergence of specialised interest groups, such as those devoted to new, authentic and ethnic musics, which increasingly are seen to require their own appropriate performing conditions and to cultivate their own exclusive publics. I believe this was indeed the right subject to have chosen and I might have done it more justice than I was able, had I approached it as a musician/critic/sociologist/contemporary historian. But I was hardly qualified to do that, and, reading it back, I am aware that I made up for my inadequacies by intruding an element of personal apologia under the mantle of objective enquiry. I really could not deal with the subject disinterestedly but used it as a vehicle for promoting what I believed was a correct reading of the composer's situation. The same characteristics may be observed in the more modest BBC talks that preceded the Reith Lectures, which are reprinted here under the title 'Modern Music and its Society'.

It is customary that the Reith Lectures be reprinted in book form (they were published at the time in successive numbers of the now defunct and lamented *Listener* magazine[1]). Patricia and Bernard Williams not only concerned themselves with the project of publishing them but offered valuable advice as to how I might improve them. Alas, to no avail, as they have been omitted from this collection.

The majority of those to whom I owe particular insights or influences appear in the pages that follow. But in addition I would like to mention the names of Edward Boyle; David Drew; Erich Fried; Amira Katz Goehr; Lydia Goehr; Sally Groves; Robin Holloway; Oliver Knussen; Thomas Newbolt; Bayan Northcott; Stephen Plaistow; Ulrich Siegele; Barry Smith; and Hugh Wood, who at various times and in various places said things that affected me deeply, and also the Master and Fellows of Trinity Hall, Cambridge, among whom I have lived for more than twenty years and who have supported me in various ways. Finally I would mention Kathryn Bailey Puffett with gratitude: after the tragic death of her husband she took on the final editing of the collection.

At the beginning of the second paragraph above I referred to the letter Derrick wrote in September and my response to the work he had done on my writings. Before the end of November he was dead. He was a brave and noble man who bore his intolerable physical burdens stoically to the end. That he should, in what were his final, agonised months, devote his attentions to these writings lends a particular poignancy to the venture of publishing them and inevitably colours it; the only available way for me to honour this is to dedicate the thing that it is to his memory.

A. G.
December 1996

1. In the issues published between 3 December 1987 and 7 January 1988.

Editorial Note

Editing these essays has been one of the most satisfying editorial tasks I have undertaken – but also one of the most difficult. In the first place, those who know Sandy as a voluble and persuasive speaker may wonder why his writings need to be 'edited' at all; several of them have, in any case, already appeared in print, presumably in a form which had the author's blessing. In such cases, it is true, a *laissez-faire* (or *laissez-aller*) policy seemed best. Writings such as 'Poetics of my Music', his Leeds Inaugural Lecture, which was printed soon after it was given; or the essay on Schoenberg that Sandy wrote in collaboration with his father (how one would like to have details of that particular working relationship!); or the 'Dialogue' with Christopher Wintle, published in a journal of which, at the time in question, I happened to be editor – these are reproduced with little alteration apart from the odd bit of bibliographical updating.

Then there are those who know Sandy as a colleague. If so, and especially if they have been on the receiving end of one of his professorial memos (which are as apt to be warm and appreciative as they are to be anything else), they will know that, as well as being voluble and persuasive, he is almost incapable of writing an unambiguous sentence. Of course I exaggerate; but I believe that in this area – and perhaps only in this area – Sandy is prone to feelings of insecurity which some might find hard to credit. How else explain his almost obsessive rewriting of earlier essays? Some, as with the 'Letter to Pierre Boulez', exist in as many as five different versions, each adding layers of richness and ambiguity to the preceding ones while at the same time losing something in directness, *un*ambiguity. In such cases 'editing' became a truly surreal experience, in which one often had to use an early version in order to make sense of (one might almost say *translate*) a later one. That is to say, sentence-to-sentence connections – not to mention paragraph-to-paragraph or even larger ones – would get obscured, sometimes the whole line of argument be lost, as the author became sidetracked by detail, seduced by a metaphor. In such a situation the *Fassung der letzten Hand* (especially if the hand in question was the author's) seemed a policy so laughably unrealistic – if these were the problems one could expect with a living author, what of a dead one? – as to be irrelevant. Every version had some claim to priority; ideally one would have liked to publish them all. But postmodernism only takes us so far; in the real world one has to make choices, to apply the knife.

I find the broader questions raised by Sandy's slippery uneditability as fascinating as the 'nuts-and-bolts' decisions one has to make when actually wielding the knife (and why this language of aggression? What is it about Sandy's writing that seems to *challenge* the editor, as it challenges the reader, making the lack of clarity seem like a weapon?). It was, after all, the difficulty of achieving a mutually agreed-upon text that led to the Reith Lectures of 1987 being excluded from the present selection. The first time I was involved in the publication of any of Sandy's writings – except for the 'Schoenberg and Karl Kraus' essay, which I had edited for inclusion in *Music Analysis* shortly after its presentation as a conference paper – was when he asked me, around 1990, to 'cast my eyes over' the text of the Reith that he had had transcribed from the broadcast tapes. This was a text he had hammered out, with the help of his radio producer and the advice of numerous well-meaning colleagues, and eventually delivered to the nation. 'A largely unappreciative nation', I almost wrote; at any rate, the critics didn't like it, though they were agreed on its breadth. Friends were polite but unenthusiastic. And now that Sandy saw the text, he didn't like it either. I could see why; it seemed like the proverbial horse designed by a committee – a camel of a text, 'scholarly' where it ought to have been provocative, circumspect where it ought to have been sharp, the whole thing bowed under the weight of 'too many cooks'. There was nothing I could do except 'leave well alone'. It would have taken more than the skills of even the most accomplished editor, which I certainly wasn't, to peel off all the layers of well-intentioned obfuscation (some of them put there by the author himself) and get to the nub of what he wanted to say.

It struck me then, and it has struck me many times since, that the best way of helping Sandy to say 'what he wants to say' is to give him the opportunity of saying it once and then fold up the microphones, transcribe the tape with the minimum of editorial interference and *on no account* give this man the chance to revise what he has said. For if you do, you will have something more opaque than the political equivocations he despises, something utterly characterless. And character is what he has in abundance. (For this reason, he is his own worst editor.) In editing his radio talks, therefore – and who, having heard them, could forget 'Modern Music and Society', his recollections of Messiaen or the radio version of the essay on Brahms? – I have tried to let him speak for himself. For it is the flavour of what he has to say, as well as the substance, that is a considerable part of its persuasiveness. I confess I hadn't fully understood this when I edited 'Schoenberg and Karl Kraus' for *Music Analysis*; and the result was a flavour-less, rather hard lump of academic prose, a brilliant piece of work, of course, but something not entirely 'by Sandy'.[1]

I want to end this note with some remarks of a 'broader' kind, remarks which may not be directly relevant to a collection of essays but which do have a place in the general sweep of things. For Sandy is first and foremost a composer. Any book of essays he produces is bound to fascinate, if only (and I say 'if only' because Sandy has never been much impressed by historicist arguments – cf. 'Is There Only One Way') because he has always been one of the most eloquent spokesmen of his generation. But there must be a sense in which words, for him – and however important they may be for him – are only a secondary form of expression. And this prompts the thought: could it be that the freedom to think again and again has a similar effect on his composing, encouraging the tendency to go off at a tangent, to get lost in detail, that one notices in some of the essays? After all, this sort of thing is easier to spot when it happens in words. And were it possible to invert the process of composition and unravel the way in which an Alexander Goehr piece comes into being, would one find a stronger, never-to-be-realised first version concealed within, a *Fassung der erster Hand* in which ideas familiar from the work we know and love would be expressed with an unsuspected force and clarity? In other words, is there a 'primitive', 'early Sibelius' figure lurking behind the urbane and sophisticated façade?[2]

The essays – or, rather, the history of the essays – suggests that there might be. Of course, such a suggestion could be completely wrong. But it is one of the functions of a composer's words to provide insights into the works in which his primary form of expression fulfils itself.

Derrick Puffett

August 1996

1. [KBP:] While I would suggest a certain degree of hyperbole in this judgement of the article as it appeared in *Music Analysis*, it is the case nevertheless that my husband discarded it and went back once again to the original script of this essay for the version that appears in this book.

2. [AG:] All through my working life as a composer, I have built up my scores from sketches, adding, extending, eliminating and, as Derrick would have it, going off at a tangent. I do in fact believe that I spoiled some of my efforts by over-elaboration and that I might have done better to leave, if not first, nearer-first, thoughts as they stood. For much of the time in which I have been a composer there has existed, at least in the artistic circles in which I have lived, a kind of virtue (or perhaps vanity) of complexity. I have not always resisted this and consequently have from time to time fallen into the stylistic trap of making things complicated. There is in the writing of modern music a notational code to which one subscribes, or does not, at the peril of being 'not taken seriously'. Today I subscribe to a remark of Stravinsky's, which I read somewhere, that all in all it is best to retain the notation in which one first wrote down a musical idea.

A Letter to Pierre Boulez

First of all, the slightly unusual title. This isn't of course a real letter to Pierre Boulez, although if, when I've finished it, it's not completely insulting I shall in fact send it. But it is in a sense a letter that I promised him. The occasion was as follows.

Ten years ago I revised a string quartet which I had written in 1956–7,[1] shortly after completing my studies in the Messiaen class at the Paris Conservatoire, and at a time when I had been seeing a lot of Boulez, who was then living in Paris. When the revised version of the piece was performed by the Arditti Quartet, they remarked a kinship between it and Boulez's own *Livre pour quatuor* (1948–9). I too recognised this and decided, rather belatedly, to offer him the dedication of it. He had encouraged me with his criticisms of it at the time when it was being composed, and had even tried, unsuccessfully, to find a string quartet to play it. So I telephoned him – he was in London at the time – and said, 'I want to dedicate this piece to you.' (I had the vague suspicion he might prefer it to one I had written more recently.) 'I'm dedicating it to you because it was written at a time when your influence upon me was very strong.'

Boulez, never missing a trick, answered quickly, 'Ah! You are trying to tell me something. You are trying to tell me that you are no longer influenced by me.'

'Look,' I said, 'it's not quite as simple as that. I'll try to write you a letter about it some time.'

I've tried at various points to write that letter to him. The purpose of it, delayed now almost as long as the dedication, is to explain what is meant by influence and the (at least partial) outgrowing of it. Like the dedication, the letter is an act of homage and gratitude.

2

It's not my intention to write the history of an important, and as yet to be documented, period when most of the compositions contributing to the concept of total serialism were being or had recently been written. These are merely the recollections of a student of that time who was extremely impressed, even over-whelmed, by what was going on. We're talking about Paris in 1955–6. During that year I was a student in the Messiaen class there, on a French government scholarship. Boulez was conducting concerts at the Théâtre Marigny, which was then the home of the Jean Louis Barrault–Madeleine Renaud Company, of which he was musical director and for which he wrote a number of scores, including a most striking Aeschylus trilogy. I remember – who wouldn't? – the premiere of Messiaen's *Oiseaux exotiques* (1955–6) and the first Paris performance of Boulez's own *Marteau sans maître* (1953–5) as highlights of that year. I frequently met Boulez; he was generous with his time, and although John Carewe, who was in Paris with me, and I would have liked to take lessons from him, he would never make a formal arrangement, just saying, 'Come round to my apartment from time to time and we'll look at music together.' So that's what we did.

I had attended the Darmstadt Summer School[2] the year before, and had had a piece performed there.[3] I had become friendly, to the extent of going to visit him in Venice when I'd finished my studies in Manchester, with Luigi Nono, at that time, along with Boulez and Stockhausen, one of the three great names of new music. While in Paris I went to Darmstadt again and had my first orchestral piece performed there.[4] Characteristically for me, I had gone to Paris in the first place to try to perform an uneasy balancing act. I wanted to attend the Messiaen class at the Conservatoire, but I also wanted to take private lessons from Max Deutsch, who

2

was one of the last remaining pupils of the original Schoenberg class, the one that had included Webern and Berg, and now an old man living in Paris. I had met him before (my father had introduced me to him), and he had encouraged my first compositional efforts. When I turned up, he asked what I was doing in Paris. I said that I had a scholarship to study in the Messiaen class and that I wanted to go to him as well for lessons. He promptly threw me out. Relations between the Schoenbergians – Deutsch and René Leibowitz – and Messiaen were already so heated that no combination was possible. (Throughout my time in Paris, however, Leibowitz could not have been kinder or more helpful, providing me with paid work as a copyist.) After a year, the length of my scholarship, I tried to stay in Paris, as Messiaen was encouraging me to remain for another year, and I did in fact manage to survive there until the following autumn. I started a song cycle based on texts by Christopher Logue, never completed, and the string quartet already mentioned. But ultimately I ran out of money and was forced to return to London. This was in October 1956. In my first years back there I completed the quartet and composed *The Deluge* (1957–8), a cantata to a text by Sergei Eisenstein after Leonardo da Vinci; *Sutter's Gold* (1959–60), another cantata, based on Eisenstein's shooting script from the novel *L'or* by Blaise Cendrars; and the *Little Symphony* (1963), which I wrote after the death of my father in 1960.

Boulez had continued to be well-disposed towards me, and he included pieces of mine in the Marigny concerts.[5] But when, some time in the 1960s, he was asked to perform the *Little Symphony*, he declined. I was told that he had said reluctantly he could not conduct 'that kind of music'. This may have been a true report, or it may have been my interpretation of it; but either way it represented a reality. Within five years my work had evidenced a decisive change of attitude: from one of very considerable enthusiasm for developments in avant-garde music – an attempt to write more or less within the paradigm set out by Boulez – to a position, if not of rejection of, at least of reserve towards, those developments. In describing this progress, I want to focus on some problems which

3

seemed (and still seem) important to me and which should not simply be swept under the carpet, especially now, when it ought to be possible to look back at them with some degree of detachment.

Post-war avant-garde music, once it had formulated itself, passed through a number of stages and predominating if contradictory influences before settling down into something like a school of Webern, who had been killed in the last year of the war and whose work was only just becoming known in its entirety. The early history of Darmstadt, and indeed of modern music in general, was to some extent a 'going through' of all the important composers of the inter-war years: first Bartók, Hindemith, Stravinsky and Milhaud, later the Second Viennese School and later still Varèse. But by the mid-1950s Webern had come to occupy a special place there, expressed in a remark of Herbert Eimert in the first number of the journal *Die Reihe*: 'There can be only one way of defining the contemporary stage of musical composition, and that is "post-Webern", a situation resulting from the discovery of the single note.'[6] (I later used this remark as a basis for a BBC radio talk, 'Is There Only One Way?', reprinted at the end of this chapter.[7])

Obviously this isn't true now when we look at it, and in fact it wasn't quite true then. There were other influences, possibly of equal importance. But in the opinion of the avant-garde composers of those years, Webern occupied a special place; he was closely studied by composers, and from many different viewpoints, even if (as it might now appear) what he stood for and achieved was in some respects misunderstood. It was, nevertheless, a creative and temporarily fruitful misunderstanding. Webern's music appealed not because of his use of twelve-tone technique, in a post-Schoenbergian sense, and certainly not for his archaisms. What seemed important was its rhetoric: its angularity, its avoidance of continuous texture, its use of 'objective' formal devices (strict polyphony, canon, isorhythm) and, above all, a kind of calculated dialogue between sound and silence, that is, the isolation of duration, timbre and attack into symmetrical microstructures articulated by and within silences. Also important was its brevity. One could say – and this is purely a common-sense thing – that brevity is the necessary precondition for the perception of micro-structures.[8] If microstructures are comprehensible at all to an audience, they certainly won't be comprehensible in fifty-minute works; they will only be comprehensible in very short pieces. To achieve such brevity demands, as Schoenberg said about Webern, a lack of sentimentality, a willingness to limit oneself to the minimum.

At the same time brevity acts as an antidote to bombast. The quasi-scientific identities assumed at Darmstadt (identities exemplified in both the compositions and the writings of these years) coincided with a distaste for subjectivism, for post-Romantic extravagance and excess. There was a rejection of pretentiousness and overblown rhetoric of any kind. If writers, especially Germans of the post-war period, distrusted words whose meanings had been debased by their use in propaganda, so too musicians would attempt to throw off the conventions of waltz, march and song in favour of more remote models, sometimes even drawn from late Medieval and Renaissance music, from Machaut, Ockeghem, Josquin and Isaac (whom Webern had in fact edited). There was a reliance upon strict device and the vigorous carrying through of compositional schemes set up at the outset, as opposed to any spontaneous or free invention. Choice, taste and style were dirty words; personal style, one could argue, is necessarily a product of repetition, and the removal of repetition is, or was believed to be, a cornerstone of classical serialism as defined by Webern's late works. Structure, relevance and purity were the ideals.

All this may well be seen as a kind of negative style precept: a conscious elimination of sensuous, dramatic or expressive elements, indeed of everything that in the popular view constitutes music. Pleasing melody, colourful harmony, the predominance of one part over others and, above all, rich orchestration for its own sake were removed as no longer relevant to contemporary sensibility. What was relevant was the drive to an objective and anonymous ideal in which the composer does not imagine his music but sets up matrix structures and performs operations on them from which the music results. If there is something distasteful about performers who consciously repeat their charming mannerisms – the sudden diminuendos, the unnotated lengthening and shortening of notes, the irrelevant pauses, the squeezing of phrases for maximum expressivity – how much worse are composers who refuse to submit themselves to the rules of language and logic for the development of their ideas, eliminating all else! (It might seem now that these high and austere ideals are somewhat cheapened when logic is automatised into serial play.) This search for anonymity, for a common language, should have led, if only through a *reductio ad absurdum*, to some kind of anonymous school of composition where music was cultivated *sine nomine*, where there were no 'great composers'. And a relic of that perhaps ridiculous idea – ridiculous, anyway, in this age of show business – might well have persisted in Boulez's ideas about IRCAM, which, whatever the reality turned out to be, was certainly set up as some kind of ambitious, idealistic research project, the sort of enterprise in which people would, as it were, don their white coats and all subscribe together towards the realisation of a great ideal – this being a language '*actuel*', as Boulez would call it, for a modern music that didn't depend upon anecdote and upon the personality differences of individuals.[9]

3

I was originally attracted to serialism – being an adolescent at the time – by the very exclusive certainties it provided. Boulez himself displayed a great confidence; there was something austere and even monastic about him which was extremely appealing.[10] But even as a student I felt a number of reservations. I couldn't share his attitude towards Webern, although I admired his analyses, especially of the Second Cantata. Having been brought up in a very Schoenbergian household I preferred to see Webern's achievement as an extension of Schoenberg's ideals. This point of view (which does not diminish its originality, but places emphasis on motivic structure and compositional logic) was anathema at this time. There was a moment, I recollect, which shocked me greatly, when Leibowitz, who was lecturing at Darmstadt, said that it was impossible to understand the work of Webern without reference to Schoenberg. This was evidently a red rag to a bull. A number of leading composers, Stockhausen and Pousseur among them, noisily walked out of the hall. Leibowitz never returned to Darmstadt. In a sense I had a lot of sympathy with his position, which I believed to be historically correct and which also corresponded to my own impressions of the music. The 'Schoenbergian' was attracted to Webern, as I was at that time, by the whole notion of musical ideas expressed in the form of motifs and rhythmic cells, these deriving, as Webern himself was at pains to emphasise, from the whole tradition of eighteenth- and nineteenth-century music. It was only when heard against a background of such a tradition that Webern's music made sense and its full complexity and beauty was revealed.[11] But at that time this aspect of Webern was rejected as not corresponding to the 'compositional situation'.[12]

I was also attracted at that time to the purely melodic characteristics of music, as I am today. I love monody, ornamentation and the articulation of word such as may be found in Gregorian chant and certain non-European musics, as well as in Monteverdi and Bach (indeed, I had come to Messiaen specifically because of his interest in those things). Purcell had already assumed great significance for English composers, in particular Britten and Tippett. I believed that, with the apparent demise of harmonic thinking, there was an opportunity to explore the refinements of such expression. From this point of view I greatly admired the vocal writing of *Le marteau sans maître*.[13] Although some of the Darmstadt composers claimed to be interested in such things, they were in fact only interested insofar as melodic ideas could be integrated into serial thinking. This necessarily vitiated against the integrity of melodic structure. I, on the other hand, regarded melodic extension (which implies a modality), ornamentation and articulative device not only as of interest in themselves but as a way of moving on from the Webernian paradigm of brevity, where ultimately a movement is just as long as the number of structured pitch-levels demands, to forms which result from an extension of these structured pitch-levels by means of inner redundancies. In Schoenberg's dodeca-phonic composition, repetitions and note-patterns serve to make the music comprehensible to an ear steeped in eighteenth- and nineteenth-century music. I believed that a synthesis of serial struc-ture and Medieval and non-European elements would throw up exciting images, so long as the serial structure did not prejudice the identity of the monodic elements by breaking them up into imperceptible fragments. In the years that followed my stay in Paris, these ideas, as well as a progressive awakening to the attrac-tions of harmonic thought, gradually took me away from the concerns and styles of the Darmstadt-centred avant garde.[14]

A third attraction was towards Viennese expressionism (as exemplified in Schoenberg's *Erwartung*), as well as towards Dada-surrealism, which featured big in Paris at that time but played little part in the musical thinking of modern composers.[15] Under the influence of a surrealist painter with whom I became friendly in Paris,[16] I grew interested in the notion of portraying 'extreme state' situations (such as you also find in early Schoenberg) and in that sense reacted against the pure structuralism and the undramatic, rather 'quietist' atmosphere that prevailed in the works of the avant garde. It was only later, in my cantatas inspired by Eisenstein, that I attempted to realise such ideas.

Lastly, there was the influence of the other group certainty of that time. This was Zhdanov, not Zhdanov in the form of the speeches he made in Moscow in 1946, nor yet Zhdanov in the romantic dress of his followers Shostakovich and Prokofiev, but Zhdanov as modified not only by known Communist com-posers like Eisler, whom I knew and who had a great influence on me, but by more local and homespun models such as Britten and Tippett (even Schoenberg in his wartime pieces did not escape his influence). These were certainly not supporters of the Zhdanov edicts, which were vulgar Marxism and, what is more, enforced by dictat and possibly worse, but idealists whose beliefs echoed in this country at that time with the basic Labour Party/William Morris ideas about art – ideas often dismissed elsewhere as straight amateurism, though this was not quite the case. England presented a more favourable musical climate in that respect: the population seemed to be open to new ideas, and it was not impossible for composers to come some way towards the public and vice versa. In the post-war period everyone was very hopeful.

I had no musical models for any of these ideals other than the avant garde. Technically I had only avant-garde techniques. Other composers whom I knew and who influenced me – particularly Nono and Eisler,[17] because of their political views – didn't really show me a way forward. However, I had two models outside music, who acted not only as an ideal to be transferred into music but also as a yardstick against which to measure other ideas. One of them was the Russian film director Sergei Eisenstein, whose films and theories I admired; the other was Brecht. In Paris, to put it crudely, I found myself in relation to the musical avant garde as a composer who technically wished to subscribe, albeit with modifications, to the new ideals, which seemed to be forceful, clear and above all definite, while at the same time I subscribed to artistic and political ideals that didn't necessarily have any connection with these things (though there were points of contact, for instance between Brecht's austere Lutheran language, Webern's preference for simple baroque poetry, or Eisenstein's techniques of montage and chronometry in the making of films and the cutting of them, and some of the structural ideas, especially the Stravinsky-derived ones, that featured in a lot of avant-garde musical thinking). An ideal for me would have been if Eisenstein had realised his dream of filming *Ulysses* and having Schoenberg to write the music for it; there we would have had another kind of art form which combined all my interests. But it didn't happen.

4

I suppose I was susceptible to intense influences because, as with all artistic developments, there was something in the air. What that something was is hard to say, but it certainly had to do with the creation of not necessarily such new music by necessarily new means. I understood the operations of the twelve-tone technique a great deal better than the music that had resulted from it, and in reality Schoenberg's own style was too difficult, for a young composer with limited technique, to serve as a useful model. Had it not been for the inspiration of Boulez I would, perhaps, have been drawn (as I certainly have been since) to writing in a simplified style owing more to non-dodecaphonic composers than to the idea of following through the implications of serial structure, leaving aside all else. In Manchester,[18] I had studied the way in which Schoenberg extended rows by neighbour-note groups and rotations – a technique developed by Krenek, George Perle and the later Stravinsky – and looked for ways in which single pitch-levels were emphasised and supported to form pseudo-cadential points. (This occurred in Schoenberg's atonal compositions and can also be observed in his dodecaphonic works, as well as in Webern, Berg and Dallapiccola.) I was aware of Hauer's and Krenek's ideas of mode (or trope), which effectively – or at least in spirit – linked dodecaphony with Medieval and Renaissance techniques. All these technical preoccupations prepared me for, but also determined the manner in which I was to understand, Boulez's most significant technical innovation, which he called the *bloc sonore*.

The *bloc sonore* relies on a mode of thinking known to the Second Viennese School and its followers as the unity of horizontal and vertical space. In its simplest form this consists of presenting a twelve-tone row as a set of (usually) three- or four-note chords, built up of row adjacencies. Boulez did the same thing, though he preferred to create 'chords' of irregular numbers of notes, e.g. chords of five, three, two and two different pitch-levels, adding up to the total twelve. These could then be transposed, inverted and retrograded in the traditional Schoenbergian manner. For Boulez, the series of chords becomes an invariant as might be the row itself, and he invents an entirely new technique, whereby, by a process of quasi-multiplication or transposition of one chord into another, he obtains a fund of chordal complexes of varied pitch-level content. The chord-types produced by this technique have something in common with Messiaen's idea of *resonance*, whereby overtone and subtone groups are utilised to colour conventional harmonies in a manner which is in its turn derived from the harmonic practice of Debussy and, particularly, Ravel. If Boulez had simply used his big chords to splash about with (as have some other pupils of Messiaen), the technique would have been of no great significance and would not have justified the new nomenclature by which he identified them. But, as it was, he fully understood that there was a great deal more to be extrapolated from the technique.

To avoid confusion, I must remind the reader that my intention here is not to explain Boulez's ideas (which are clearly discussed in his own writings[19]), but to describe my own view of them and the way in which they led me to a kind of music far away from anything imagined or likely to be approved of by him.

The derivation of *blocs sonores* from an original twelve-tone row has the effect of relegating the row itself from the foreground of the music into the position of a not-to-be-heard matrix determining long-term relationships, while allowing for the reintroduction of locally determined types of foreground composition.[20] A duality results which may be expressed as an interplay between strict (serial) and free diminution. In theory, at least, this looks like a regression to a Bachian situation, where ornamentation in the narrow sense and harmonic and melodic diminution are applied to a pre-existent quasi-background composition. It is not for nothing that Boulez is attracted by the idea of the *double* form, or of bracketed interpolation (as in the Third Piano Sonata). It certainly is the antithesis of any continuation of the Beethovenian tendency to insist increasingly on a motivic or some other specific function for each and every note of a composition in the belief – to use Schoenberg's terms – that a composition is based on a single, determinant 'idea'. Probably Boulez believes this too. But I observe that when in his music he moves on from an ideal of continuous and total foreground, as in the First and Second Piano Sonatas, *Structures I* and to some extent *Le marteau sans maître*, to such conceptions as *Structures II*, *Pli selon pli* and *Doubles*, he introduces what he might be prepared to accept as an interplay of strict and free elements, or, if not that, a distinction between long-range organisation and the refinement of detail.

It may be regarded as paradoxical that Boulez developed such ideas in the name of a search for a total polyphony, following an ideal which Leibowitz (perhaps incorrectly) attributed to Schoenberg.[21] In the music itself, which Boulez wrote in the late 1950s and after, the structural duality not only makes possible a virtuosity and free flow which differentiate it from the stiffness that characterises some post-Webernian dodecaphonic music, such as, for example, that of Dallapiccola, Sessions or Babbitt, but shows a way in which registral disposition (pitch as opposed to pitch class) and the organisation of real temporal durations may be connected to the background structure of the row-derived *blocs*. For me, this seemed a more promising move of thought than the automatic coupling of row interval or ordinal and duration (as well as, perhaps, timbre, mode of attack and dynamic level) first found in Babbitt's work and Boulez's *Structures I* (1951–2). The fact that structural/serial operations of various types operate in the background guarantees proportion and at the same time leaves open the attractive possibility of free, short-term activity in the areas of orchestration, rhythmic diminution and timbre-composition.

I believe that Boulez's model made available the possibility of an increased variety of stylistic elements and even a new interplay of strict dodecaphonic structure and the atonal-motivic legacy. After a period of musical history in which structural rigour was admired above all else, and at the cost of most other considerations, there is today a healthy whiff of spontaneity and anti-dogmatic anarchy to be felt. While recognising the self-restricting narrowness of the 1950s posture, it ought to be understood that Boulez himself, commonly regarded as the arch-priest of that posture, has opened the way to a practice which offers the possibility of greater and freer expression. By freeing surface phenomena from the direct and tiresomely literal forms of the series, he showed a way in which the free manipulation of shape, without recourse to traditional thematicism, may be connected with the organising potentialities of the series.

The actual compositional results may vary widely. If Boulez was critical of Schoenberg for putting 'new wine in old bottles', and he himself put 'new wine in new bottles', I might describe myself as putting 'old wine in new bottles'! In the essays that follow I attempt to describe why, and to a lesser extent how, I do this. In the late 1950s and early 1960s, I substituted a combinatorial method of my own, simpler and aurally more limited and consequently more easily perceptible than the Boulezian *bloc sonore*, for it, and by this means obtained not only a serial-structural background, but also a way of getting away from the dodecaphonic notions of transposition, inversion and retrograde into an area of thought which differentiates between 'real' interval and shape identities on the one hand and quasi-'tonal' transformations on the other, both equally strictly derived from the series.[22]

It would appear that Boulez interpreted the material he created by means of manipulations carried out on an original dodecaphonic series as a multi-dimensional sound universe, which he now proceeded to elaborate in manifold ways, inspired less by the musical models he admired than by the late work of Stephane Mallarmé. This poet utilised the relationship of free-standing word or words on the blank page, and differing type sizes, to make a book which might be contemplated and read in differing ways: the page and the symbols placed upon it might be treated as one picture; then again, capitals might be 'read' through the entire text, in a kind of simulation of music, where one may follow a simple voice within a complex network of voices. The work appears to be a labyrinth, but one to be followed in a finite number of ways. It is a mandala, an object of contemplation, a symbol for a religious, possibly pantheistic, world view, where all apparent phenomena and changes are to be observed as having no extrinsic implications and – in contradistinction to earlier poetry – lacking connection the one with the other. Such a work leaves an overwhelming impression of a mirror-universe, from which the observer is either excluded, or within the bounds of which he is contained, so as no longer to sense a distance between the purposeless and inconsequential events in the book and himself.

Mallarmé's conception is transformed by Boulez into a crystalline sound-world in *Pli selon pli* (1957–62), his portrait of the poet, and in his Third Piano Sonata (1956–7). It suggests a composer not unlike the poet Mallarmé is reputed to have been, an artist of intellectual austerity and rigour, detached from the everyday world. But no such detachment is carried over from Boulez the composer to Boulez the writer, the conductor, the lecturer and the entrepreneur. In Paris in the 1950s, and subsequently in the various stages of an extraordinarily successful career, he gives the impression that the public world of music has to be rebuilt according to ideology. Subjective preference and imagination determine the compositional methodology from which works are created. They require appropriate external conditions for their realisation. So new institutions must be founded, or old ones reformed, to provide such conditions and to re-educate the public.

Although any unilateral intention will obviously be modified by practical realities, all this sounds a little like a Marxist position. Systematic socialism too attempted a reform of social institutions and the re-education of the people according to its theoretical tenets. But when it came to cultural institutions, tradition coloured by *Volkstümlichkeit* was to be respected. According to a more conventional model, popular taste and respected institutions were to determine the shape and contents of works of art, except only that these were, by virtue of a conscious empathy on their creators' part, to embody the aspirations of the proletariat as defined by the Communist Party. Here the world was to be changed but art retained in its traditional shape. But an avant-garde artist, as Boulez was and is, can get along with society while at the same time wishing to change its artistic institutions.

I do not believe that Boulez is merely doing more successfully what in fact every artist dreams of but is unable to realise. We have here, in all its aspects, a unique and peculiar vision differing substantially from the beliefs in a two-way process, in the institution of the work of art as a synthesis between individual perception and the demands of society, implicitly or explicitly expressed by artists as different in their natures as Schoenberg, Eisler and Britten. The extent of this difference was now to be brought home to me sharply, and through personal experience.

5

Returning to England in the late 1950s, and observing a perhaps unglamorous but at the same time rapidly and positively developing musical life, I felt that Boulez's position and his implicit rejection of compromise and synthesis were both unrealistic and theoretically incorrect. Extant institutions with all their peculiarities and material limitations determine the development of culture and the progressive expansion of the forum in which music and its audience meet. Here, there is a demand for the composition of new works of art, expressing new perceptions by new means, so long as they may be realised within the forum. To provide such works requires the mastery of appropriate techniques, based on suitable attitudes, and these in their turn colour, limit and even change the individual creative imagination. As an aspiring composer, I either accept this situation or reject it, turning my back on its inevitable risks, compromises and disappointments. In the second case I have to try to find ways and resources to realise my own works in the most appropriate manner. An inescapable conflict arises, whatever the position taken.

It was really the effort to deal with this conflict that determined what I did in those years. I sought (temporarily, and generally with limited success) to reconcile the ideals of new music and new society. A more cautious or canny person than myself might have hesitated to deal head on with the situation I have described. But I read it as a personal challenge which I felt I had to accept. Following the favourable impression made by the performance of my cantata *The Deluge*, I was asked to compose a work for large chorus and orchestra[23] for the Leeds Triennial Festival. The chorus was an amateur one with a tradition of performing new work, most recently Britten's *Spring Symphony* and Fricker's *Vision of Judgement*. It was understood that what was sought was not an *à la carte* Festival event, but a genuine attempt to meld a new vision with available talent. This was a formidable and perhaps imposs-ible undertaking.

It soon became apparent that the expressionist fragmentation of the narrative did not produce the kind of writing that the singers and the experienced but traditional chorus-master could manage. It was not just that the singers were required to perform rhythms and pitch-patterns that were beyond them: it had to do with the fact that a huge gulf had come to exist between their and my kinds of musical experience.

Of course, the situation is not always as black and white as it appeared to be in 1961, when, following the performance, *The Times* in its fourth leader (it was a time when such matters were still regarded as of some national interest) declared that this work, *Sutter's Gold*, marked the end of the British choral tradition.[24] I didn't know whether it marked the end of the British choral tra-dition or not – I got a rose named after the piece – but my feelings were really those of shame, because the singers had met every day for a year to battle with this intractable material and hadn't had a good time at all. I felt that this was a situation which was too harsh and which I couldn't cope with. But I learned from it how compositional imagination and technique have to be modified by social considerations. If one wishes, one can just say that music has to be autonomous and self-sufficient; but how to sustain such a view when people who sing for pleasure are deprived of true satisfaction in the performance of new work?

This sort of social argument draws attention to a deeper issue which confronts any and every composer. It is in the nature of a philosophical problem, which really is to ask the question: In any particular fashion, development or musical school, exactly where does the music live? Where is the music in a particular style? We can talk about music in terms of the ideas that inform it; we can talk about structure and techniques; we can talk about aesthetics or ethics or politics. But we have to remember that while all this, realistic or not, is of great importance to composers and to anyone who likes to follow what composers are doing, what is being discussed is not the music itself but the location of the music, the place where it exists. Perhaps I couldn't have formulated it like that in 1955, but I felt it that way.

One day John Carewe and I were sitting with Boulez and talking about Debussy's *Jeux*. Boulez did a kind of analysis of the introduction and about twenty-five bars further. After these bars the technique he was pointing out to us seemed to disappear. We said to him, 'What happens now?' He was sitting fiddling at the piano, and he started playing the music and said: 'Oh well, these techniques don't go on, but it is marvellous music, isn't it?' One wanted to say, 'That's not the point.' But on the contrary, that is precisely the point: that the techniques aren't the music. The techniques inform the music, but they aren't the music itself. Cornelius Cardew once said to me, 'You mustn't have a bad conscience about techniques.' He said it because I did have one, and because I felt that for every composer some techniques contribute to the appearance of music and some prevent the appearance of music. One of the criticisms of the avant garde that is bandied about today is precisely that their techniques sometimes seem to prevent the appearance of music.

6

In the 1950s I believed that I was witnessing, even participating in, the creation of a new musical language: that is, not a personal style of composition, but a common practice working for composers in general and gradually seeping through to performers and public. This 'language' was to be assembled, partly by 'beginning again', as I understood the intention of the Bauhaus to have been, partly by a re-examination of the materials of music, and partly by a critical dissection of that music of the past which seemed relevant and '*actuel*'. This was the music in which the structural dimension was of most obvious interest (Ockeghem, Machaut,

Bach, Schoenberg, Webern and Stravinsky), as well as that music which appeared to embody a new expression of time or sound-type (Debussy, Varèse, Messiaen). At the same time the work and ideas of Mallarmé, Joyce, Kandinsky, Klee and Mondrian seemed often to have more to do with new music than did the bulk of the Classical, Romantic and even twentieth-century repertoire.

I was both attracted by the apparent nobility of this high aspiration and repelled by its exclusivity. It should be our aim to understand the music we love and the intentions of its makers as far as is possible truthfully, which means in all its dimensions. But creative composers do not necessarily function like that: there is always a tendency to select what is useful and ignore what is irrelevant. Every artist knows this quandary. If Schoenberg wished 'to breathe the air of other planets', he also wished to revitalise the classical and romantic tradition. But even there he emphasised those elements of past musical language which he believed were innovatory and personal, saying, as it were, that the Classical–Romantic tradition is of its nature continuously evolutionary and that its achievement lies in its innovations, which would have been only a partial truth had it emanated from a lesser man.

Certainly the idea of making things anew was in the air in the optimistic post-war period. The idea of a new musical language seemed modest and sober then, and not overwhelmingly arrogant, as it may appear to be now. It seemed reasonable that, after the atrocities of recent history, new beginnings would lead to a better world and a new world, and that such a world required a totally new art. There had been a brief period of reconciliation between the ideal of a new society and modern art after the Russian Revolution, but this had been rapidly destroyed by the doctrines of Socialist Realism, which put artistic innovation out of court. As a consequence there was, after the Second World War, no analogous reconciliation between modernists, avant gardists and Socialists, except as a form of private wish-fulfilment.

Yet there were similarities between Socialist Realists in the Soviet Union and the West European avant garde. Both sought to rewrite history; both set up a canon of relevant models; and both were authoritarian and party-line in nature. If it is widely accepted that a doctrine such as is Socialist Realism can only be practised, if it is practised at all, in a centralist state, it is equally true that avant gardists will inevitably remain a collection of individuals, and that they will have little access to the wider public and few chances for performance of works demanding large forces without special outlets set up and financed by public subsidy. It was state radio, especially in post-war Germany, and later the conquest of higher education, that provided, as it still provides, the platform for the dissemination of new music. With these came the bureaucracy, the systems of ranking and evaluation, which seemed to me then, as they do now, to stand for everything that modern art exists to oppose.

In the 1950s I admired the post-Webernian ideal of a purified, crystalline musical structure, self-sufficient and non-referential in nature. But at the same time I wanted to contribute, if I could, to a wider, more democratic development of music which, in those years, seemed to be a practical possibility and which in most European countries, especially Britain, and in America, has actually taken place. As far as the actual writing down of music was concerned, this demanded a synthesis or a set of ever-changing compromises. It was the attempt to effect this synthesis that provided at once the motivation, or part of the motivation, for my compositions and the choice of forms, words and subject matter that seemed appropriate for them. I recognised in myself, on the one hand, a desire for abstraction, for formal innovation and for systemisation, and on the other a wish to express human feeling in a realistic manner as it has existed from Monteverdi to Janáček. I always preferred the dynamic expression of the crowd on the Odessa steps in Eisenstein's *Potemkin* to the static contemplation of figures on a vase in a perfect poem of Mallarmé. Furthermore, as in life, so in music I wished to lay claim only to the space and time that I actually required and to do no more than adequately and personally inhabit that space and time.

The practical implications of such apparently contradictory

ideals and the various partial attempts to reconcile them that I have described led me away from what was later to be seen as the 'classical' avant-garde position and make my music of no interest to, though not free of the influence of, Boulez.

7

At the height of the Cold War, Hanns Eisler, who fully recognised and was probably broken by the path of conflicting ideals, made two observations which I'd like to repeat here. Speaking of the great innovators of the twentieth century, he suggested that they were Schoenberg, Stravinsky and Janáček. 'Everybody will agree to the first two, but why Janáček?' Schoenberg and Stravinsky, he said, achieved new musical forms and languages. Janáček did not, but he was a genuine innovator in expression. He was a Realist innovator.

Eisler also said, on another occasion, rather ruefully and in pain after the rejection of his libretto for an opera on Johann Faustus by the Party in the DDR, 'The only music worth writing now is one not easily performable or acceptable in either East or West.'

(1987)

Appendix: Is There Only One Way?

The German musical theorist Herbert Eimert has recently made the following pronouncement: ' . . . there can be only one way of defining the contemporary stage of musical composition, and that is: post-Webern – a situation resulting from the discovery of the single note.'[25]

For my own part, I can't see that post-Webernism, or any other stage of musical development, represents the 'only way'. It's a fallacy to suppose that at any given historical point there is a unique solution to the problems of composition, and that musical evolution is ascending to an ever higher order of revelation. By that argument, a composer need only, as is so often said, be alive to some sort of musical law of progress in order to take his place on the train of 'serious advance', to write music which is legitimate because it is 'aware of its time', 'contemporary'. In point of fact, the best new music has already belied this kind of historicism.

There has never been a common denominator of musical style. The assessment of style in terms of historical necessities is inadequate. If you say that a piece of music is stylistically pure, you merely acknowledge one of two things: either that the piece is very narrow in its field of references, or that it successfully fuses any number of diverse and even contradictory elements. Artistically speaking, *the concept of style can only be used with reference to quality.*[26] According to Schoenberg, style is the result of a well-balanced relation between the effect and the resources employed.

The development of music in Europe is unique because it is cumulative. The present-day composer has the widest possible choice of models, the largest number of possible influences at his disposal. In what way, then, does the music of the past influence a composer? I can only suggest that the composer, like any other listener, will tend to be attracted by anything that is irregular in the context of the piece he hears. Our textbooks are full of examples of exceptions: strange harmonic progressions, odd contrapuntal combinations, which, we feel, enhance the expression. In the composer's mind, vague memories fuse and grow into a new, conscious, creative idea. An artist is related to the tradition from which he comes, and this bond has little to do with time or progress. There is no common 'only way' to any future stage; *all art is new art and all art is conservative.*

Apart from Messiaen, the composers who reached their maturity in the 1930s and 1940s have had only a limited effect on recent developments. The primary influences have been Schoenberg and Webern and Berg on the one hand, and Debussy and Stravinsky on the other; but the composers whose attitude Dr Eimert represents[27] have chosen Webern alone as the key figure for the development of new music. They ignore Webern's traditional attitude towards musical continuity, which owed a great deal to

Schoenberg. They apply a kind of statistical analysis to Webern's music which bears no relation to musical reality. They isolate single events, durations, pitches and dynamic levels; they analyse statistical ratios in the minutest detail – and so they ignore the audible development of complex forms. *Analysis should only have one single purpose: to explain why a particular work of art makes its specific effect.*

Serial composers of the post-war era cite Webern in an effort to show that the single note can be a structural entity, like a motif. The isolated note, they say, forms the only *'historically correct basis for the creation of musical form'*. We are told that 'the situation resulting from the discovery of the single note brings us to the threshold of a new era'. In support of this view, Mondrian and Malevich are dragged in. Malevich defined painting as the logical development of the empty canvas. Accordingly, we now hear that 'music is a logical development of a certain duration of silence'.[28]

This outlook amounts to a complete neutralisation of musical character. The creative idea is replaced by mere procedure. There is no *material* in the traditional sense, but only a pre-compositional abstraction of the intended course of events. This musical attitude reaches its climax in the *Structures [I]* for two pianos by Pierre Boulez, written in 1951–3.[29] The pieces are an attempt at total serialisation of all elements. Every element is filtered through the original series. Rhythmic durations are measured, absolute dynamic values are attached to each individual note. Any free thought is submerged in the wholly serial form.

The work has been hopefully compared to Bach's *Art of Fugue*. A French critic writes as follows: 'Boulez intends to complete the three existing structures by adding a further nine . . . when the twelve structures are complete, they will be the sum total of all serial possibilities on the levels of pitch, duration and dynamic intensity. For serial music, this will be a great achievement, comparable to *The Art of Fugue* or *The Well-Tempered Clavier*.'[30]

Well, it's hardly worth pointing out the flaws in this comparison.

Suffice it to say that Boulez himself, in an article written not very much later, referred to the unwieldy monster of total serialisation.[31]

Indeed, this music is dull in its lack of formal complexity, of dramatic gesture. No amount of technical ingenuity can break the monotony of regularity – even though this regularity can be shown to contain, within itself, the widest possible degree of isolation and differentiation. The dull impression is simply due to the fact that all serial possibilities are continually present in the work. Musical interest is always produced by the restriction of possibilities – a restriction which is determined, in its turn, by the character of the material, by individual invention.

And so the carefully erected world of total serialisation collapses like a house of cards. History already winks at the optimistic belief in a fresh start, the illusion of a 'Brave New World'. *Musical reality has moved on.*

It is, as I've said, Boulez himself who now rejects the impracticable aspects of serialisation; he is inspired by a new ideal of musical sound and form. In two works for voice and chamber ensemble, *Le marteau sans maître* and the *Improvisations sur Mallarmé*, we find a musical style which is new, which does not rely on the so-called 'situation of the single note', nor for that matter on purely statistical theories. The various discernible influences are indicative of broad musical responses. The compositions succeed because they are based on enriched and characteristic material; the forms are variegated, complex and therefore expressive. Most important of all, Boulez has created a new kind of sound, by way of an ensemble in which non-sustaining instruments predominate.

The return to subjective preference, to individual judgement, in the formulation of a musical idea is a return to genuine musical thought. There is some ground for optimism here. Boulez, through his recent development, counters the impoverishment of artistic sensibility which has for too long been considered the 'only way'. To achieve anything of lasting value, we shall have to widen our terms of creative reference, and break the shackles of contemporaneity. We shall have to free ourselves from an historical approach based on insensitivity and stupidity. Let us, as musicians, beware of the over-simplifications of our self-appointed dictators and our non-playing captains.

(1960)

1. String Quartet No. 1, Op. 5 (1956–7, rev. 1986), performed in the revised version by the Arditti Quartet during the Almeida Festival, London 1987.
2. Kranichstein Musikinstitut, Darmstadt.
3. Piano Sonata, Op. 2 (1951–2), performed at Darmstadt in 1954 by Else Stock-Hug.
4. Fantasia, Op. 4, written in 1954–5 and performed in Darmstadt by the Hessische Rundfunk Orchester, conducted by Otto Matzerath.
5. *The Deluge* and the Suite Op. 11 (1961) were conducted by him.
6. 'What Is Electronic Music?', *Die Reihe*, No. 1, 'Electronic Music' (Bryn Mawr: Theodore Presser, 1958), p.8. I was the (anonymous) translator of this volume. [The exact wording used is: ' . . . in the contemporary phase of music only one way can be seen of determining the compositional situation, that is: "after Webern", the situation resulting from the discovery of "the *single* note".']
7. The talk was first reprinted in *The Score*, No. 26 (January 1960).
8. [A term used in Eimert's article 'What Is Electronic Music?', pp. 3ff., and common in Darmstadt-oriented writing of the time.]
9. [AG's differences with Boulez over technology surfaced publicly as early as 1977, when an article by the latter – scarcely more than a 'plug' for IRCAM – drew an unexpectedly sharp response. See Boulez, 'Technology and the Composer', *Times Literary Supplement*, 6 May 1977, p. 570, and ibid., 10 June 1977, p. 703.]
10. I am not speaking here of Boulez's personality (though he did appear to me as I describe him) but of what seemed to me his calm confidence about the act of composition. He really seemed to believe (and the publication of his correspondence with Cage supports this) that his 'charts' of pitch levels, durations etc. would of themselves, if suitably realised, produce significant music. [Cf. *The Boulez–Cage Correspondence*, ed. Jean-Jacques Nattiez, trans. Robert Samuels (Cambridge: CUP, 1993).]
11. An accurate performance without awareness of a traditional hierarchy of strong and weak beats renders it one-dimensional and arbitrary in effect. It is as if one attempted to read Kafka for the images alone, without reference to conventional grammar and syntax. The result might be evocative, but the essential ambiguity would disappear.
12. Cf. Armin Klammer: 'Our investigation will not take in the thematic structure of the piece, since that is something quite foreign to serial thought, and has nothing to do with Webern's personal achievement.' See 'Webern's Piano Variations, Op. 27: 3rd Movement', *Die Reihe*, No. 2, 'Anton Webern' (Bryn Mawr: Theodor Presser, 1959), p. 81. I remain mistrustful of any attempt to separate the so-called progressive and traditional aspects of a composition, as originality inevitably arises from a personal synthesis of old and new elements. In music, as in the fine arts, there must necessarily be a compromise between the desire to portray reality and

the tendency to abstraction. Cf. Bianchi Bandinelli: 'Realismus und Abstraktion sind zwei Modi, die nahe Umwelt des Menschen durch Formen darzustellen, die er selbst schafft' etc. in *Wirklichkeit und Abstraktion* (Dresden: VEB Verlag der Kunst, 1962), p. 11. [The actual phrase 'compositional situation' is used by Eimert: see note 6 above.]

13. As in the beautiful movement 'L'artisanat furieux' for voice and flute alone, perhaps modelled on 'Der kranke Mond' in Schoenberg's *Pierrot lunaire*.

14. From the vantage-point of today many of my musical enthusiasms and view-points of those years appear as somewhat theoretical in nature. I certainly had not heard chant of any kind; nor was there access to any non-European music, other than a brief exposure to Arab music, which I had heard in Israel in 1952. (I had also heard Tippett and Britten's Purcell performances and, like everyone else, was profoundly impressed by my father's Monteverdi Vespers at York.) Nor indeed were there many opportunities actually to hear any new music of the serial school other than piano solo or small chamber works. Today, with much more available on tape and disc, the young composer will receive his inspirations from the physical sound of the music and perhaps then try to discover how it is created. But I had access only to scores and articles about them (apart from some occasional success in picking up a broadcast from Germany). Consequently I was primarily excited by technical ideas, with a most inexact picture of what their applications sounded like. To this day I can invoke the effect that the sight of the score of Boulez's Second Piano Sonata (1948) or of the examples in his article 'Eventuellement' (1952) had upon me. As I later observed in China, shortly after the end of the Cultural Revolution, a glimpse of a single page of score could suffice to set off a susceptible young composer into a whole new development. [Cf. 'Eventuellement', *La Revue musicale*, No. 212 (May 1952), reprinted in Boulez, *Relevés d'apprenti* (Paris: Le Seuil, 1966); this has most recently been translated by Stephen Walsh as 'Possibly . . .', in *Stocktakings from an Apprenticeship* (Oxford: Clarendon Press, 1991).]

15. The direct influence of artistic movements of the twentieth century – Futurism, Dada and Surrealism – can only be observed in rather peripheral composers (Cage excepted). Varèse, in *Offrandes*, sets a surrealist text, as does Boulez in *Le marteau sans maître*, and Messiaen's own words in *Harawi* are influenced by Eluard. But, Satie apart, there has been little successful music exploiting surrealist discontinuities.

16. Louis de Wet.

17. [See below, pp. 286–7]

18. I was a student of Richard Hall at the Royal Manchester College of Music from 1952 to 1955.

19. Notably 'Eventuellement' ('Possibly . . .'), referenced in note 14 above, and *Boulez on Music Today*, trans. Richard Rodney Bennett and Susan Bradshaw (London: Faber, 1971).

20. The use here of the terms foreground and background is a deliberate invocation of Schenkerian terminology; which is not to suggest that a Schenkerian model could ever be made in which the twelve-tone row was attributed background functions. Such an analogy would be confusing. What can be applied here is a profoundly anti-Schoenbergian notion of compositional levels.

21. In the 1950s Leibowitz's books provided almost the only technical information about the Second Viennese School and were widely assumed to have emanated from the Master's (A. Schoenberg's) voice. In fact this was not the case. Leibowitz believed in the primacy of polyphony as the engine of musical development (which is something that Schoenberg nowhere states), and it would appear that Boulez, a pupil of Leibowitz (but later his enemy), carries on in this fundamental belief. See Reinhard Kapp, 'Shades of the Double's Original: René Leibowitz's Dispute with Boulez', *Tempo* No. 165 (June 1988), pp. 2–16.

22. These procedures are described in 'Poetics of my Music' and 'The Composer and his Idea of Theory: A Dialogue': see below, pp. 58–76 and 236–71.

23. *Sutter's Gold* was performed – once, on 9 October 1961 – by James Pease (baritone), the Leeds Festival Chorus and the Liverpool Philharmonic Orchestra conducted by John Pritchard. [The difficulties surrounding the premiere are also described in *The Music of Alexander Goehr: Interviews and Articles*, ed. Bayan Northcott (London: Schott, 1980), pp. 14–15.]

24. 'A dying tradition?', *The Times*, 28 October 1961, p. 9c; reproduced in the Appendix to this book, p. 305

25. [Eimert's exact wording, together with the bibliographical reference, is given above, note 6.].

26. [These and subsequent italics are all AG's.]

27. [AG is referring to those composers who contributed to the first two numbers of *Die Reihe*, which Eimert (along with Stockhausen) edited.]

28. [Quotations unidentified. The remark about Mondrian and Malevich is probably a reference to Heinz-Klaus Metzger's article 'Webern and Schönberg', in *Die Reihe*, No. 2 (English-language edition, p. 45).]

29. [1951–2 according to the catalogue of Boulez's works in Dominique Jameux, *Pierre Boulez*, trans. Susan Bradshaw (London: Faber, 1991), p. 370.]

30. [Quotation unidentified.]

31. ' "An der Grenze des Fruchtlandes"', *Die Reihe*, No. 1 (1955); trans. as ' "At the Ends of Fruitful Land"', in English *Die Reihe*, No. 1 (1958), pp. 19–29.

Manchester Years

I

There is something faintly specious about reminiscences. They are
a sign one is getting so old that one cannot talk about the present,
only about the past. But it isn't my intention to muse affectionately
about those distant days, to be precise 1952–5, which I spent in
Manchester; I wish to deal, perhaps more substantially, with
musical conditions then, and how people thought about things. In
part this might overlap with what is thought about now, in which
case it will be 'relevant'; but some things which are no longer
thought about will be relevant too. I wish to talk from a personal
point of view. So this is not an attempt to present a complete
chronicle of a particular time in Manchester; but merely an account
of my experiences and my feelings about studying composition
there – why I did, and how I did, what I did.

Some sort of personal prehistory is necessary. I didn't come to
Manchester for the music, actually. I came for something completely unconnected with music, which was a sort of political
movement. When I left school I had been a conscientious objector,
and had been ordered – as we were at that time – to do alternative
service, which meant being an agricultural worker. Through a
combination of events I became very interested in the Socialist–
Zionist movement. At that time the state of Israel was new, and
emissaries came from there to recruit Jews from England (and
other countries) to take them to Israel to join collective farms.
Mine was a Marxist organisation, but deviating from the British
or any other Communist Party which opposed nationalism and
consequently the state of Israel. Political movements and houses
were set up in the various towns where there were large Jewish
populations. I came to 100 Bury Old Road in Cheetham Hill. By

day I was a ward orderly in Crumpsall General Hospital, doing some fairly unsavoury things, and in the evening I was a lecturer in politics, reading Marxist pamphlets and trying to persuade. At the same time I wanted to be a composer. I came from a musical family and had studied a little. My father, who was a conductor,[1] knew a pianist in Manchester called Iso Elinson.[2] Through him I met Richard Hall[3] and became his private pupil; and, as a result, I gave up a scholarship to Oxford to study Classics and stayed at the Royal College of Music in Manchester.

At that time this was eccentric behaviour. There were not many people from the south in Manchester, and southerners generally did not know anywhere north of Barnet (on the old A5). Although I didn't come to Manchester for musical reasons, it later became musically important to me. This was because of the personality of Richard Hall, who was obliquely responsible for a lot of my musical development.[4] He wasn't a firebrand, though he had managed to quarrel, for one reason or another, with most of the musical establishment of Manchester. He was originally a priest, who had left the Church and worked with the unemployed during the 1930s. He was of a speculative turn of mind, very different from the kind of people who normally taught music in colleges or universities. The alternative would have been someone like Lennox Berkeley (at the Royal Academy in London). Hall was a different kind of man.

Were he still alive, he would probably remember me as extremely opinionated. I had a lot of strong views not entirely supported by reason, and a lot of negative feelings; there was a great deal I was against. I had difficulties with my family and was committing myself to becoming a musician against their advice and without their support. There was little enough evidence at the time to suggest any particular reason why I should study music. But as so often is the case, the decision to 'go it alone' and the siege mentality masked grave personal misgivings and (justifiable) lack of confidence. Looking back at that time, and seeing myself on my soap box, I fear I must have appeared slightly ridiculous and certainly very aggressive to the dull Mancunians of the time, but I do recognise in the hectoring promotion of contradictory views the same person I am now. My political views and my musical views didn't go hand in hand. It wasn't just that art ought to be written in such a way that people could understand it, whereas as a composer I was attracted by things which seemed to be comprehensible to only a tiny minority. There was even a basic clash of intention: whether to become a composer or to do something of a more political nature. This clash expressed itself in my having strong views on subjects, each possible, but not obviously combinable. The working out of such views forms one of the recurring subjects of my activities as composer, teacher and writer.

Richard Hall was superficially a gentle and slightly ironic man who had the knack of deflating one's strongest views. He also had invented techniques of teaching composition which, at that time, were very unusual. He had observed that many people who desperately wanted to compose or study music were, from the conventional point of view, confused and unsuccessful students. While ordinary music students, aspiring teachers perhaps, were moderately good at harmony and counterpoint and at doing the various things you were meant to do as a music student, just those who had the most promising ideas about composition had enormous difficulties with these things. So he started young composers off with a pentatonic method of his own devising. He gave you only the five notes of the pentatonic scale, and you had to invent melodies and counterpoints and derive harmonic systems which mainly consisted of sevenths and fourths and seconds, and which consequently were not triadic and quite fresh in sound. This was, in embryo, a systematic way to compose. It's still a good way of starting composers off, because, although I didn't realise it at the time, it reproduces in an extremely simplified form some of the objective criteria of intervallic (or even twelve-tone) technique, in that, like it, it offers a simple combination between horizontal and vertical: the same mode of construction provides the chords as provides the melody notes. Also like twelve-tone technique it offers simple euphony without tension. In a limited sense everything sounds 'nice': you can't make pentatonic music not sound 'nice' (this of course is its severe limitation). The chords produced were never of the 'nasty' kind caused by bad tonal voice leading.

The method continued by taking two pentatonic scales (effectively black notes and white notes or some transposition of them); now more complex harmony resulted from the combining of the notes of the two modes. I wrote piano pieces and songs in this way, and, although I didn't know it at the time, I was being prepared to understand principles such as hexachordal twelve-tone systems where six-note sets are combined with each other. Pentatonic thinking made it much easier for me to understand the twelve-tone technique than it would have been if I had been writing tonal pieces, harmonising by figured bass. Richard Hall's simple 'carpentry' techniques enabled me to achieve some fluency, and to apply objective criteria of good and bad.

When it was time to go to Oxford, it no longer seemed a good idea. Richard Hall managed to arrange the Jeanne Bretey Composition Scholarship for me, and I found myself enrolled for three years at the old Manchester College. At that time it looked terrible – I'd never seen anything that looked quite like it – but it had certain advantages. By comparison with the London establishments it retained a certain Central European feeling about it. Many of the teachers had been pupils of Egon Petri, and they had attended Busoni's summer classes in the years between the wars. There was a Busoni tradition which survived both in piano playing and in composition, the last scion of which was Ronald Stevenson, who was there just before I was. With a number of other students he had started a kind of Busoni cult. The Henry Watson Library is extremely well provided with Busoni scores bought during and after the First World War. There was a lot of music available, and quite a lot was performed. And it was not only Busoni, but also the composers who form a kind of alternative musical culture: Scriabin,[5] Van Dieren, Sorabji. John Ogdon was, until his last days, an admirer of that musical culture, never really believing in what we were doing at all. It was Peter Maxwell Davies who owned a copy of the *Opus clavicembalisticum* by Sorabji and wanted to get rid of it. He gave it to John Ogdon, and in that way seems to have infected him for life.

I think I moved the dominant influence in the Hall class away from Busoni and towards Schoenberg, which was not so far distant as the two overlapped in a lot of their thinking.

2

I want now to describe what was considered interesting and what was not in that composition class, and also the people who were in it. There were, in fact, two composition classes in the old Royal Manchester College of Music: the one run by Richard Hall, and the one run by Thomas Pitfield.[6] The Pitfield one was a Nadia Boulanger class. I don't think Pitfield was himself a pupil of Boulanger, but his was very much a Stravinskian, French musical culture. The Richard Hall class, partly as a result of the difficult relationship between the two men, was anti-Stravinskian, anti-Nadia Boulanger. It didn't express itself like that – more by a not so polite scorn of a mutual kind than in any conversations between the two. The composers in the one class (each numbering about ten) were hardly recognised as existing by members of the other. For instance, a composer who later became Head of the BBC in Manchester, David Ellis, who had been in the Army in Germany and knew a great deal about modern music, never, or very rarely, talked to me or Harrison Birtwistle or anyone from the Hall class. We simply belonged to a different circle; there was no communication of any kind. I am not proud of this snobbery.

Neither I nor Harry Birtwistle nor Peter Maxwell Davies was the compositional star of the College at that time. In fact we were hardly taken seriously. The 'star' was a composer – I don't know what became of him – called Roy Heaton-Smith, who had his works performed in college concerts. He wrote in a style very much influenced by the Britten of the Serenade and Nocturne. He was highly thought of, was even getting a few public performances around Manchester and looked like becoming a successful composer. Another good, highly thought-of composer was James Pye, who wrote what we called Manchester Spanish. He was a fine pianist and composed in the style of Albeniz. It seemed very striking indeed, and is one of the reasons why Albeniz is still one of my favourite composers.[7] I often do a touch of Manchester Spanish myself when I can get round to it.

At that time British modern musical culture was Vaughan Williams (by then an old man, appearing in Manchester once a year to conduct the St Matthew Passion with the Hallé), Bax, Walton, Bliss, Moeran, Finzi, Britten and Tippett. There were premieres of several symphonies in the years I was in Manchester, including the *Antartica* (1949–52) and Walton's Second (1959–60), as well as 'Cheltenham Symphonies' by Arnold, Rawsthorne, Berkeley and others. The more progressive side of this traditional English establishment, of which Richard Hall was a peripheral part, preferred Delius. The University professor, Humphrey Procter-Gregg,[8] was a great fan of Delius, to the extent that he, like Delius, scorned Bach and the Viennese classics. I remember him saying in public that he thought Bach 'trundled along'.

The principal prevailing influence upon modern music in the 1950s was, however, not Schoenberg, not Busoni, but Hindemith. Hindemith was what was new. Not only was his music admired, but his attitude of mind (as expressed in his book *A Composer's World*, 1952) provided an inspiration for modern musical practice. In the 1950s there seemed to be an enormous gulf between London, Paris and New York and our provincial world. The problem for people in it was how to combine an interest in all sorts of advanced and esoteric matters (not just musical but spiritual and numerological) with musical life in the community, which was on a restricted scale. Hindemith seemed to offer an appropriate example, teaching how new musical ideas might be applied in a practical way so that amateurs could become involved in them. A lot of Richard Hall's work was for pipe and recorder players; he composed music for amateurs, and had to do it in such a way that they could play it and sing it. But it was not *à la carte*. It contained *Gebrauchsmusik* applications of advanced ideas, such as tone or durational series, inversions and retrogrades. The relative demise of Hindemith as a major influence marks the distance from then to now. Nobody in the early 1950s could conceivably have predicted that Hindemith would not be rated in the same way as Bartók or Stravinsky. He now appears much less frequently in programmes. But I'm always bemused when I hear some of the quartets of Shostakovich that are currently so highly praised. Somebody should listen to Hindemith's Third and Fourth String Quartets to try to hear how they influenced Shostakovich.

Hindemith's intellectual position appealed to me because of my political views. But in practice most of the students rebelled against the combination of experiment and practicality, aimed at producing work which was designed for choruses to sing and amateurs to play. We had a passionate interest in theories of any kind. For the composition class, which used to meet once a week for two or three hours, Richard Hall, basically an idle man, wouldn't have prepared anything very much. It was a case of waiting until one of us advanced a theory or showed something; or else Richard Hall would mention something he'd been reading. We went through all the speculative theories of composition at that time, the more abstract the better. We spent time on the work of Joseph Yasser,[9] who redivided the octave into twenty-three; we speculated about the possibility of applying it and also the micro-intervals of Hába.[10] We were also fascinated by the theories of Joseph Schillinger, the Russian mathematician who had gone to America and invented the Schillinger Method of Musical Composition, in which he attempted to apply mathematical principles to composition.[11] He had taught George Gershwin and Glenn Miller, but I don't know whether in practice he had influenced anyone in the USA other than these jazz musicians. The only composer I know who seems to have studied his method is Earle Brown. But I suspect that his ideas were more influential, and that Elliott Carter and Conlon Nancarrow might have looked at his books, because the methods they later used are implicit in Schillinger's discussions of the application of number to tempo and to metre. I was particularly interested in one chapter of the book called *Strata Harmony* which outlined a method of finding common denominators to organise simultaneously sounding harmonic strata. This resembles a number of Carter's musical ideas (for example, that of intervals being confined within certain areas and sounding simultaneously in different strands of a texture). Such ideas were keenly studied and had an effect on all of us, in some cases a ridiculous effect. I remember an unending viola sonata which consisted of mathematically calculated rhythms and chords (which were unplayable, having always a different number of notes, thirteen, twenty-three, etc.). Richard Hall applied Schillinger to Blacher's[12] variable metres, which is to say, he invented artificial rhythms and developed them according to serial principles.

This background prepared me for Schoenbergian theory and twelve-tone technique, which came to us partly through the publication of the first edition of *Style and Idea* (1950), then a collection of about eight essays. We now take this book for granted; it has become standard academic fare. In fact, quite apart from Schoenberg's music, it revolutionised musical thinking in this country. It, and the same author's *Structural Functions of Harmony* (1954), brought a number of new insights: it introduced analytical method and a different approach to harmony, and in some senses replaced what at its best beforehand was expressed by Tovey's essays. Almost overnight the publication of these books in the early 1950s changed the terms of reference and introduced ways of thinking about music which were new and fruitful.

It is odd that Schoenberg's influence should have come through his essays and not through his music. The situation was that we very rarely heard any Schoenberg, and that everybody (except me) seemed to dislike it intensely. Schoenberg's ideas were liked, the twelve-tone technique was liked, but not actually his music. Richard Hall disliked it strongly, as did most of the other students in the class. I was probably the only enthusiast (and remain so). They found it too abrupt, harsh and hysterical; to this day I believe that audiences find the intense physicality of Schoenberg's work hard to take. The technical devices, however, helped us; their application immediately made our music seem more sophisticated. But we still had our modest but real musical world to take into account. How do you take these twelve-tone rows and turn them into recorder pieces or choral pieces which 'ordinary' people can sing? The big influence on us here, matching that of Hindemith, was Krenek. We didn't know many pieces by Krenek, but his theories provided a way of deriving an artificial modality out of twelve-tone hexachords which made it possible to write a modified twelve-tone music in such a way that amateur recorder players could play it. Again, social and experimental aspirations join together. Deriving artificial modes is an aspect of the twelve-tone culture which comes not from Schoenberg, but from Krenek and Josef Matthias Hauer. Hauer was another composer Richard Hall was interested in and whom he rather resembled, sharing a number of his preoccupations. The most important event of my student life, however, was the impact of Messiaen. Messiaen, whom we became aware of at that time, represented (but in a much more palatable way, in that it was soft and religious) a kind of music which incorporated all the different ideas that concerned us: artificial modes, non-retrogradable rhythms, metrical experiments and number-generated structures. All these things I found later in the Messiaen class; but I had already picked them up from the prevailing ideas of that time, though the aesthetic was quite different.

3

In the Hall class was Harrison Birtwistle. He wore a small hat with a feather in it, and had a fishing fly in his pocket. One day he came up to me after a lecture where I'd misbehaved. The teacher tried to analyse the classics in a very schematic way, and I quarrelled with him throughout the lecture. Harry asked, 'Were you serious? Do you really believe what you said?' I said, 'Of course I do. Why shouldn't I?' We became firm friends.

He, in fact, had been at the other Manchester college, the Northern School [of Music], and had had a compositional career there; but by the time he came to the Royal Manchester College he had almost completely stopped composing. In all the years in Manchester he was a clarinettist, trying to write pieces but never finishing anything. He wasn't interested in academic technique, or any of the other things that were on offer at the College. He and I once went to the Whitworth Hall to sit a rudiments exam. I don't think either of us lasted more than about twenty minutes, and that was the only time either of us participated in the official doings of the institution. It offered no degree in composition, so it wasn't necessary to take it seriously.

Harry and I learned the Berg Clarinet Pieces (Op. 5). He was a good clarinettist, in that he made a very nice sound, but he was not too hot on the counting. Nor indeed was I. We got a performance together which was really an anticipation of aleatoric composition; we made a lot of marks on the copy and waited for each other to reach certain points – it sounded quite impressive really. People liked it; it was through the Berg pieces that we met Peter Maxwell Davies, who was a student at the University on the joint course with the College. He came up to us after we had played the Berg pieces and said in a sardonic tone of voice, 'Do you like that sort of thing?' We thought he was another enemy, and I remember being rather sharp with him, saying, 'Yes, we take that sort of thing absolutely seriously.' He later wrote to me, expressing interest in composition and asking to meet me.

We arranged to meet at the Kardomah Cafe by the Free Trade Hall. He was rather intense. I said to him, 'Do you compose?', and he snapped back, 'Only when I want to.' It seemed a stupid reply, and I said that was true for all composers I'd heard of. Anyway, he got involved with us, and I remember the first meeting with him as, retrospectively, a rather nasty occasion. He'd written a piano sonata which was about forty minutes long, and he played it to a group of us. I remember we criticised him rather harshly; years later I remember it as a kind of kangaroo court. I don't know what gave us the right to do it, as we were only students. I suppose it was my didactic streak trying to move the others towards some sort of an artistic movement. I was trying to state what was and what was not real modern music; what was not was to be expunged. Later in Darmstadt I observed the same style of discussion of new music and modern art: didactic and party-political. People were excluded from the circle of the elect simply for having the wrong views and not paying lip service to a party line. I don't say this entirely with regret, because there is value in having a firm canon of judgement – it moves you on, and removes a lot of rubbish from view – but it certainly was a harsh way of proceeding. Max, who had had a completely different musical life before he met us, simply stopped composing that way and his piece disappeared.

There then followed a time of intense collaboration and discussion. We formed a group to give concerts, which I paid for from my grant. There were five of us: a cellist, John Dow, who was in the Hallé (and who composed badly but played the cello rather well); the pianist John Ogdon, who could play anything and therefore was extremely useful; Gary (Elgar) Howarth, for whom Max wrote his trumpet sonata; I was a sort of non-playing director; and Harry played the clarinet. We had a very unpleasant encounter with Humphrey Procter-Gregg, on which occasion John Ogdon played him the Second Sonata by Boulez – from sight, it should be added. The man, who was a sensitive soul, was swooning and making awful noises. He couldn't bear it and was getting some sort of masochistic delight from John's bashing away at the piano. But as a result of it I was invited to conduct the Ricercar from the *Musical Offering*, which at that time I was very fond of (as I still am), as a prelude to the University's opera performance of *A School for Fathers* by Wolf-Ferrari, which seemed a very odd bit of programme-building.

It is worth mentioning that there was a modern music society in the Manchester College which met every now and then, and was run by one of the piano professors, Lucy Pierce. It was there that we managed to put on our first performance as students. The people who played at the Society's evenings were a strange bunch. For example, I remember a parson from the Lake District played his piano compositions, which were ramblings in the style of Cyril Scott. These were juxtaposed with our first works. It was because Lucy Pierce insisted on playing the *Goldberg Variations* and other avant-garde pieces of that kind that we originally decided to secede and do our own concerts. So the so-called New Music Manchester group was formed. We rented rooms in the City Art Gallery and in the Whitworth Gallery, and gave several concerts (attended by around twenty people) in which we tried to do new music by ourselves and the continental avant garde. We weren't warmly supported by the administration of the College, who viewed our efforts as a form of sinfulness. There was at that time a moral objection to modern music. (I find it hard, growing older, to point out to people that to call yourself avant garde has not always been a passport to success. At that time it was actually a form of abuse.)

Our student careers ended rather rapidly because we all went off in our different directions. We had a final concert at the Arts Council Drawing Room in London, put on by William Glock, which became quite a well-remembered event. It was widely reviewed, as it was regarded as astonishing that there was an avant garde, so-called modern music movement in Manchester which contained people who had already been to Darmstadt. The *Daily Mail* called us the 'dull young things of the 1950s', a designation which I still treasure. At that time I'd written a song cycle which had been performed in London, and then a piano sonata for Margaret Kitchin and some clarinet pieces for Harry;[13] Max had written his trumpet sonata. These were the pieces done in that concert, together with pieces by Elizabeth Lutyens and Richard Hall. I then got a French government scholarship and went off to study with Messiaen. Harry was called up for his National Service and, I think, played the violin part of *Tristan und Isolde* on his clarinet in the army band at Oswestry. Max had a short career in the army but was soon released. He alleged they told him that the country needed him as a composer rather than as a soldier, which seemed implausible at the time but proved correct. He then went off and studied in Italy. John Ogdon won the Moscow Prize and became a famous pianist; he led a tragic life, as did John Dow. Elgar Howarth, who was rather removed from us as a composer – he had a brass band background – went on to become the great trumpeter, and later the excellent conductor, that he is.

It was a short chapter in the life of the Royal Manchester College of Music. In general the 1950s were good years for the College. There were a number of fine pianists, instrumentalists and singers who later did well in the profession. For the composers among us, these were years of experiment and the trying out of various syntheses. But there were then few resources available. Later, in Darmstadt, ideas became less abstract. As countries (at least Germany) grew richer, and possibilities for performance and for avant-garde music-making became more frequent and luxurious, composers could afford to be less concerned with abstract intellectual ideas and in applying them to conventional surfaces. Now composers developed the possibility of physically realising their sound ideals in more complex instrumental and vocal combinations, and of exploring an interest in new techniques of playing instruments. It was a move from the purely and abstractly intellectual to the more immediate, rather like a move from drawing to painting. Complicated things can be done with a pencil on paper, but drawing will always lack the pure physicality, immediacy and sensuousness of oil paint. Analogously, our musical ideas at that time were conditioned by the relative poverty of our performing resources: a 'drawing with a pencil' was the best we could hope to do. Such limitations mould one's way of thought, and I can never entirely throw off a belief in the primacy of intellectual activities over sound fantasies.

These are a few reminiscences of the people and the ideas of that time. Obviously they don't tell much about the music in any kind of detail, and there's a lot I've left out. The origins of medievalism, for instance, particularly in Maxwell Davies's work, came very much from the course at Manchester University and Procter-Gregg's insistence on correcting false relations in Byrd, which was Max's main concern at that time. Max became quite well known for singing the original while everybody else was singing the corrected version, causing havoc in the performances. Also, the interest in orientalism was a new thing which concerned us at that time. All these interests are things which don't necessarily fit together in a simple way. But I think that nowadays, when we analyse music so much, we shouldn't forget that we ought also to study, for any particular period that concerns us, the set of influences and conditions that causes a young composer to choose what notes to put together, what is relevant and what is not, and so forth. It is in this spirit that my reminiscences of those three years in Manchester are offered.

(1990)

1. [Walter Goehr (1903–60). German conductor and composer. Studied under Schoenberg in Berlin; brought his family to England in 1933, one year after AG's birth. Conducted the Morley College concerts from 1943 until his death. Gave the first performance of works by Britten (Serenade for Tenor, Horn and Strings, 1943) and Tippett (*A Child of Our Time*, 1944), among others, and the first performance in modern times of Monteverdi's Vespers.]

2. Russian émigré pianist and professor of piano studies at the Royal Manchester College of Music.

3. [Richard Hall, b. York, 1903; d. 1982. Professor of composition at Royal Manchester College of Music from 1938 to 1956, when he became director of music at Dartington. Left Dartington in 1967 to become a Unitarian minister.]

4. [See AG's article, 'Richard Hall: A Memoir and a Tribute', *Musical Times*, Vol. 124 (November 1983), pp. 677–8.]

5. It seems eccentric to place Scriabin in this list, because he seems to me to be a much more important composer than either Busoni or his followers. In fact Richard Hall, who came from York, had been a founder member of the local branch of the, at that time (in the 1920s), avant garde British Music Society under Dr Eaglefield Hull, the British biographer of Scriabin. [Arthur Eaglefield Hull (1876–1928). Editor, teacher and writer. Founded Huddersfield College of Music in 1908. Author of many books, including *A Great Russian Tone Poet: Scriabin* (London, 1916) and *Modern Harmony: Its Explanation and Application* (London, 1914).] One of Hall's colleagues was William Baines, a gifted composer who died very young. The Cambridge theology student Hall was deeply attracted by the theosophically inspired technical innovations and vague orientalism of Scriabin. It was the pianists, rather than he, who inspired the Busoni cult.

6. [Thomas Pitfield (b. 1903). English composer, poet and teacher. Taught at the Royal Manchester College of Music from 1947 to 1973.]

7. Later my warm regard for Albeniz was further encouraged by Messiaen's enthusiasm for *Iberia*. It is a model for *Vingt regards* and the *Catalogue des oiseaux*. I was not particularly impressed by the musical material itself but by the subtlety of the way in which Albeniz colours the harmony with finger work, probably in imitation of guitar writing. This linked with Messiaen's interest in the keyboard techniques of Scarlatti and Couperin, and later of course Debussy and Ravel. The *acciaccatura* technique had a colossal effect on Messiaen's harmony.

8. [Humphrey Procter-Gregg (1895–1980). Founded Music Department at Manchester University in 1936, was Professor of Music there 1954–62.]

9. [Joseph Yasser (1893–1974). American conductor and writer. Author of *A Theory of Evolving Tonality* (New York, 1932) and *Medieval Quartal Harmony: A Plea for Restoration* (New York, 1938).]

10. [Hába's books included *Harmonické základy čtvrttónové soustava* [The Harmonic Principles of the Quarter-Tone System] (Prague, 1922) and *Neue Harmonielehre des diatonischen, chromatischen, Viertel-, Drittel-, Sechstel- und Zwölfteltonsystems* (Leipzig, 1927).]

11. [Joseph Schillinger (1895–1943). American composer, conductor and theorist. His theoretical works included *Kaleidophone: New Resources of Melody and Harmony* (New York, 1940), *The Schillinger System of Musical Composition* (New York, 1941), *The Mathematical Basis of the Arts* (New York, 1948) and *Encyclopedia of Rhythm* (New York, 1966).]

12. [Boris Blacher (1903–75). Composer and professor of composition at the Berlin Hochschule.] He had evoked considerable enthusiasm with a technique of variable metres, influencing Daniel Jones, especially in his sonata for timpani solo. Blacher visited the composition class in Manchester and was most encouraging (as Hermann Scherchen was not when he came there!).

13. [*Songs of Babel*, Op. 1 (1951); Piano Sonata, Op. 2 (1951–2); Fantasias for Clarinet and Piano, Op. 3 (1954).]

The Messiaen Class

I am not sure whether this is in fact about Messiaen or whether it is about myself at the time [1955–6] when I was a member of Messiaen's class at the Paris Conservatoire. But it may well be that to write about something as technical as the proceedings of a composition class will throw some light not only on Messiaen himself as a composer, but also upon the nature of his influence on a younger generation of composers. Much has already been written about Messiaen's class, but little of it accords with my own recollections of him or it.

My father gave the first English performance of the *Turangalîla-symphonie* in 1953. As a student in Manchester I had become acquainted with some of Messiaen's music – the *Préludes*, *Visions de l'amen*, *Vingt regards* and the *Ascension* – and in Richard Hall's composition class we had studied (and tried to imitate) the ideas contained in *Technique de mon langage musicale*. But this perform-ance made a huge impact upon me (and upon English musical life in general). It was a marvellous concert, given in the Royal Festival Hall by the London Symphony Orchestra as part of a series of important modern works, promoted by the BBC (Leonard Isaacs, the producer, it is said, lost his job as a result). Yvonne Loriod and Maurice Martenot were the soloists in the *Turangalîla-symphonie*. I have rarely witnessed, in London at least, a work which so divided an audience, at once arousing enormous enthusiasm and considerable distaste. The tone of the press reception was summed up in one of the by-lines, which described Messiaen as 'Madman or Mystic?'. The press was quick to seize upon the apparent vul-garities of the style, but not so quick to evaluate the genuine innovations contained there.

After the performance I was taken along to a gathering at the home of Felix Aprahamian in Muswell Hill, at which Messiaen

Fig. 1. Messiaen extracted this analytic example from the development section of the last movement of Mozart Symphony No. 41 K551. It demonstrates his figuring and explanation of what he considered harmonically 'equivocal' chords. These, he would say, 'cause a shadow to fall over the music'. (A transcription is provided in the Appendix on p. 307.)

was present, and there, among other things, we played a strange clapping game,[1] suggested by Messiaen and apparently discovered by him on his travels in Papua, New Guinea (where he had also found inspiration for his *Île de feu I* and *II*[2]). Later that evening Yvonne Loriod played the whole of Boulez's Second Piano Sonata, which was, in the small confines of the drawing-room, a stupendous noise. I was, for the second time that evening, completely overwhelmed, not least because, when she had finished playing, the piano was covered with blood. She had cut her finger on a key, and had not stopped but continued to the very end – a kind of persistence typical of both Messiaen and Loriod, as I was later to discover, and a quality important in explaining the development of Messiaen's composition (and the more observable when one particularly lacks it oneself!). On the spot I determined to become a pupil of this man, to see if I too could learn to 'draw blood' by my composition.

I duly turned up at the Salle Gounod of the Paris Conservatoire in the rue de Madrid. It was so called because of the bust of the composer which stood on a plinth behind the lecturer's stand. When, in the course of the classes, it grew dark, the reflection of the bust in the window made it seem that the composer was looking in at us, never entirely approvingly. The classes took place three times a week, on Tuesdays, Thursdays and Saturdays, from four to eight in the evening without any break. We sat round a table, about fifteen pupils, with Messiaen at one end. About ten of the students were French, coming through the classes of the Conservatoire, and the remainder visitors to France, at this particular time all from America, Canada and Britain. The class had been called Musical Analysis, but at this time was called, rather pretentiously some felt, Musical Philosophy, in order to allow Messiaen to generalise and widen the topics discussed. There was a considerable disparity in standards between the French students, often prizewinners from the composition classes and thus very distinguished technically, but in many cases unaware at the time of the special talents of Messiaen himself, and the more motivated but more dubiously equipped students, like myself, who had come especially for him.

As a result there was a certain amount of tension between the teacher, the French students and the more motley crew of foreign visitors. This was partly due to the teacher's extreme impatience with those who could not speak French at a reasonable speed. We were, consequently, made to feel that we were boring everybody. But it also resulted from the great differences in standards. The French student best known today, as a composer and conductor, was Gilbert Amy, who was a *premier prix* of Milhaud's composition class, and who at that time wrote what we, the more technically dubious avant gardists, described disparagingly as 'mi-Fauré mi-Franck' (a description taken from the rubric of one of Messiaen's own exercises in stylistic composition). I had been to Darmstadt, had been performed there,[3] and thought I was coming to the most advanced composition class in Europe. So I was a bit scornful of the French students, who, though extremely able, seemed nevertheless to have no idea what was happening in the world. The best composer in the class (and also the nicest man), in my opinion, was a former pupil of Varèse, the Canadian Gilles Tremblay. I think Messiaen shared this view.

The first impression of the class was disappointing, partly because Messiaen, whom, in my adolescent fantasy, I had seen as some sort of dangerous revolutionary in the mould of the Second Viennese School, turned out to have conservative, even bureaucratic tendencies. The very first hours of the class consisted of a reading of the 'Règlements du Conservatoire', which took me very much by surprise. He spent the rest of the time dictating a syllabus which, though it was not taught in all its detail each year, is still worth recalling, as it gives a valuable insight not only into French thinking but also into his own musical personality.

First, he said, we were to talk about Psychology, which consisted of Acoustics, Memory, Time and Imagination. Then, Physiology: physiology of the ear and the 'effects' (*pouvoir*) of music, which at that time aroused a certain ironic mirth (as reflected in my notebook). This led directly to the 'Basis of Music in Nature' (acoustic properties, periodicity, rhythm in nature, the stars, the tides, the seasons, the movements of waves and mountain chains, 'natural melody', birdsong, the sound of wind and water). If an English composer had been interested in any one of these things, as indeed some were, it would have been regarded, certainly in the positivistic ethos of that time, as an extramusical concern, at best, something of biographical and general cultural interest – as opposed to the 'real' and technical musical concern with harmony, counterpoint or form. But here, as I was to find out throughout my year with Messiaen, such things were all bound together. There were often very surprising leaps from general observations about natural phenomena, described quite impressionistically, to purely musical ideas. So, clearly, it was not possible to ignore or at least categorise Messiaen's interests as 'beside the point' musically. For him, and this he perpetually emphasised to us, there was no dividing line between the observable world and the microcosm of music.

Having talked about the basis of music in Nature, he turned to 'Human Music'. First came rhythm and accent – Greek and Hindu rhythms, 'irrational values' – then ancient and exotic modes (again Greek and Hindu) and pentatonicism. There followed the 'Ethnic Study of Music': antiquity and exoticism, world folklore, South America, China, Japan, Mongolia and Korea, Hungarian and Russian folksong, and finally Gregorian chant, which remarkably enough came under the same heading.

The section devoted to 'Musical Analysis' consisted of a long and fairly comprehensive list of works, some of which were and some of which were not studied that year. At the end of the year, candidates for the *prix* (the degrees of the Conservatoire) were required to write a thesis which had to be defended before a jury of French composers. I wrote (and defended) a study of the finale of the Jupiter Symphony, based on Simon Sechter's essay.

The year more or less followed the same general plan, although some of the more abstruse-sounding scientific subjects, which when treated nowadays assume a considerable preliminary knowledge, were here dealt with quite practically, as if they were ear-training.

In fact all the classes we had, whatever the subject matter, were constantly interrupted (if that is the right word) by practical tests. The French students, all of whom had completed the study of solfège, were extremely versatile here. They had very highly developed senses of both pitch and duration. They were not just better than me; they were in a completely different league. In the middle of an analysis Messiaen would go to the piano, mention a student's name, and ask him to identify the pitch levels of a chord or an arpeggiation, or the constituents of a rhythm. The French students could inevitably rattle these off, while I was still stumbling to identify the bass note. The repertoire of ear-training included Schoenberg's *Erwartung* (in which Messiaen particularly admired the chords built on alternate perfect fourths and augmented fourths, with major thirds to break the cycle), Stockhausen's *Klavierstücke I–IV* and, for rhythmic purposes, Jolivet's solo flute pieces. The only examples I got right were the rhythmic ones, which one could work out with the mind on the basis of likelihood.[4] Messiaen was absolutely predictable: more than any musician I've ever come across he had very strong aural preferences. He had an extraordinarily refined ear himself,[5] and attached to this was a set of absolute likes and dislikes. He liked certain chords or even durations, and disliked others, purely physically, not according to how or where they occurred in a piece. For him they were, as he says in another context, *personnages*: they had personalities of their own. The effect of this on the ear-training was that he always played the chords he liked. It was quite possible, after a short time, to predict what he would play at any given moment. For me a moment of truth came when once I was actually able to identify a chord correctly before he had played it. He was surprised.

The pieces of music analysed were chosen from a varied repertoire, beginning with Beethoven's Fifth Symphony. This first session came as rather a shock to me. In London and Manchester at that time, ideas which were later to become established as methods of musical analysis were already floating around. There were people talking about motivic and even structural, Schenkerian analysis, and I had become familiar with some of these ideas from my father (as indeed had my co-student in Paris, John Carewe, who had written a most interesting Schenkerian study of the introductions to Beethoven symphonies). So when Messiaen pointed to me to answer the question, 'What is the form of the first movement of Beethoven's Fifth Symphony?', I thought to myself, 'That's a profound question', and remained silent. I did not dare venture an answer in that environment. Messiaen repeated the question, this time addressing one of the French students. Quick as lightning, the answer came back: 'Sonata form with two subjects.' 'Bien, Monsieur' – and so much for that. I jumped to the conclusion that the analysis to be received was superficial, but this first negative impression was soon contradicted by the session spent on *Prélude à l'après-midi d'un faune*. It was this and the other pieces of Debussy that came under his scrutiny which made the most profound impression upon me. The strength of his analysis lay in his ability to combine his own different interests in a single study. The harmonic analysis was purely academical, following the French tradition, in which each individual chord is analysed. There is little overall interest in the long-term workings of tonality, nor in the relation of individual phenomena to the whole. Each chord is identified according to its constituent tones and then described, as, for example, a dominant seventh (implying but not necessarily receiving a tonal resolution), a modal chord or pair of chords implying a mode, a whole-tone chord, etc. Analysis thus progresses from chord to chord. It seemed to me then, as it does now, that there is limited validity in this approach to harmony in music such as the Viennese classics, which were obviously conceived in a different spirit, but that it reveals a great deal about music by French composers and, curiously enough, about music that particularly interested them, such as Wagner.

More striking and personal was Messiaen's ability to analyse melody and also to relate the music to literary and visual images. It's best simply to repeat individual examples he gave. In Debussy's *Pelléas et Mélisande* Messiaen proceeded from scene to scene, explaining the relationship of text to musical setting, scene to harmonic development. Some of his points were so vivid that they have remained with me over the years. For example, at one moment Golaud says, 'La joie, on n'en a pas tous les jours' (joy, one doesn't have that every day). Messiaen pointed out how Debussy places this high in the tessitura, emphasising the banality as much as the melancholy of the sentiment from the mouth of an old man, and found the repetition in the melodic phrase deliberately trite, thereby characterising the intended banality. This is musical realism; and, like Musorgsky, Messiaen was absolutely committed to it. So that a waterfall or a bird was, as far as Messiaen was able to realise it, a real waterfall or a real bird.

For me this constituted a difficulty: I was no great naturalist (despite passing my six birds and six trees recognition test as a Wolfcub), and could not take this essential ingredient of his composing entirely seriously. I could not imagine how one could, as it were, compose from nature without falling into a bathos, analogous to Strauss's *Symphonia domestica* or Honegger's *Pacific 231*. Messiaen retorted, in response to my ignorant tittering, that for his part he certainly would not take me for a walk in the forest, as my giggling would upset the birds. But I had to realise the superficiality of my view when it came to the premiere at Boulez's Marigny concerts of *Oiseaux exotiques*,[6] which, as we now know, is a classic of transitional Messiaen, moving from the first style of *Turangalîla* to the works of his later maturity. It came after he had completed his one great and influential flirtation with 'structuralist' music, the group of pieces including *Quatre études de rythme* and the *Livre d'orgue*, especially in the domain of duration and timbre, which had had an important influence on nascent Darmstadt avant gardism. But the new composers of this avant garde, Boulez and Stockhausen, at least, most certainly influenced him. But now he was to some extent distancing himself from these younger composers, many of whom had been his pupils.

The students in the class asked Messiaen to tell us something about his new piece, a thing he immediately refused to do. He never talked directly about his own work (though it certainly seems to me now that he was talking about it implicitly all the time, and that is why I am writing this account of his class), and scorned those who did. 'What are you writing now?' he would mimic, and answer, 'I've just reached the bridge passage of the slow movement of my *tel-ou-tel oeuvre*.' 'Listen and use your ears,' he said. At that time he even deplored the following of scores in performance, believing they got in the way of true perception of the sound. He arrived at the following class with an even larger mountain of books than he normally brought with him. These turned out to be ornithological treatises of various sorts, and the lecture, lavishly illustrated at the piano, was a factual description of the countries of origin, habitat, physical appearance and song of a large number of birds. Some pages contained Red Cardinals, Blue Popes and a 'Singer from South America' which, as I recall, aroused some mirth among us. However, when the performance came, we realised he had taken us at our word and provided us with what he thought an appropriate introduction to his new work. What he had played on the piano were none other than his own transcriptions of bird-song, taken down by him all over the world and combined into what he probably considered an idealised, but nevertheless true, portrayal of nature. He often said that he found it odd that painters went out to paint landscapes while musicians did not. Musicians should use their ears in the way painters used their eyes. But he could not really be drawn about the music itself. I was bowled over by the piece then (as I am now), not only because of the extraordinary colours and the masterly instrumental writing, but also, more conventionally, by the continuity and form, which seemed quite original. To this day, few commentators have paid attention to the way in which the dawn choruses, consisting of many independent and overlapping parts, have been built up rhyth-mically and harmonically, and no wonder, because here technique at the highest level hides technique. You hear the final harmony and the balancing combinations of voices, but you cannot say how it's done. Questions about such matters elicited no response at all from Messiaen.

I learned an important lesson about composition here. Mes-siaen liked to pretend that he was merely transcribing what he heard when he went to the forests, and I believe we were being encouraged to do likewise. In reality it hardly mattered musically which particular bird he thought he was transcribing; his inventiveness and supreme musical personality revealed itself in the way he set down his transcriptions. Imagine the famous 'Epode' dawn chorus from *Chronochromie* if it had been composed by, say, Schoenberg or Prokofiev: the inspiring birds might well have been the same ones, but there would have been no similarity of musical effect.

He would never talk of such things, but he was prepared to talk about philosophical and psychological aspects of the work. He did this by reference to the work of Gaston Bachelard,[7] whose books had greatly influenced him. In Bachelard he had particularly admired *L'air et les songes*, which deals with the symbolism of flight. At that time I did not understand the phenomenological nature of his thinking, and saw it as little more than a collection of colourful poetic images. But I was wrong. Later, when I came to read the work of the philosopher Vladimir Jankélévitch,[8] I came to understand the way in which observed images could be categorised and broken down into sets of minute variants: for instance, in the way Debussy portrays falling water, Mélisande's hair, a tennis ball bouncing away, by means of various kinds of falling arpeggiation. The greater the differentiations of detail, the more like a detailed musical analysis the result. But characteristically such inquiry takes the form of a catalogue, with subheadings and increasingly detailed distinctions. A fine example of this mode of musical inquiry is contained in the comparative study of Debussy's and Fauré's harmony by Messiaen's pupil Françoise Gervais.[9] Think of the theme of *L'après-midi d'un faune*, which Messiaen said fell too slowly and rose too quickly. By observing its continuity and shape, and the variations of mood and setting to which it is submitted, we may obtain an understanding of it as a whole, without reference to any *a priori* notion of musical background structure or depth. Messiaen recognised no idea of musical levels: all was surface. To some of our primitive Schenkerian ideas, badly expressed in poor French – we might say: 'Mais,

Maître, le *Urlinie* dit . . . (that such or such a note is structurally significant)' – Messiaen would respond quizzically, 'Qui est ce Monsieur Urlinie dont on parle?' He had no knowledge, as few had at that time, of the seminal works of musical theory, and he was not, in fact, to any great extent aware of non-French thinking.

Probably the aspect of Messiaen's teaching that made the strongest impression upon me was his concern with time and duration, a concern which seems to be unique in the history of recent music, certainly of recent Western music. Being a realist, and concerned with the real world, he perceived real time: clock time. We spent a long time doing tests to develop our consciousness of time. He would bang on the table and, after a longish silence – possibly twenty seconds – bang again. We were expected to identify the duration between the two bangs and compare it with others often only minutely longer or shorter than the first. This was done by counting, but I think he himself supposed that he could, and that we might learn to, recognise durations of silence as if they had specific characteristics (at least when they were constructed as short chains). The longer the silences, the harder it was to perceive their durations. This kind of test was locked together in Messiaen's mind with number. He was concerned with the Golden Mean and Fibonacci series (among other series), which he knew from the books of Matila Ghyka.[10] But, as always with him, numerology was neither merely mathematically nor merely symbolically fascinating. As with natural phenomena, numbers had personalities, some of which he liked and some of which he disliked. Thirteen was not just one more than twelve. It was a prime, with a personality of its own, a different thing. He would rarely use durations of even numbers as examples for us.

In analysing music, he implied that a sequence of absolute durations could be in its way as expressive as could be a melody of pitch levels. So in 'Scarbo', from Ravel's *Gaspard de la nuit*, he drew our attention to the passage beginning in bar 121,[11] which he analysed as a sequence of durations. In conventional, 'metrical' music, he observed duration without regard for metre or accent, or regarded accent as the beginning of a duration and continuing silence as resonating sound, the whole all together comprising a single durational identity. This was the principle behind his analysis of the *Rite of Spring*.[12]

Such ideas are of great importance for the understanding of Messiaen's own work. When he selects a sequence of durations, as for example in the *Mode de valeurs et des intensités*, or in *Livre d'orgue*, he composes them by arranging them in a specific order. The result is to be understood as a kind of melody of duration, coloured by chord and repeating figuration. In this way time is 'coloured', as is implied by the title of his – in my estimation – greatest orchestral composition, *Chronochromie* (1959–60).

From this notion of duration, or side by side with it, arises the concept of the rhythmic cell, so important in his analysis of the *Rite of Spring*, in his own work and in the early work of Boulez. A 'cell' is not, as for example in metrical music, or even as in Berg's *Hauptrhythmus*, a rhythmic motif, but a complex of durations to be constructed and continued independently of metre. By analogy with feet in prosody, cells were built up into lines, with caesura and abbreviated final, and into verses, combining like with variant and unlike. These cells were not only categorised according to durations (long and short) but were assumed to have personalities, by analogy with those Greek prosodic identities that had names – dactyl, anapaest – or those Hindu rhythms with exotic and evocative names which referred to qualities and aspects of the real world, and which Messiaen found in the article on Hindu music in the *Encyclopédie Lavignac* of the Paris Conservatoire. These Hindu 'cells' had for Messiaen the advantage not only of being an example of a symbolic system but also of containing durations arithmetically related as two to three to five.

The study of duration naturally included the study of silence. But silence was not to be evaluated merely as negative sound or as duration. In music, different types of silence could be distinguished. Messiaen had seven kinds of silence. I can remember only the silence that precedes sound (anticipatory silence), the silence that follows a sounding event (resonating silence), the silence that is interpolated rhetorically between two sounds, and the empty silence that is indeed a negative sound. I don't know where the other three went.

Messiaen was very much attracted to lists and catalogues, and found categorisation a useful aid to his poetic thought. This even extended to a visit to a Chinese restaurant. By Chinese, or today's London, standards, this was a fairly touristy place, not far from the old Opéra. Messiaen always ate slowly, and, as we worked our way through various vaguely Chinese dishes, he liked, together with Gilles Tremblay, to see how many separate taste experiences he could distinguish in one mouthful of food. In Asia he particularly admired, and took as his example, the meditative perception of sequences of tiny detail; he had special affection for his Chinese and Japanese pupils.

But Messiaen was, both in the restaurant and in his more serious concerns, perfectly satisfied to perceive isolated events, or to imagine and compose them. He did not, like most other composers of our time, feel any desire to construct them into organic wholes. This is particularly noticeable in comparing his works with those of the young Boulez that are influenced by him. Inevitably and systematically Boulez takes something that in Messiaen stands on its own in free association or in counterpoint with musical ideas drawn from quite other sources, and gives it a functional significance as a matrix. It was always tempting, and then frustrating, to try to find a key to Messiaen's work by assuming that there was an intentional system just below the perceptible surface. In the fifties and sixties, the concept of matrix-structure was so firmly implanted in our minds that really it was assumed that it, and only it, constituted the interest and ultimately the value of music. It was this that drove Messiaen away from the Darmstadt avant garde, whom, in an unguarded moment, he described as '*tous fous*'. In the discussion of music he felt no urge to try to combine the different parameters by means of which music – his own and other people's – existed. Here was harmony, here formal counterpoint, here durations. They all coexisted, in Cage's telling formula, as if different objects in the same room. But they did not necessarily have anything to do with each other, or, if they had, it was not a fact of any particular interest or value.

Perhaps the most surprising and even shocking aspect of the Messiaen class, for a young man coming to it – and expecting it to be the equivalent of what one imagined (probably quite wrongly) a Schoenberg class would have been like in 1916 – was the absolute and unbroken continuity it evinced between tradition and the study of the most advanced concepts and sounds. For Messiaen there was no split between the tradition of the French organ school, of which he formed (possibly the greatest) part, and the new concerns with which he was in sympathy. He often referred to the *Traité d'orgue* of Marcel Dupré, and to his 'secular' teachers, Maurice Emmanuel and Paul Dukas. In dealing with the most complex new music, he saw no reason to learn new techniques or concepts of analysis, and was quite satisfied to listen and describe what he had heard in the technical language he was accustomed to use. I laughed at the fact that he proposed to deal with compositions of the Second Viennese School, dodecaphonic or otherwise, as if each chord could be catalogued by the rules of the harmony book (added sixths and the lot). But then, why not? One may learn a great deal about the Berg Violin Concerto by examining its row structure, but it may be that to listen, perceive and describe, in whatever language one considers appropriate, is just as good a way of approaching the unique nature of a masterpiece.

Messiaen did not really appear to me to have much in common with the composers of the post-Schoenbergian, or post-Webernian, avant garde. He seemed to be part of an unbroken tradition, and one cannot imagine that the issue of his relation to the past constituted the kind of guilt-laden if fertile problem that one knows it was for Schoenberg and even for Brahms (to mention two composers for whom Messiaen had only lukewarm enthusiasm, if not actual dislike). At the time he seemed to me to stand, in relation to modern music, rather as the Douanier Rousseau stands in relation to Picasso: a 'naif' and a lover of the brightly coloured exotic, perhaps, but not one to be ignored for his novel ideas about pictorial space. Messiaen recognised his affinity most of all with

Varèse, whom I heard him describe as 'my brother, who does for the urban landscape what I try to do with Nature'.

I think that the year I spent in Paris was a critical and unhappy time for him, for personal as well as artistic reasons. Face to face with his sometimes obstreperous students and opinionated hangers-on, he was even reduced to tears. We sat in silence for long periods, especially after an aggressive attempt by one of us to argue with him. Here we were, before one of the most perfect musicians of our times, combative and argumentative, in tense, unbroken silence. And he would say, 'Gentlemen, let us not argue like this. We are all in a profound night, and I don't know where I am going; I'm as lost as you.' He had achieved a great deal at that time, but he had no defences. He had accepted no systems. As an artist he was stark naked and incredibly humble. We were just a bunch of adolescents. But in the years since then, when I have gone my own way, I remember that: that a man of that kind of ability, of genius, needed no positions or systems but retained always his new and open relationship to sound, and a humility which many would like to have but few can hope to achieve.

(1988)

1. I describe this in detail in 'Music as Communication': see below, pp. 220–221.

2. These are the first two of the *Quatre études de rhythme* (1949), to which I will return below.

3. See above, p. 24, note 3.

4. Superficially Messiaen's rhythmic tests were not unlike those of Hindemith's *Practical Musicianship*. But Messiaen particularly liked durations involving portions of irrational groupings. In *La mer* he would stress the last beat of a triplet tied to a quaver as a durational entity. The *locus classicus* of such 'durations' was for him the *5 incantations* (1936) for solo flute by André Jolivet. 'To get the right answer', I always found it helpful (and still do) to imagine the possible written notation, because in reality the durations Messiaen particularly liked could only be perceived contextually, a view he strenuously opposed, believing as he did in the absolute identity of a durational value.

5. The only more extraordinary demonstration of 'good ear' that I ever met was that of Alois Hába, who liked to analyse the exact pitches (to the sixth of a tone) going up an ordinarily tuned piano. Fat lot of good it did him!

6. See above, p. 2.

7. Gaston Bachelard (1884–1962). French epistemologist and philosopher of science. 'Scientific hypotheses, and even scientific facts, do not present themselves

passively to the patient investigator, but are created by him. The investigator's reasoning and the natural world on which it operates together constitute a second nature over and above the crudely empirical one . . . He saw both technological and imaginative thinking as issuing from reverie and emotion into practical expression. His works on the psychological significance of the four elements, earth, air, fire and water, illustrate this . . . Our science and our poetry have a common origin accessible only to psychoanalysis.' Colin Smith in *The Encyclopedia of Philosophy*, ed. Paul Edwards et al. (New York and London: Macmillan and The Free Press, 1967), vols. 1–2, p. 234.

8. [Vladimir Jankélévitch (b. 1903). Author of *Debussy et le mystère* (Neuchâtel, 1949), *La musique et l'ineffable* (Paris, 1961), *Fauré et l'inexprimable* (Paris, 1974) and other works.]

9. [Françoise Gervais, *Étude comparée des langages harmoniques de Fauré et de Debussy* (Paris: Éditions de la Revue musicale, 1971).]

10. Matila C. Ghyka, *Esthétique des proportions dans la nature et dans les arts* (Paris: Gallimard, 1927), and *Le nombre d'or (Rites et rhythmes pythagoriciens dans le developpement de la civilization occidentale*, 2 vols (Paris: Gallimard, 1952).

11. Durand edition, p. 26, second system.

12. 'Le rythme chez Igor Strawinsky', *La revue musicale*, No. 191 (1939), pp. 331ff.

4

Poetics of my Music

I wish to deal with things to do with the making of music, and not primarily with questions which arise from listening to it. The majority of those who are not professional musicians, or (even more narrowly) professional composers, will ask why this should be so. 'Surely', they might say, 'it is simpler and better to leave questions of craft to craftsmen and to attempt to study music as an aesthetic experience.' One may indeed be uncertain whether 'craft' questions can have any independent validity or interest for the non-composer; and, even if they have, whether these can alter the way he hears and what the music means to him. But the problem of a composer is that he is often unable to identify the reactions and so-called problems of his public with what he knows to have been his experience while composing. So he may well doubt 'what the papers say' (without necessarily subscribing to the idea that they are all fools) and begin to feel that, technical matters apart, there is very little to be said about, at least, new music – except 'I like it' or 'I don't like it'. The kind of general talk with which it is customary to surround new music, and which generally has to do with extramusical matters anyway, is, I feel, an impossibility because, unlike listener or critic, the composer cannot separate his own work from the experience of making it. He knows in his heart of hearts that an abundance of factors comes into play when a piece is made, and that the final form in which he delivers it generally falls far short of its original aspirations; consequently, he may feel that expository talk always disguises the work and helps to form distorted impressions.

One would like to convey to an interested audience what it is like to struggle with the material (and where the rewards come).

But here words fail one; and every time one tries, one is aware of the impossibility and, finally, the absurdity of trying to re-create an experience.

What, then? If we are not to talk about experience arising from the listening to music, what is there to talk about? What can a composer reasonably ask of his listener in the way of preliminary knowledge? Every composer is aware of problems that arise in the making of music, and there are attitudes and divergencies of opinion about priorities and in matters of taste. But these only arise out of the interaction of technical procedure and material. Commentators and critics talk about atonality, serialism, aleatorics and other -isms and -ologies as if they were familiar to everybody. You will find such terms included in magazines lazily read in doctors' waiting-rooms. But what does this mean? Do people really hear with deeper understanding if they know to what ideological faction a piece allegedly subscribes? All the extramusical trappings may colour our aesthetic impressions. But in the end, surely, we should limit our researches to the notes and the way these are arranged. It is in these that music exists.

I want to talk here about the relationship between what Schoenberg called heart and brain in music. I want to try to isolate the portion of the music that results most directly from the creative imagination – what we normally call the 'musical idea' – and give some indication of how such an idea relates to its wider context in the stuff of music. This will bring to our attention a special problem of our own times, a problem which has not been frequently discussed but which is a begged question in much exposition of contemporary problems: namely the difference, if there is one, between spontaneous musical gesture and choice in the generating of musical form. To illustrate these things, I have isolated a few technical procedures to do with the relating of musical ideas to musical space, or, to put it another way, with the interrelationship of the personal and the general. I shall attempt to describe these procedures in some detail and try to hint at the way in which they contribute to outward musical forms. (These procedures, or compositional operations, are, as far as I know, my

own property and not anybody else's, though they derive principally from the work of Schoenberg and Webern and do
consequently indicate basic agreement with the attitudes of these
men to their materials and their traditions.) In doing this, I propose,
in the case of each of the selected procedures, to outline a historical
introduction and only then to isolate the precise operation.

2

The imagination expresses itself in the form of gestures and defined
musical ideas. We may isolate a musical idea, or 'bit', by identifying
its characteristics, but at the same time recognise that this 'bit' is
also a part of a whole. Take a piano keyboard as a metaphor for
musical space. The distance from bottom to top (as we would
say, although these do not correspond to physical thresholds of
differentiability) may be divided in a variety of ways: into octaves,
into cycles of fourths and fifths, and into tones and semitones. Nor
is the usual arrangement of our piano regular, for it is made to
converge upon a centre. This arrangement of sound-space is a
historical development which need not necessarily have taken the
form it does. One can perceive this total space most simply by
hearing all the notes sounding simultaneously.

The historical development of music does not, however, suggest
that musicians were aware of a theoretical abstraction like sound-
space-time, which is, after all, a purely physical phenomenon. Like
researchers and explorers in other fields, composers and instrumentalists worked outwards from a limited area. Even today, the vast
majority of those who play an instrument, string or wind, know
only a tiny number of the sounds that can be drawn from it. At
no time did a music exist which started from a perception of a
total space to be filled in and divided up, in the way in which one
supposes a painter might initially block out the limited dimensions
of a canvas. Sound-space was organised and reorganised from a
centre, into regular systems, by means of calculations such as those
that produce cycles of fourths and fifths and ultimately the regular

tonal system with its manifold hierarchies of triadic relationships. However, the development of such organisations resulted not only from the speculations of musico-scientists, but also from the practices of ordinary music-making. For example, the human voice has relatively few natural divisions in the projecting of a continuous sound-space. But the invention of the simplest pipe with holes imposes discrete steps and a system of regular divisions, with intervals, a well-defined lower threshold and a practically definable upper one.

This simple relationship to musical space gives rise to a considerable superstructure. Take a fairly simple example from classical usage. In the classical eighteenth-century orchestra, instrumental groups are built up in a regular manner, with compensatory adjustments designed to create an evenly balanced instrumentation. The total sound-space mirrors, in augmentation, the structure of the sound-space of each instrument, i.e. a middle range with extensions. This is represented in classical pieces by the formal unit known as the *ritornello*, in which each instrument plays approximately in its middle range. The classical composer gives a function to this necessary general sounding of the whole and characterises it with musical invention that lacks individuality and might almost be interchangeable from piece to piece.

In the exposition of the classical symphony we find not only a sequence of themes, their developments and restatements (*ritornelli*), as is customarily observed, but also a succession of vertical partitions of the total sound-space. The music is likely to be most individual at those places where the sound-space is most characteristically partitioned and, conversely, least individual where the sound-space is least partitioned (that is, in the *tutti* and *ritornello* sections). A musical idea in a classical piece is in any case merely a few notes with some internal repetition and some characteristic rhythmic form. It must not be too long, because it has to be easily recognisable, and by definition it contains no kind of development. The important thing is that it possesses a flavour, a lilt, even a rhetorical character. It may be a whole melody, but it may also be a short signal.

Where does this come from? It is hard to say. Some believe that music relates to itself and that inventing is a process of half-remembering. Something like this must have been in the mind of Anton Ehrenzweig, who derived an idea from Ernst Gombrich in suggesting that the background, semi-articulated figurations and motifs of one artist might provide the foreground ideas of another;[1] and in his last book he cites an experiment which he and I once made connecting *Le marteau sans maître* by Boulez with *La mer* by Debussy in this way.[2] I am not quite sure about this; but we can say that a musical idea, like the initial factor of a series, is a beginning which has no 'left-hand side' or, more appropriately for music, no 'before it'. Because it has no 'before it' it differs essentially from everything else – except another new idea – that may happen in the course of a piece of music.

In order to survive, this spontaneous gesture of the imagination must worry the composer until he is able to find a continuation for it. This stage of the process has been nicely described by Stravinsky. He says:

> Composing, for me, is putting into an order a certain number of these sounds according to certain interval-relationships. This activity leads to a search for the centre upon which the series of sounds involved in my undertaking should converge. Thus if a centre is given, I shall have to find a combination that converges upon it. If on the other hand, an as yet unoriented combination has been found, I shall have to determine the centre towards which it should lead. The discovery of this centre suggests to me the solution of my problem. It is thus that I satisfy my very marked taste for such a kind of musical topography.[3]

I would like to put two more composers' views beside this penetrating description of Stravinsky's. They indicate two further aspects of the matter.

Tchaikovsky, writing in 1888 and reacting – the context suggests, negatively – to a performance of Brahms's Double Concerto, also speaks of the nature of spontaneous melodic invention. He comments, disparagingly, that the majority of the Germans construct their melodies with the understanding rather than discovering them intuitively. 'Brahms juxtaposes two fourths to obtain a theme and Wagner deduces the motifs of the Nibelungen from the perfect chord. Even Beethoven constructs rather than sings.'[4] This may be considered a somewhat jaundiced point of view, but it says something about the difference between spontaneous invention and calculated choice of musical material.

The musical idea is expressive insofar as it is spontaneous and irregular, on the one hand, and insofar as it is self-contained, itself a form, rather than an element of a series (such as a scale or an arpeggio), on the other. Talking about the primacy of the idea, or motif, Webern says:

> To develop everything . . . from *one* principal idea! That's the highest coherence. Everything is doing the same thing – just as it is in the music of the Netherlanders where the theme is sung simultaneously in all possible variations, augmentations and diminutions. But how to do this? That is where art begins. Always thematicism, thematicism, thematicism![5]

Webern always emphasises the importance of the musical idea. He sees here a characteristically Goethean relationship of artist to material as man to the natural world. He quotes Karl Kraus on language, from *Die Fackel*:

> Everything in it can be literally taken as applying to music. Karl Kraus says in this essay how important it would be for people to be at home with the *material* that they are constantly using, so long as they are alive and able to talk. In the last sentence he even says about language, 'Let man learn to serve her!' Kraus says – and note this very carefully, it's immensely important and we must clearly be agreed about it – that it would be foolish to set about dealing with this material, which we handle from our earliest years, as if the value involved were aesthetic. Not, then, because we want to be artistic snobs and dilettantes. What he says is that our

concern with language and the secrets of language would be a moral gain.[6]

The spontaneous expression of the imagination, the melodic idea, does not seem to alter its form significantly through the ages. There is not such a great difference between a fourteenth-century melodic idea and one by Webern. But the organisations of the total space undergo continual change, and, as in other fields, character-istic and arbitrarily irregular orderings are gradually rationalised and replaced by symmetrical and automatic networks. The idea sends out shoots which reproduce itself; and this process expresses an overall ordering which implies a centre, or a network of com-measurables and relationships of which the generating, original idea is now merely a bit.

The technical history of our music can be told as the ways in which composers have increased the influence of their ideas from foreground relationships to the most trivial aspects of background. First we have horizontally expressed, melodic-rhythmic ideas. Gradually these come to extend to the vertical dimension. The famous *Tristan* chord stands as an idea in its own right and is used as such by Wagner. However we explain it, in its many contexts, it is an independent musical idea. So are the Scriabin *Ur*-chord and Schoenberg's chord of fourths in his first Chamber Symphony, which are imitations of its effect. Here is an idea which to the greatest extent determines the continuation of the music; and while it destroys older and more familiar ways of organising music, it suggests the possibility of new ways of extending its influence on its continuations.

3

Some composers are able to express themselves and even find intuitive new solutions within an inherited musical framework. They have the advantage of a common practice against which to work, and their music has a greater chance of success in its own day. When they fail, they are described as eclectic or neo-archaic by their critics. Other composers feel a conflict between traditional expression and the inwardly changing nature of a developing style of writing. Many of the most important composers of this century, from Debussy and Schoenberg to Webern, Messiaen and a few of our own contemporaries, have struggled and do struggle to create expressive forms in the traditional aspect of music while at the same time realising the changing requirements of the material.

The eclectic composer and the explorer-type avant gardist have it in common that they concern themselves with the manner of presentation. In a sense, they may see 'old objects with new eyes' or find the contemporary relevance of new and unprecedented sound-materials or ways of working them. In either case the ego is of great importance. These attitudes tend to provide the fireworks of our musical culture – and often burn out quickly. Often they have changed the sensibility of their own time before they do so.

Yet I feel that these attitudes can only provide the new music of young men. The breakthrough in all dimensions which characterises the mature style of the great masters from Bach to Webern is achieved in another way. The problems of language, meaning and form must remain central to the composer, and he has constantly to set himself up against the history of his own art. At the same time he has to retain the freshness and spontaneity of intention that made him a composer in the first place.

For some time now, from Schoenberg onwards, a number of composers have been dealing with their situation in terms of the relationship between traditional modes of organisation and the operating of the twelve-tone or dodecaphonic technique. Today, this might legitimately be called a system of composition rather than merely a technique (it is certainly not a style). The technique was evolved by Schoenberg and others to deal with a musical situation where tonality as a background organising force had almost ceased to function. In fact, the technique of using up all twelve notes of the chromatic scale before repeating any of them had appeared long before the formulation of the ordered row. Schoenberg extended the influence of his musical ideas by increasing the amount of thematic variation and derivation; and, more important still, he increased significantly the area where this influence was felt. When he defined the principle of ordering the twelve semitones, it seemed possible that all dimensions of pitch organisation should be subjected to the one principle. Had Schoenberg not been of a particular German Romantic tradition which had already widely extended the concept of a musical idea – had it, for instance, been Stravinsky or Bartók who had formulated this technique – the likelihood is that it would have remained a technique of melodic derivation and not have altered rapidly into a developing system of ordering and partitioning of the total sound-space, operating beside and together with traditional but decaying tonal systems. Schoenberg suggested that the inventing of a twelve-tone row should of itself be the continuation of a spontaneously invented musical gesture. That is, he might invent a little melodic idea of five or six different notes and then continue it with the remaining semitones to make up a full twelve-tone set. Later, this turned into the idea of six different semitones followed by an inversion of these six semitones, the whole adding up to the total twelve – like an antecedent and a consequent in tonal music. Schoenberg explored the characteristics of twelve-tone ordering in the context of tonal and pre-tonal aural habits and conventions: transposition (sequence), inversion and retrograde, antecedent and consequent, leading note. In this way, the initial ordering functions as an idea extending regularly over the whole sound-space but also allowing some of the choices open to the traditional composer. Schoenberg's sketches demonstrate that he did this consciously and that he was aware of some of the applications of hierarchies of transposition and combination that were only formulated theoretically somewhat later.[7] The influence of tonal Romantic practice remains in the way he formulated his musical ideas and in the way he developed them.

Webern did not follow the practice of his teacher. He constructed a twelve-tone row by choosing and combining tiny segments of two, three or four notes which generated a network of symmetrical relationships; and he often made these resemble some of the functions of the tonal system. This divergence of practice reflects not only personality, but a change of situation. Like Schoenberg, however, he cast his inventions in a formal rhythmic pattern in which short motifs, phrases and accompanimental figures may be realised in performance (albeit in a highly fragmentary form) and understood musically as a sequence of ideas together with their continuations and developments – despite the fact that the pitch-level structure of many of his compositions makes it hard to distinguish between the musical idea and the different types of continuation and development. In Webern, as in some pieces of late Brahms, the musical idea *as pitch* is not genuinely expressive because, to put it vulgarly, it is too much like everything else in the piece. The idea is only a combinable segment of the series. This historical-technical – let me say it frankly – defect does not, however, make Webern a lesser figure, precisely because of the compensatory developments of other aspects of his musical invention. Webern is, above all, a rhythmic composer. Fragmentation, analytical orchestration and, above all, the word heighten his rhythmic invention in a unique and magnificent way.

If we examine an arbitrarily constructed ordering or row, we will see that it has certain internal tonal relationships. For example, in the following, the first three notes, the descending semitones F♯–F–E, are followed by a leap up of a fourth to A, and notes 5, 6 and 7 (C–B–A♯) are the same sequence of three adjacent semitones followed by a leap of a minor third up to C♯:

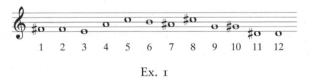

$$1 \quad 2 \quad 3 \quad 4 \quad 5 \quad 6 \quad 7 \quad 8 \quad 9 \quad 10 \quad 11 \quad 12$$

Ex. 1

Transposing the original row an augmented fourth, notes 1, 2 and 3, which are now C–B–A♯ are at once a transposition of the original sequence F♯–F–E and the same as 5, 6 and 7 of the original. Now compare the two orderings. In the original, C–B–A♯ is

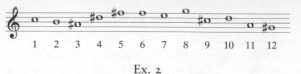

1   2   3   4   5   6   7   8   9   10   11   12

Ex. 2

preceded by an A, a minor third lower than the C, and followed
by a C♯. In the transposition, C–B–A♯ is preceded by a G♯ (taking
the twelfth note as preceding the first in a circular ordering), which
is a major third lower than C, and followed by a D♯, a fourth
higher than A♯.

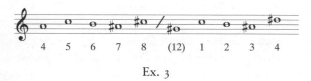

4   5   6   7   8   (12)   1   2   3   4

Ex. 3

The same relationship is reproduced in the corresponding pair
of inversions; the inverted motifs F♯–G–G♯ and C–C♯–D now act
as pivots.

Notes 9 and 10 of the transposed inversion are B and A♯. These
are preceded now by F, a fourth below A♯, but followed again by
D♯.

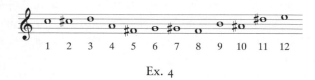

1   2   3   4   5   6   7   8   9   10   11   12

Ex. 4

Together, these three segments combine to make an 'idea'
involving the motif of three adjacent semitones, as a pivot, twice,
with a partial repetition a third time, moving on through the
inverted ordering so that the final note is the same as the first.

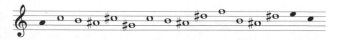

Ex. 5

It exists only where these three forms, or transpositions or inversions of them, are associated in this order. In this way I formulate 'ideas' which are irregular in relation to the symmetrical sound-space mapped out by a twelve-tone row. They generate specific hierarchies and categories of variation and development.

Conversely, I can invent freely (without reference to rows) and build up some analogous network of hierarchies.

Compare this idea with the beginning of the slow-movement melody of the Mozart G minor Symphony. A similar three-element structure (with varying intervals) and the use of notes in common act as a basis for an intervallic structure.

Ex. 6. Mozart, Symphony in G minor, K550, 2nd movement

A considerable number of my own pieces are based on ideas and melodies of this kind, e.g. the opening Cantus of my Violin Concerto (1962):

Ex. 7

From my String Quartet No. 2 (1967):

Ex. 8

69

The thorniest problems of dodecaphonic composition have to do with the vertical combination of sound, that is, harmony. Tonal harmony as a means of regulating the formal structure of music had already weakened by the beginning of this century. There was greater interest in personal and exotic modes, and from them there followed changes and blurrings of the traditional functions of harmony and melody in a dissolved polyphonic idiom. In classical twelve-tone technique, the vertical combination of sounds is considered as horizontal sequencing with a time distance of zero. If two notes which follow each other in the row are performed simultaneously they become a chord. Strictly, a harmonic dimension, with all its important traditional attributes, no longer exists. This way of working caused difficulty, because, as a result of the projection of the tones over the whole sound-space of the traditional orchestra (and other instrumental groupings), the technique became ambiguous. The rotation of tones was too rapid. Schoenberg and Webern attempted to deal with this problem rather in the way a cook uses flour to thicken a sauce. Taking advantage of old rules about doubling, they duplicated and trebled row forms so that a two-note chord automatically thickened into a four-note or a six-note chord. This in itself led to some very remarkable compositional applications, especially in late Webern (Cantata No. 2,[8] fifth movement). But the Viennese composers did not seek to evolve much more than a practical, rule-of-thumb, imitation of functional harmonic practice in the twelve-tone system. Only where vertical sound combinations actively affect what goes on around them (as in the tonal system) can we properly talk of harmony. Less than that, it is just a question of accompaniments, doublings and settings.

When twelve-tone practice was combined with the ideas of modal composers like Messiaen, with their personal but quite systematic ways of generating harmony, real progress was made. Boulez was the first person to put these two traditions together in the formulation of what he called the *bloc sonore*.[9] Earlier attempts in this direction had been made by J. M. Hauer and Ernst Krenek; a contemporary making a similar attempt, at roughly the same

time as Boulez, was George Perle. By a process of intervallic multiplication Boulez generated groups or clusters of notes from the
factors of a single row. He operated them partly according to
principles culled from traditional twelve-tone practice and partly
(and more significantly, I think) according to new principles generated from an observation of the characteristics of the *blocs*
themselves.

I have operated in the following manner. Taking once more the
basic row:

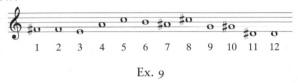

1 2 3 4 5 6 7 8 9 10 11 12

Ex. 9

Divide it into two halves. Then combine these two halves, note
for note, so that the first note combines with the seventh note and
the second with the eighth, etc., giving a sequence of vertical
intervals: a major third, an augmented fifth, etc. (This is an arbitrary combination.)

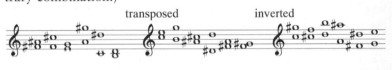

transposed   inverted

Ex. 10

Treat this now as the matrix of a structure which, with certain
redundancies in the superposition of members of each hexachord
above their matrices, creates two- to twelve-part vertical structures
that replace single pitch levels in the row, i.e. pitch level x is
replaced by a vertical complex ($x + n$) of pitch levels. The new
version of the row is identified not only by the order of its pitch
levels but also by the order of vertical intervals. When an ordering
(of this combined type) is transposed or inverted, the contour is
reproduced; but the order of actual pitch levels is rotated. Alternatively, the ordering of vertical intervals may be reproduced but the
pitch levels that combine to make each vertical interval will be

redistributed. Taking pitch levels common (in their sequence) to more than one row form (as was done above to create the 'melodic idea' out of three row segments), and comparing these with their respective partners in the vertical structure, each tone can be attributed a limited number of different partners so as to create the possibility of 'alternative harmonisation'. In my work, I have seen this alternative harmonisation as analogous to the varying harmonisation resulting from a change of mode in earlier music.

Ex. 11

Principles of systematic distortion have been well known to painters at various times, but are known to musicians only in the techniques of rhythmic augmentation and diminution. There are not really any forms of systematic intervallic procedure of this kind other than those found marginally in the tonal answers of fugue and the like. One can find a great variety of decorative and variational devices. But there exists little formal interest in the comparison of approximate shapes and their regular and irregular distortion.

This has a great deal to do with the use of conventional instruments in music. Were resources limited to the human voice and string instruments, which have few discrete steps in their structure, it is possible that music might have retained a greater interest in shapes, disassociated from precise intervals and pitch steps. The same is true of music generated by electronic means (tape manipulation). Messiaen has interested himself in these things, e.g. in the symbolic use of expanding intervals to express growth towards the Word of God. But the most significant achievements of this kind have been in the rhythmic domain, in the work of Stravinsky and Messiaen. Boulez, in his important article 'Eventuellement',[10] hints at a technique of pitch distortion by filtering. He proposes to reduce and increase the sound-space of a particular piece of music so that by enlarging and contracting the proportions he might change the basic intervals. It would be necessary to use electronic means of filtering to achieve this, as Boulez does not propose that it could be done within the semitonal system. However, I believe approximations would be more interesting, as they would magnify the effect of the irregularities.

I have used a technique of progressive and systematic distortion based on the extensions of the dodecaphonic interval system demonstrated. Taking again the diagram of the two-part structure of six elements:

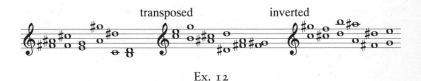

Ex. 12

To recapitulate, we have A♯ on F♯, a major third; C♯ on F, an augmented fifth; etc. In this ordering system, call the major third factor 1, the augmented fifth, factor 2 of the row. We obtain a row of vertical intervals which may be defined as the six first factors of the series. Now, reconstruct these six vertical intervals successively on the lower unit of each (two-part) chord so that each lower unit corresponds successively to the first factor, the second factor, etc., of the row. (This makes the lower part a pedal: six repetitions of a single pitch level.) The vertical intervals constituting each two-part chord, now transposed, identify the factor of the series; but above there is a new ordering of pitch levels.

Ex. 13

F♯–A♯, the first factor, is retained. In the second, below, F becomes F♯ so D replaces C♯. In the third below, F♯ replaces E, so A replaces

73

G. Continuing the process means that a new upper row replaces the old one, reading A♯–D–A–F–A–A.

Performing the same operation, using the lower note of the second factor, a new resultant row, above, reads A♯–C♯–G♯–E–G♯–G♯. Observe that functional note repetitions result from this operation. This causes it to act as a bridge between regular dodecaphonic rotation and more limited, filtered, tonal areas. I have found, in applying this procedure, that it is possible to come upon a surprising and often aurally fresh range of musical connections.

I do not believe that the days of organising musical material are over. New ideas appear and new styles are born, both of rigorous application of formal principles and of arbitrary strokes of fantasy and imagination. When one is lucky, these two coexist. A new ordering of heart and brain thus suggests itself. A piece of music is brought into being by a free act of the imagination. This single stroke, involving as it does the man, his beliefs and his memory, ensures something other than the result of choice. Take this irregular thing, and upon it make operations of one kind or another as elegantly as possible. This produces an order of brain following heart. But better still when the results of the brainwork themselves become new gestures and new images for development. A group of notes is transformed by the brain and a new image fires the imagination: a *trouvaille*, or quotable gesture, in the sense that it suggests its own continuation. Suddenly a new association of harmonies or a new melodic tag interrupts the regular plan of a piece and sets everything out of joint. The composer must obey this ebb and flow, apparently exposing himself to the operations of chance as the painter reacts to the free movement of the paint that he himself has brought into play. Francis Bacon is quoted as saying, 'What I really love is the way, of its own accord, paint makes things. The way that, in Constable, the flakes of paint as they happen to fall, make a horse.'

The operational aspects of the compositional process only make sense within such a hazardous and dynamic context, where a beginning image suggests a conscious working out, this in turn throwing up a new image and a new beginning . . .

4

I have tried to demonstrate very primitively the way in which shapes and gestures are developed in time to become a continuous musical argument. Reducing things to such seemingly simple technical operations fairly suggests that the personality of the composer is best expressed in his relationship to the stuff of music. The music of the past, too, is made of spontaneous elements built out according to systems. As students of music, we listen to and look at the great monuments of our past, and by systematic (and sometimes inspired) analysis try to reveal coherent thought processes in them. We construct models for organic forms, and today these are sharper and more detailed than some of the crude systematisations of some old textbooks. But all this still gives a dangerously incomplete view of musical creation. Leave out of account so many of the things that are customarily associated with music – love of nature, religion, romance, concern for our fellow men, feelings for third dimensions – and you give a false impression of having set up a sort of constructivist ideology, as it were, against these things. The critic will say, 'Heartless and dry intellectual'; and the layman will say, 'All this has nothing to do with real music,' and, 'What about music being the language of the emotions?'

The seasons, the relationships and the experiences of each with the other and with the soil, the quality of our lives, our defence of freedom – all these things affect our state, our thought and our actions and create the necessary emotional intensity for our work. Our work has no meaning without these things; and, where men oppress each other, there is no time to observe the intimate workings of either nature or art.

But what has been described here is merely an extreme elaboration of most primitive music-making. Give a child a pipe with a few holes to produce a few sounds. The child interrupts the silence and blows a note; it embellishes it to form a spontaneous phrase, a melody; it repeats it many times and varies it in many ways. The child explores the world and the material of the instrument, finding the different notes with different fingerings, colouring them in different ways, being moved by them and moving with them. People sigh, dream, dance. For the little things that the child does, and the oneness of the child with its material, form a model of its universe: a microcosm, in the words of the ancient philosophers. The child expresses the world and itself, and, as it does this, it exists within a system of finite means . . . of infinite uses.

(1972)

1. Anton Ehrenzweig (1908–66): *The Psychoanalysis of Artistic Vision and Hearing: An Introduction to a Theory of Unconscious Perception* (1953; 3rd edn London: Sheldon Press, 1975).

2. Ehrenzweig, *The Hidden Order of Art: A Study in the Psychology of Artistic Imagination* (London: Weidenfeld and Nicolson, 1967), p. 75.

3. Igor Stravinsky, *Poetics of Music in the Form of Six Lessons*, trans. Arthur Knodel and Ingolf Dahl (London: OUP, 1947), pp. 39–40.

4. Quoted in Richard H. Stein, *Tchaikowsky* (Berlin: Deutsche Verlags Anstalt, 1927), p. 227.

5. *The Path to the New Music*, ed. Willi Reich, trans. Leo Black (Bryn Mawr: Theodore Presser, 1963), p. 35. Translation modified.

6. Ibid., p. 9.

7. Most meaningfully by Milton Babbitt and least meaningfully by European composers associated with Darmstadt.

8. [This was one of the works analysed to AG by Boulez.]

9. [See above, pp. 10ff.]

10. Translated as 'Possibly . . .'. See full reference in note 14 on p. 25.

5

Modern Music and its Society

A Pebble in a Pool

In these talks I want to talk about modern music. I want to talk about the way composers have thought about modern music, and the ways in which they have composed it; and I want to say what modern music is. At the same time I'd like to talk a little about the way modern music has been organised in the seventy or eighty years that it's existed. Because I think I can show, by looking at the history of the making and organisation of modern music, that a considerable transformation has taken place over what is after all the greater part of the twentieth century. What was then is not now; and we really have to look at the whole thing in a historical light.

We use the terms 'contemporary music', 'new music', 'modern music' and 'avant garde' almost interchangeably, and nobody is quite clear whether they all mean the same thing; and it's worth remembering that there was a time when these terms were not used. They were probably first used in the way we use them in connection with the founding of the International Society for Contemporary Music in the early 1920s. Interestingly enough, the original German title for the society was the *Gesellschaft für neue Musik* – 'New Music' – but in English it was changed to the much more general title 'Contemporary Music'. Now of course a great deal that was performed in the early festivals of the Society wouldn't today be considered modern music: much of it has passed into oblivion, and a great deal of it has gone into the normal concert repertoire. 'Contemporary', or 'new', in that sense, merely meant something chronological: it was written at that time. Nevertheless the Society was founded, by composers principally (although the first President was Edward Dent), to serve the needs of a certain kind of composer who wrote modern music, and it's about that kind of modern music, as opposed to merely 'new' or 'contemporary' music of any particular time, that I'd like to talk.

Composers have indeed always found it hard to get their pieces played and listened to – even nowadays, when there are a lot of mechanical aids (radio, record, cassette) and when there are many more opportunities for hearing music. But during the time I am talking about – after the First World War – there was a somewhat special situation. There had been, through the war, a great backlog of music collected which people hadn't heard, and one of the primary considerations at the end of the war, which had divided artists both politically and geographically, was how were they going to get together again. This was one of the reasons for the founding of the ISCM. Another reason was that, even before the war, composers had run into difficulties with their publics. To some extent, of course, this gave them pleasure: I can't think that Stravinsky was terribly upset by the fact that his *Rite of Spring* caused a scandal, although Schoenberg might have been more upset at some of the scenes that took place at the performance of *his* works before the First World War in Vienna. But in Moscow, Paris, Vienna and Berlin, which were the principal centres of modern music, composers did feel that they wanted to break away from the conventional concert hall, with its rather formal set-up, and form societies in which they to some extent considered themselves an elect: they were breaking with everything that was old, looking towards some sort of new world. The best example of this is the Society for Private Musical Performances started by Schoenberg during the war, in which the audience was to some extent excluded, so that people could really hear what the composers had composed without the paraphernalia of public concert life. A lot of this spirit went into the founding of the ISCM. The first festivals – in fact, it was a principle that lasted quite a long time – were festivals of compositions by composers and friends of composers (like the conductor Hermann Scherchen, who figured prominently in those festivals) and principally for composers and students of music; they weren't directed at the broad audience.

In fact quite a similar situation existed after the Second World War. After the long period of Nazism (or Fascism, in Italy), followed by the war itself, there was again a great backlog of music, and the re-forming of the world of artists after the war had something in common with the re-formations after the First World War. Again we had a number of artists and friends of music – pre-war enthusiasts of modern music – who observed that all the important composers of the early part of the century had been ignored while lesser figures had been promoted; and at the end of the war there was again a spirit of 'Let's start anew', followed by an enormous boom in the 1950s. But there was one significant difference. Many of the people who were interested in modern music before the war, people who were not themselves composers but teachers, critics and writers, now found themselves, as opponents of the Nazi regime, in positions of great power – in the radio stations, the press, the universities and elsewhere – and they, in saying 'Never again', also said, 'We will now do the thing as it always should have been done; the institutions which are there to disseminate culture will now be put at the service of the new.' Heinrich Strobel, the Director of the Südwestfunk, said, 'We got it all wrong before the war; this time we're going to get it right.' And it was he more than any other who promoted new music after the war, first of all in reviving the composers who had been banned by the Nazis – Schoenberg, Stravinsky, Bartók, Hindemith – and then, as it were, bringing into being a new generation of composers who also were informed by the spirit of modern music.

What is particularly noteworthy in discussing the development of the ISCM is that we have here a complete transformation of organisation and purpose. Because, in the early days of modern music, the artists who were informed by this spirit of newness, whether they were painters (like Kandinsky, Franz Marc) or composers (Scriabin, Schoenberg) – I mention only those who feature in the publication of the *Blue Rider* almanac, which figures prominently in the thought of this time – these artists stood for the truth of individual experience as opposed to bourgeois, or for that matter proletarian, society. Their individual consciousness seemed to them a kind of truth which had to be defended against the collective – the collective taste of the time, collective organisations of the time (in this they were truly avant garde). And this was the reason why they set up private societies. But looking at the other end of the transformation, we see that what was private has now become the public domain, and that the modern art which broke away from society and the organs of society is now the official art of society: modern music, and a great deal of the rest of modern art, exists thanks to the tax-payer, thanks to organisations sponsored by the state in this country and elsewhere, and many people have seen and do see it as an official art. I suppose that for many of us the culmination of this feeling came when we watched the opening of the experimental music centre in Paris, the Beaubourg,[1] where the French state has created an official centre, sponsored by the money of the state, for the making and developing of new musical languages. In a sense this transformation can be seen as a strange irony indeed; one could say that the piper calls the tune. But I wouldn't want to be too mechanistic about this irony, because it's not said that this is necessarily a bad thing. We can look with some pleasure at the fact that the way we spend our money is more enlightened rather than less enlightened: it doesn't automatically follow that, because modern art is sponsored by official organis-ations, it's therefore all bad. Whether it's good or bad, or what it is, can only be determined by looking at the material itself, and really we can't talk about modern music without looking at the history of that music.

Now when we say 'modern music', as opposed to contemporary music or new music, what do we mean? Is this modern music?

Ex. 14: Ravel, *Valses Nobles et Sentimentales*

Or is this modern music?

Ex. 15: Schoenberg, *Kleine Klavierstücke*, Op. 19 No. 2

Quite clearly the example from the Ravel waltzes would not be considered modern music; the example from the Schoenberg little piano pieces, on the other hand, clearly would (although the two works were written within months of each other). But why? Why would we all agree that the Schoenberg was modern and the Ravel not? The Ravel's not conventional; it doesn't sound like a Schubert waltz or anything very old-fashioned; nor does it use particularly conservative means – the chords used are quite advanced, in some ways as advanced as the chords used in the Schoenberg. So it's not really a question of grammar and syntax: it's not that composers who are modern write more dissonant music than those who are not modern, as is often vulgarly assumed. What, then? Is it the composer's intention? Is it whether he wishes to please or shock, or something of that kind, which determines whether or not a composition is modern? Well, it's extremely hard to tell what a composer's intention is. We can read his letters; we can talk to people who remember him; but really there's no way of knowing exactly what a composer's intention was at the time when he wrote a particular piece, an intention which would enable us to determine the purpose of that piece and thus its nature.

No, I think the way we determine what is modern in music is different. It's not a question of grammar nor a question of intention. It's a question of omission: it's what a composer leaves out that is important. Now in the nineteenth century this tendency already demonstrated itself. For example, in a piece like *Funérailles* by

Liszt[2] the effect of the music, which is a sort of hyper-expression – it's aiming to be very striking and very moving – is achieved not by any particular innovation in the grammar or syntax of what is played but by the fact that the composer insists on the same music again and again. It's a vulgarisation, if you like, in relation to Classical music, and academically it might be regarded as not very good; but the effect is very, very strong.

A new sound: that's what Liszt aimed to create. And that, quite simply, is what modern music is: it's the aspiration to create a new sound. This is the essential ingredient of Modernism. And it contrasts with other musical attitudes, especially with that attitude exemplified by a composer like Mahler, who thought of music, and especially of the symphony, as a world, a world of darkness and shadow, of contrasting moods, of different characters walking across the whole rich tapestry of life. In modern music the characteristic expression is achieved by the elimination of everything that is not essential to the composer's vision. The symphonic form is replaced by something that could almost be called a spiritual telegram. External form is the reflection of internal reality, and internal reality is obsessive and repetitive; the elements of obsession and repetition create new sound; and this new sound is modern music.

In my next two talks I'm going to try and describe the development of new sound. First I'm going to talk about those composers who actually tried to imagine a new sound, who heard it with their inner ear and who tried to notate what they heard; then I'm going to talk about those composers who developed new languages, new systems of composition, in order to achieve new sound in that way. These two categories are not only contrasted, but chronologically the second follows the first. In examining the development of these two attitudes towards composition, I hope to be able to throw some light on the question that is at the centre of these talks, and that is: where we are now.

New Sounds

Making modern music is quite simply inventing a new sound:

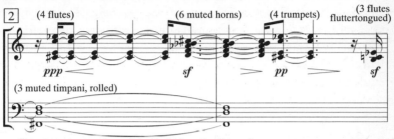

Ex. 16: Webern, *Orchesterstücke*, Op. 6, No. 4

In the first of these talks I drew a distinction between the kind of new sound that results from an act of the imagination – when the composer actually imagines the sound or imitates it from something outside himself, something in the world of nature or in the urban world – and the kind of new sound that results from mental operations, from systems of construction, from new ways of doing things. These are two different aspects of the creating of new sound, although they do of course overlap in the same composers and chronologically the second type of procedure follows the first. I want to discuss the earlier in this talk and the later in my next.

When talking about art, one could say that this is an arbitrary distinction and so not necessarily true. For instance, Edgard Varèse would not have agreed that one could divide types of music according to the intentions of the maker; he implies as much when he says that Schoenberg and Webern are great composers *despite* the invention of their systems of composition. On the other hand, I really believe that the external sound of a piece of music is the direct result of the thought processes that went into its making. An example is of a piece, for example Schoenberg's Fourth String Quartet (Ex. 17), where the sound as such isn't particularly attractive but the mind very rapidly latches on to the kind of motivic working that is going on; and even if one doesn't know what this is, the sound soon becomes differentiated and comprehensible.

Ex. 17: Schoenberg, Fourth String Quartet, Op. 37

At this point I ought to say what I mean by the word 'sound'. Of course every music – every kind of music, in every time – has its own sound, and some of the sounds that were once new are today familiar and accepted. And some of the sound owes its nature to the manner of its production: as instruments change, so the sound changes. Electronically generated sound is automatically new by comparison with instrumental sound (which is automatically familiar). But that's not really what I'm talking about. By a 'sound' I don't mean the sound of the Hallé Orchestra, or something of this kind. I mean a particular constellation of sounding events which results from acts of imagination or mental processes. Consequently it's not to do with instruments as such but to do with the mind.

Now there's a very big difference between the way new sound was created in the past and what I mean when talking about modern music. In the music of the past you can almost always diagnose a new chord or a new resolution of harmony behind a new sound, behind something which was in its own times against the rules. The explanation was generally that a composer's desire for expression made a rule temporarily inapplicable, and that that sound then established itself in the repertoire and was used by later composers without its creating the shock that it had on its first appearance. This is quite a usual theory of the evolution of musical style, or at least of one ingredient of it. But in our times new sound is something fundamentally different. As I said in my last talk, it's not now entirely a question of syntax, because those chords of fourths and fifths, those whole-tone scales that once seemed so new, are today the stock-in-trade of all commercial music. It's not that. New sound in this century represents an inner imagination and a moral attitude. I don't know, actually, whether I'm right to say 'moral attitude', but what I mean by this is that artists taking themselves very seriously thought they could invent an external form for their imagination or picture of the world, and that they used images from the world outside to isolate them and their attitude from the world around them. By repeating the same kind of image over and over again they made it impossible for the work to spread out, to encompass other musical images, and strengthened the original image almost to breaking point.

Nature imagery: water, sky, mountains. The paraphernalia of death: cortège, funeral bells. Night moods. These are to a certain extent of course the legacy of the nineteenth century. But this kind of imagery, which characterises the first composers of the twentieth century, becomes joined with a transcendental idealism, often tinged with oriental ideas, and a mystical, rather than ideological, espousal of what is new. These people believed in renewal, a rebirth for the world, but not in the sense that their political confrères did; they saw the new more as a sort of transcendental spring/rebirth of truth and purity. The composers who shared this point of view – Scriabin, Schoenberg, Ives, and later Webern and Berg and Bartók – felt that they had to get away from what was old, visualising a new and crystalline world in which this transcendental idealism would be made flesh. These artists were not concerned with any practical solutions to the problems of the society in which they lived: they were concerned with making sound out of their spiritual experiences. And they weren't, consequently, concerned only to describe their innovations in terms of grammar and syntax.

I should give an example of this. In the *Blue Rider* almanac, in which Schoenberg and Scriabin were the main musical contributors among a group of painters, there's a very good article about Scriabin's *Prometheus* by L. Sabaniev, in which he writes: 'In analysing Scriabin's work it is difficult to distinguish its individual forms from the general idea, from the ultimate "artistic idea" that has now become completely explicit in the composer's consciousness. The artistic idea is a positive, mystical action that leads to an ecstatic experience – to ecstasy, to the perception of more elevated dimensions of nature.' And of the actual piece *Prometheus* he says that 'all the main themes . . . from which the composer creates his texture derive from a "single" harmony [which] has the capacity to include the most diverse nuances, beginning with a mystical horror and ending with a radiant ecstasy and caressing eroticism.'[3]

Such modes of thought were characteristic of modern art prior to the First World War in Vienna, Moscow, Berlin and Paris – and even in the New England of Charles Ives and Ruggles. People have made comparisons of Ives and Mahler, but I think they're quite erroneous, because in Ives's piling up of different musical modes – the popular band marches, the ragtime and that particular mystical style connected with hymns and chromatic harmony – the important thing is surely that they *are* piled up, one on top of the other, to create an imaginary sound world. In that way, what Ives does relates much more closely to what was characteristically new in a composer like Scriabin. These ecstatic and pantheistic visions, this mystical welcoming of some unidentified and generalised new, is to be found in the writings of the composers of this time and, of course, even more characteristically in the writing of the poets. The Christian mystic Alexander Blok, welcoming the Russian Revolution in his poem 'The Twelve', the writings of Stefan George, with his imagining of a kind of elect, the visionary poetry of Constantin Balmont: all these are indications of the spirit of new art. And in a simple sense this can be identified with the Russian Revolution.

But the arrival of the Russian Revolution heralds another strand of Modernism, which has at first little but ultimately a great effect on music; and that is Futurism. Now we go to the opposite extreme. In listening to Ives and Scriabin one is struck by the genuineness of their expression, but also by the slightly nineteenth-century and dated character of the clothing the images wear. But the Futurists espoused the new world. Their central image was one of speed; they were concerned not with nature imagery but with town imagery; and the art form that was most characteristic of their thought was architectural drawing. It's the new town-scape, with stations for trains and aeroplanes, that characterises their world. At first the influence of the Futurists upon music tended to be superficial. The composers who made use of Futurist elements – Prokofiev in *Le pas d'acier*, Stravinsky a little, the notorious Antheil and the Mossolov of *The Iron Foundry* – tended to use superficial images culled from Futurist ideas. Perhaps a more important part of Futurist musical thinking is contained in the painter Russolo's 1913 manifesto, when he advocated a music based not on the traditional harmonies and counterpoints of classical music but directly on noise. Here for the first time you get the idea, later developed by Cage and others, of the artist embracing the whole world and using *all* the sounds which are available to him. The funny little noise machine that Russolo constructed to create this kind of music now looks as silly as the eighteen bulbs that were Scriabin's light organ; but the idea was more important than the machine.

These transcendental, mystical attitudes characteristic of the pre-World War I years, and the newer, more typically modernist Futurist ideas emanating from Russolo, come together in an amazing way in the figure of that composer whom one most immediately thinks of when one is talking about the creation of new sound *per se* as an integral element of modern music; and that is of course Edgard Varèse. Varèse has survived better than many of his confrères, and his music seems stronger and fresher today than one would have thought when it was mocked in the years before the [Second World] War. Both the tendencies I have tried to describe join up in Varèse. Composers such as Stravinsky often said, quite cynically, that a lot of Varèse's technical ideas were taken from *The Rite of Spring*, but that was absolutely to miss the point. And that's why Varèse's work is best described by non-musicians. It is Louise Varèse, his wife, in her biography, and Henry Miller who seem to me to put the finger on what is remarkable about Varèse. I think the easiest way to describe it is to quote a description of a new piece Varèse is proposing to write given by Henry Miller in *The Air-Conditioned Nightmare*. Miller writes:

> The world awake. Humanity on the march. Rhythms change: quick, slow, staccato, dragging, treading, projecting itself into space. Voices in the sky. Invisible hands were turning on and off the knobs of fantastic radios. Shooting stars. Words recurring like hammerblows. I should like an exultant, even prophetic tone, incantatory. Also some phrases out of folk-lore, from the most primitive to the furthest reaches of science.

Those phrases from 'Varèse's Program' were chosen at random. But they tell us – and I can't underline this too frequently – that the new sound of a composer is the embodiment of a stance, of a moral position and of an attitude to the world around him. You hear it at its most characteristic in the work of Varèse, and sometimes also in the work of Messiaen (who described himself in class as Varèse's brother).[4] Scriabin, Ives and Ruggles; the Schoenberg of *Jacob's Ladder*; Webern; Edgard Varèse; Henry Cowell, Stefan

Wolpe and John Cage (in the early part of his career, at least): these are the composers who attempted to invent a new sound, directly out of their imagination or through listening to the sounds of the world around them.

What about the others? Where are Boulez, Stockhausen, Nono and Carter? I think that these are a different kind of composer; these are people who really believed that they would create a new sound out of the reconstruction of the musical language. And this, I think, is another subject.

New Structures and Secret Languages

In my last talk I suggested that the creation of new sound in music embodied a stance, an attitude towards the world. I tried to show that it had evolved out of two fundamental elements: on one hand, the kind of mystical transcendentalism that we find at the turn of the century and in the years before the First World War, a spirit associated in music with Scriabin, Schoenberg and Ives; and on the other hand, after the Russian Revolution, the influence of Futurism, first of all rather superficially and then linking with the transcendental welcoming of the new in the work of Varèse. Varèse's creative career falls into two halves. The pieces which we remember him for principally were written in the 1920s and 1930s, in New York. He then lapsed into a long silence; but he did compose again after the war, in the 1950s. There's no greater contrast possible than between the reception that was accorded his music up till 1945, which was mainly cynical, and the enthusiasm with which he was greeted after the war. The same can be said to some extent of the other principal modernists, Schoenberg and Webern (by this time Scriabin had fallen out of the modernist canon).

But the years after the Second World War were very different from the years after the First World War, although there were certain elements in common. At both times you have a great deal of leeway to be made up: I described it, in the case of the First War, as being a desire on the part of artists to get together again, after the political and geographical divisions which the war had created. But in the case of the Second War the situation is different, because we're not talking about four years, we're really talking of the period from 1933, when modern music had tended to disappear in Central Europe, until 1945, which is much longer. Like the period after the First World War, the period after the Second is characterised by the amount of leeway that has to be made up. There are a lot of composers whose works haven't been heard. First of all, the Bartóks, Hindemiths, Milhauds and Stravinskys; then the composers of the Second Viennese School; and only then Varèse, Ives and others who were greeted almost as new discoveries in the late 1940s and early 1950s.

But there's another great difference, and I think this one is even more important. The young composers, especially on the Continent, who emerged in the years following the Second World War were by training, outlook and experience of quite a different type. Educationally and technically there was not much difference between the composers before the First War and those after; it was after all only four years. Educational traditions, the ways in which composers were trained, remained roughly intact throughout the First War. But after the Second, things had changed considerably. Composers who were born into those pre-war years and reached their first maturity in the years after the Second War hadn't really been submitted to the kind of technical training that was characteristic of European music earlier on. Now, although there was the same urge to compose, the same urge to take on a stance in relation to the world, it was one in which the composer's inspiration was mixed up with the desire to get to grips with a technical tradition that was alien to him. So that the idea of writing new music, while based on the achievement of those earlier composers who were considered modern and interesting, was also a way of finding out how to compose. The old ways didn't seem to work any more – they were alien and foreign – and young composers saw in the work of the masters of modern music, as they now came to be known, a gateway into the world of technical composition; so that they were not only interested in the aesthetics and metaphysics of those earlier composers, they were also interested to cull from them technical devices and ways of doing things which would come together to form a new style of composing music as well as a new content.

The easiest way to understand the various attitudes of the composers who came into prominence after the Second World War is simply to examine the attitudes of the three who were grouped together, as a kind of troika, in those years: Boulez in France, Stockhausen in Germany and Nono in Italy. Two of these composers were pupils of Messiaen; the third was a pupil of Hermann Scherchen. They really came together for the first time in the Darmstadt summer schools, and that's where their attitudes to music were formed. They came, and they declared themselves to be, under the influence of the work of late Webern, more than that of Schoenberg, and although they soon grew tired of the very limited range and technical mastery of Webern, they always thought that they were basing their developments on the work Webern did in the latter part of his life (the years of the war), when his music was totally unknown.

Of the three important post-war composers that I have mentioned, Nono does to some extent seem to me to fit into the pattern of modernity as I've described it, albeit with some substantial differences. I'm really talking about the Nono of the pre-electronic works. Nono tries – as did Varèse, whom Nono very much admires – to create by the elimination of all sorts of musical material a single, monolithic effect. In this he resembles his painter contemporaries – some of the American abstract expressionists, Klein in particular and Soulage – in trying to make in his work one big sign for us to look at. His political motivation has a lot to do with this. But what concerns us principally is his technical means, because unlike Varèse he does not actually imagine a new sound-type but creates one by the kind of technical means he has learned from his studies of Webern. He uses these in a simplified (some would almost say a crude) manner, and there is a great disparity between the little detail of his pieces – what happens from note to note – and the general effect they make. But here we do have a composer who creates a sound of his own, a form of his own, which corresponds precisely to a particular [aesthetic/moral] stance.

Nono's monolithic position is very different from that of Boulez and Stockhausen. These are composers of a quite different type. They, like Nono, also originally based their ideas on that idea of Webern which tried to identify a technical process with the final form of the work – by which I mean that the means used to organise the notes, the rhythms and the phrases of the music are themselves the form of the music, this being emphatically not the case in earlier composers. But Boulez and Stockhausen kept to the spirit of Webern rather than to the letter. Tiring of the limited range of his work, they tried to develop his technical means to include the whole gamut of what they rightly considered the striking and progressive elements in the modern music of the past fifty years.

Implicit in Boulez's thinking is a kind of evolutionary ideal, in which a composer isolates by selection from the music of the past those elements which are technically 'actuel' – one of Boulez's favourite words – and aurally striking, with the object of integrating them into a systematic structure. Old-fashioned choice, the potential for intuitive combination and development, it is implied by him, is arbitrary and will not contribute to the building up of an objective, multi-dimensional language for the art of the future – for nothing less than this is his aim. He wants to separate Debussy's achievement of composing in a kind of flux of tempo, Stravinsky's harmonic blocks and rhythmic cells, the expressive fragmentation of early Schoenberg and the sonority of Varèse, combining them in one systematically controlled composition. It's a most impersonal ideal and a very ambitious one. But it is not really like scientific research. It's a kind of individualist version of the vision of Mallarmé at the end of his life, the Mallarmé who tried to break up language into something where the elements of space, the word on the page, all contributed to one general, poetical effect.

Stockhausen, similarly – but less methodically from work to

work, and with a broader range of cultural and scientific interests – has pursued this same ideal of systematic integration. As early as 1952, in discussing Varèse, who clearly does not fall into the twelve-tone canon from which Stockhausen stems, he suggests that Varèse's sound remains inessential as long as people are unable to integrate single sound-events into a meaningful total order. So rather than excluding noise and other elements that traditionally don't fit into the world of our music, as Webern would have believed, he wished to find new, systematic extensions for ordering *all* sound characters. This often moved him into the area of acoustics. And this in fact has been the continuous aim throughout his apparently tortuous and varied development.

Naturally these are very general remarks and don't tell the whole story. But perhaps they're sufficient to demonstrate three points. First, the way of thinking that has characterised the work of Stockhausen and Boulez has been enormously influential. It's been influential in raising the standard of talk about music and, superficially at least, the standard of composing music. Whereas thirty years ago only a few of the pieces that were written by young composers showed a high standard of writing, today throughout the world the discoveries of Stockhausen and Boulez, and their preoccupations, have caused a comparatively sophisticated and differentiated type of thinking about music. This type of thinking has spread out, from the small Darmstadt summer schools, which were attended by composers from all over the world, to a very broad culture; and universities and music colleges of the world, wherever people are interested in composing and the teaching of composition, have taken on these ideas and made them into a kind of canon. And I think it's generally believed that this is a new aesthetic.

My second and third points contrast, perhaps somewhat alarmingly, with this first one. The gist of the first point is that the discoveries of young composers have led to a new aesthetic. But as far as the public is concerned, they do not accept any new aesthetic in the same way; and those works of Boulez and Stockhausen which have made the greatest impression upon them –

Boulez's *Le marteau sans mâitre*, his Second Piano Sonata and *Pli selon pli*, and Stockhausen's *Gruppen, Momente, Refrain* – are heard not because they integrate such a huge gamut of sounding materials into one systematic whole, but, on the contrary, because they achieve, within the tradition of modern music, an exclusive and characteristic sound.

And my third point leads on from my second point. Those composers who have been influenced by these original models and by the attitudes of Boulez and Stockhausen to advanced music of the pre-war period have managed to establish their own artistic identities in just this traditional way. The composers we recognise as interesting are, again, *not* those who create all-embracing systems (they may create them, but that's not why we find them interesting) but those who have taken a very narrow area and explored it thoroughly, eliminating everything else. Those composers are Xenakis, Ligeti, Carter and Birtwistle: they make a strangely assorted group, but they have it in common that they too, though working generally with systematic means and certainly maintaining that kind of stance for the public, have managed to create an identifiable sound-world which puts them, at least in this respect, in the tradition of Modernism as I have defined it.

I think that over-characteristic, limited and newly invented images – even noise as conceived by Varèse and Stockhausen – is artistically usable, but not, as Stockhausen suggests, insofar as it can be integrated stylistically but insofar as it can be projected as shock. Modernism in art conveys something insofar as it challenges convention and expectation. Integration – systematic organisation – is aimed at creating new convention. Creating new convention is the inevitable fate of all modernisms, but it also marks the end of them.

Modern music, like all modern art, represents an ideological stance, and its characteristic ideas can easily be related to the moral ideals of its creators. Its force in society is of its nature oppositional and critical, and its proposed alternatives deal in the flash of momentary revelations. We've seen how the ideals of pre-World War I modernity were a shock, a pebble in an apparently tranquil pool; they've become absorbed into a social and cultural framework. We've seen a correspondence between the way composers thought before, characterised by an exclusive radicalism, to the way they think now, aiming at an inclusive systemation of all modern means. And we've seen how, in society, they first withdrew from conventional ways of music-making – from the life of opera houses and orchestras – only to find themselves reintegrated into new, conforming social organisations. I'm afraid that this development accounts, on the one hand, for a great propagation of new ideas, which is a good thing, [and], on the other, for a decline in the intensity of these ideas. Once the pool was disturbed by the pebble; but now only the ripples are left.

Ripples in Ever-Spreading Circles

In my previous talks I have in the most general way tried to describe the development of a modern music in this century. I've tried to show that Modernism might be seen as embodying a kind of moral stance, a philosophical position, as opposed to any concern with the contemporary, the merely new, at any particular time. Modernism may be seen as representing a philosophy which says that an individual experience, an individual perception of truth, is to be set above the collective values of society; and in this way modern music has come into conflict with society, first of all withdrawing from the public domain into a created, private world of its own, with its own societies and its own organisation, and then, paradoxically, coming round, through the influence of the wars, to a situation where the public domain has apparently taken on the values of modern music as its own and organised it in that way.

In our time, when modern values in art have become generally acceptable, at least in academic institutions and in organisations for the propagation of art, the artists have tried to adapt the values of Modernism – those values that emerged from the much admired early creations of innovators at the beginning of the century – into some kind of general language, a general mode of thought, and have tried to base some sort of a new academicism upon it. All this implies a *volte face* from the original, individualistic position to what must be described, without any pejorative meaning to the word, as a conventional position. Today modern music, like most modern art, it seems to me, is a kind of convention, a convention based on certain values, certain beliefs about the way we live, and in particular on the belief that by carrying on and developing these values we are doing something that is relevant and a good influence in the world around us.

These conventions have spread amazingly. What I've described as a pebble thrown into a pool has now spread over the whole pond; and from the furthest parts of the world – from Iceland to Japan, from Eastern Europe to South America – similar values have been admired in modern music. People travel throughout the world, to festivals and congresses, exchanging works, and by and large, although local differences between ways of thought and ways of composing remain, there is a generally agreed convention. And all this has come from these few centres, from these few individuals at the beginning of the century who set themselves up against the convention of what was then available and commonly pursued. This has created a totally new situation, which I have described as an inversion of the previous one.

Well, what does it all matter? Does it in fact help us in any way to make some diagnosis such as I have attempted, and does agreeing with such a diagnosis make it more likely that we're going to write better music, or enjoy modern music more than before? The answer to that is both yes and no. In an obvious sense, no: the biological element is always the most important – composers will compose something urgent and interesting if they've got some-thing urgent and interesting to compose. But on the other hand, yes, because I think it's of the greatest importance for young com-posers (and not-so-young composers too) to understand where fruitful land lies, where it is useful for them to work. Composers in our time have perhaps been too ready to accept the conditions of the artistic world around them as they find it. Putting it at its most negative, they have been quite happy to walk into their subsidised ghetto and exist within the protection of its walls, little concerned with whether what they do is really being greeted with any kind of comprehension by whatever small part of the general public is concerned with modern art anyway, and scrabbling around within these walls as if this were a permanent and final condition for the art that they pursued.

Because we shouldn't kid ourselves: after the war – after the Second World War, that is – the musical public was very positively inclined towards modern art. It was a time, not when everyone who went to a concert understood what all the composers were doing, but when (probably under the influence of the horrors and the war that had been) people were prepared to accept something new. They were looking for something new, and they were prepared to give artists and musicians a chance. I think it's true to say that the audience no longer feels this. There is now a considerable hostility to what modern musicians are attempting to do, and the incomprehension does not help any future comprehension if it isn't matched with good will. As a result, the real interest in the content – the philosophical content – of modern music has disappeared, and I am afraid that very often all that remains is a sort of personality cult, centred on the flamboyant imitators in the high arts of the much more genuinely challenging pop or punk personalities. These last people, like so many self-styled Dionysian liberators, actually frighten us; but we're not nearly so frightened of their imitators in the high arts when we know that the work they're doing is actually on commission from some state organisation or other. 'These people hold no terrors for me.'

It seems to me that the attitudes of a composer are expressed in his choice of forms, artistic images and material, and I believe that in order to speak to and for his time, which must be his aim, his attitudes must take into account the characteristic attitudes present in the world around him. The 1970s, which are now ending, can in fact be seen to be a time of considerable change. It's not appropriate for me to play the role of a social historian; there are people better qualified to do that. But it is useful, perhaps, to suggest that the deep ideological changes that have [taken] and are taking place might actually have some influence on our particular world – the world of composers and modern music.

I think it would be true to say that in this decade, under the influence of our present and continuing crises, the belief that our society will improve itself by means of technological progress has been considerably shaken; I wouldn't say more than that. Now doubtless those who criticise what has become the conventional idea of technological progress can be accused of having thought up some very fanciful, and even hysterical, modes of life. But nevertheless I think something important has changed. Today we are genuinely more concerned than before with the preservation of what is useful, pleasant and beautiful in our world and less eager to knock down anything we see around us. We're eager to revive and relearn skills which for one reason or another have almost, if not completely, disappeared, and as always, when looking at the spirit of our time, we can see it at its best in the work of the buildings around us. We see today that architects, under the influence of austerities and the necessity for working on very limited budgets, and in answer to public demand, are turning away from the kind of utopian ideals associated with Le Corbusier, which conditioned a great deal of thought earlier on in the decade, to a simpler approach, a less complicated technology, in which they try to eliminate complicated running costs and preserve the world and the environment around the new building. It is not appropriate for me to go into the proposed economics of Dr Schumacher's 'small is beautiful' movement, nor to discuss the improvements possible in bread and beer. But nevertheless, although the details of this are unimportant for our present purposes, I think we can say that this non-political (or apparently non-political) revolt has important political and philosophical ramifications; and it's the application of these to the world of music that I would like to touch on a little.

In this situation, the new technological institutes, and the belief that a new musical language is going to be created by thinking about its technological bases, seem very odd indeed. It would seem to be more appropriate that one concern oneself with the invariants, the common bases, of a musical language – perhaps somehow in the way that was attempted for painting by Paul Klee in his *Pedagogical Sketchbooks*, when he returned to the very bases and conventions of his art. I think, looking critically from this point of view at the modern musical culture around us, we could say that it's a very narrow culture, taking in only a very small area, although this is frequently betrayed by its less scrupulous and more commercial adherents in the interest of greater impact. Also, and more to the point, that as a culture it's hopelessly ethnocentric in a world that is considerably less ethnocentric than it used to be. We tend to look at the world too specifically from our own point of view. It's true that we show some interest in other than our own music; but this is generally seen for its unusual colours and devices, which may from time to time be synthesised with our own artistic ideas.

To really learn about other musics, and to open heart and mind to them, means neither to be a tourist nor to be a collector. It means to put oneself in the position of a pupil. In our urgent need to rethink the bases of our own music we have to learn to understand how other, and apparently less developed, ethnic and classical musics work. In studying the music of others, we learn the way their minds work and we find out again how ours works. As dull as I find the majority of the metalanguages and unprovable hypotheses that are pumped out in the journals dealing with modern music, so interesting do I find the writings of the ethnomusicologists in their concern with the very basic and invariable qualities of music. For we find here the sort of rigorous thinking that formerly characterised thinking about classical music. Here we learn the real meanings of words like 'mode', the relationship of modes to the range of a particular melody, about instruments and about the relationship of word to music. I say 'learn' because in the welter of the virtuoso figuration and the intense fragmentation which our own art has undergone in these last fifty years we've forgotten it, quite frankly, and the opposite values are what we cultivate.

It's not a far cry from this concern with other musical cultures to think again about the basic skills of our own culture; not as it's now done, in universities and colleges, as a kind of doffing your cap to tradition in order to move on as quickly as possible to what is 'relevant', but with the idea of finding the *raison d'être* of the procedures of the past. The harassed peoples of our times have indeed taken flight into nostalgias, and superficially one would think that some such claim, or some such invocation to study the music of the past, is one of these nostalgias. But a nostalgia can be a positive and a negative thing. It's a negative thing in the way little bits and quotations from the music of the past have been picked out of context and put into new musical surroundings, because this has merely been done to arouse stock reactions; it is a form of stylistics. Positive is to learn how things worked in the past: to learn how technologies worked, how things operated, not for the purpose of reconstituting them in any way, which is an obvious impossibility, but for the purpose of understanding the relationship between what is an invariant in art and what is a personal choice, the fruit of personal imagination.

And the aim of all this, I should add, is emphatically not to create some kind of new neoclassical style. Nor would I in any way like to predict what kind of musical style *might develop* with such concerns: it would be a foolish man who attempted to predict how any particular art develops. No, the object of reinstating the traditional bases of music, rather than spending our intellectual energies on trying to form new bases, has a simpler, and yet more wide-ranging, significance. Because in examining the traditional bases we find that the individual musical works created on these bases, in different places and at different times, vary very greatly; that an understanding of the traditional bases allows for variation, fantasy and a cancellation or postponement of an expectation aroused; but that in music which is based on new hypotheses, on new conventions, the greatest thing that it can be is coherent, adhering to the system which has been set up, because new systems in themselves do not arouse expectations in listeners. It is impossible to invent a new technological system on which to base one's art and then to contradict it in order to introduce the element of surprise; and yet it must be stated that what is needed of art, in the world and in the psychology of people, is not adherence to systems, not logic, not inner coherence, as high ideals, but rather the opposite: the sudden momentary perceptions, the flash of insight, the jumps in logic – all these things.

Refinding the values of the old, then, is not a kind of neoclassical fantasy, nor any form of arch simplicity. We can't alter our condition, though we can alter our understanding of it. But I truly believe that with a relearning of the relationship between a rich and varied content, in which fantasy and rigour combine, and a simplification of the external means, we can on the one hand move a little towards the reinstatement of the traditional bases of our art and, on the other hand, free ourselves to some extent from the control which society has taken of us.

(1979)

1. [AG is referring of course to IRCAM. See above, pp. 6 and 24, note 9.]
2. [From *Harmonies poétiques et réligieuses* (1848). See also below, pp. 196–7.]
3. *Der blaue Reiter Almanac*, ed. Wassily Kandinsky and Franz Marc, rev. edn ed. and with an intro. by Klaus Lankheit, trans. Henning Falkenstein et al. (London: Thames and Hudson, 1974), pp. 127, 139–40.
4. [See above, pp. 55–6.]

6

[With Walter Goehr]

Arnold Schoenberg's Development towards the Twelve-Tone System

I

Although the conditions and problems facing a creative artist vary at different times, an ethnic culture imposes a certain common tradition and leads to a fundamental similarity of outlook. An understanding of the roots and historical development of a culture is essential for an assessment of any individual artist. Assuming this fact, we have the opportunity of seeing the comparative value, the parallels and divergencies of individual composers, seemingly unrelated, in a logical and responsible manner. For example, Brahms and Wagner were for decades believed to be antipodes, whereas we today, in comparative detachment, are able to see the affinities in the common national character of their work.

The German school of music at the threshold of the twentieth century based its teaching upon the study of German music from J. S. Bach to the Romantic masters, virtually neglecting earlier music or that of other nationalities. The melodic and rhythmic idiosyncrasies, the harmonic subtleties and the freedom of expression attained by these composers were measured by comparison with arbitrary prototypes of so-called normality (or regularity) created by the theorists. Mastery over technical material was obtained by a study of traditional harmony and academic counterpoint, based upon Fux rather than upon Palestrina and his Italian and Flemish predecessors. Although the music of France, Russia and other nations was studied, a fundamental schism had developed between the outlook of German musicians and those of other national schools. Heinrich Schenker, in his illuminating article 'Rameau or Beethoven' (1930), heads his discussion with a quotation from a letter of C. P. E. Bach: 'You may loudly proclaim that the fundamentals of the art of my father and myself are anti-Rameau.'[1] This divergence of attitude continued and grew, and even when German composers were influenced by the works of other national schools, their attitude remained sharply differentiated (as it remains today). The very nature of the German tradition is a dialectical one, and its development is one whereby each successive composer builds upon the technical achievements of his predecessors. There was little place for eclecticism. French composers, eclectic by nature, were much more open to newly discovered technical possibilities and to influence from hitherto unknown types of music. The German remained comparatively little affected by the new experiences made possible by a rapidly improving system of communications and the consequent opportunities for cultural exchange with remote parts of the earth. The teachings of Vincent d'Indy and Paul Dukas illustrate the eclectic and experimental tendency; the influence upon Debussy of Eastern music at the Paris World Exhibition is well known. The differences in method between the two traditions are clearly seen at times when Debussy and Schoenberg work with similar musical material, but with utterly different approaches and results. The German attitude of mind, one that can hardly be found in any other cultural sphere of the West, results in a cumulative style steadily and logically progressing to great subtlety and complexity.

One must remember that the German musical language was already in a state of advanced development at the time when Schoenberg entered the field. Brahms and Wagner, the former with a subtle juxtaposition of new asymmetries of form and rhythm beneath a surface of the traditional,[2] the latter with his liquidation of the old formal divisions and functions into a dramatically coherent whole, founded the style which composers like Wolf, Mahler, Reger and Strauss developed towards a flowering in the art of music completely original in its plasticity and powers of free and largely asymmetric construction. The developments of Wolf and Mahler in the elaboration of the melodic line (continuing what Wagner had begun), together with the widespread adoption of

Brahms's great developments in the variation of harmony, brought the musical language to a point at which Schoenberg's principles of 'varied repetition' and 'musical prose' can be considered a realistic assessment of the musical style of the time. It is our purpose to demonstrate the processes by means of which Arnold Schoenberg, in the period of his creative life until 1923, was to bring this musical language towards its logical conclusion and subsequent, seemingly revolutionary, development.

Development of artistic style involves a dual process. On the one hand, it entails an accumulation of increasingly varied elements, an extension of the means of relating previously unrelated material, and consequently a persistent replacement of comparative regularity and symmetry by asymmetry and irregularity. On the other hand, it stipulates (and this must be particularly emphasised) restriction, reduction and simplification, seemingly retrogressive habits, and the deliberate neglect or sublimation of traditional elements arising from new aesthetic considerations. There results a positive process of addition and accumulation in the creative mind and a quasi-negative restriction determined by choice and individual preference. When we consider the various facets of the progress of Schoenberg's music, we see that the balance between these two contrasting elements of development more than anything else distinguishes him from his contemporaries and marks him as a great composer. The further his style progressed (seemingly away from the German past), the more he concerned himself with analysis and the more he thought upon the fundamental problems inherent in Classical and Romantic German music. His particular path as an innovator was largely determined by his unusual powers of perception to understand and analyse the problems that had faced Mozart, Beethoven, Brahms and many others. Although his musical language was from the beginning one of great originality, the technical means that he used were, to a great extent, derived from the processes of his predecessors in German music. Aware of the continuous striving towards a new musical language, Schoenberg wrote in a letter at the time of the completion of *Das Buch der hängenden Gärten*, Op. 15 (1908): 'I have succeeded for the first time in approaching an ideal of expression and form that had hovered before me for some years ... I may confess to having broken off the bonds of a bygone aesthetic ...'[3] Seemingly contradictory is the famous sentence in his article 'Brahms the Progressive', first published in *Style and Idea* (1950): 'Analysts of my music will have to realise how much I personally owe to Mozart. People who looked unbelievingly at me, thinking that I made a poor joke, will now understand why I called myself a "pupil of Mozart", must now understand my reasons.'[4] These two quotations (and many similar ones can be found in Schoenberg's writings and sayings) are characteristic of the duality of his purpose and his development.

2

In attempting to trace the continuity of musical thought employed in Schoenberg's compositions from the *Gurrelieder* (1901) to the Serenade, Op. 24 (1923), we shall deal separately with the different aspects of construction: first, with his treatment and subsequent dissolution of the functions of tonal harmony; then with the significance of his return to the use of counterpoint; and, finally, with the character of his rhythm and with other elements that contribute to his conception of form and the novelty of his expression.

Throughout his life, Schoenberg occupied his mind with the problems of tonal harmonic structure (his two main works on this subject were the *Harmonielehre* and *Structural Functions of Harmony*[5]). His system of describing structural harmonic processes may be said to be based on the progressive theories of Simon Sechter, who was Bruckner's teacher and the master with whom Franz Schubert had decided to study counterpoint a few weeks before his death. In his *Die richtige Folge der Grundharmonien*,[6] Sechter greatly extended the harmonic vocabulary by acknowledging, describing and analysing chords and harmonic progressions which, although used for a long time by individual composers (even as early as J. S. Bach) for certain purposes of expression, had not previously been granted a theoretically clarified inclusion in the system of tonal harmony.

Schoenberg (like others before him) developed the theory of harmony, following Sechter's pattern of incorporating into the system of functional harmony increasingly complex harmonic phenomena which appeared in the works of contemporary composers, sometimes for reasons of freer part-writing and sometimes with the aim of achieving ever more subtle expression. At the beginning of the century, composers like Reger, Mahler and Strauss wrote in an idiom which went very far in the elaboration of harmony and, while adhering to the basically diatonic construction of tonal harmony, included in their vocabulary more and more chords of a chromatic character or chordal combinations of intervals not primarily connected with diatonic harmony (intervals of the whole-tone scale, chords built on fourths, combinations of the tritone with other intervals, etc.). Some of the harmonies used, especially passing chords in vast prolongations, are of a nature only loosely connected with the idea of diatonic harmony. Schoenberg, feeling that here the limits of tonal harmonic analysis were reached, started calling certain types of chords 'roving harmonies'. He saw in these novel chordal phenomena, quite rightly, the source of astonishing new developments and, at the same time, the danger of over-development and of obscuring the basic cadential structure. Wagner had already seen this danger and after *Tristan und Isolde* largely withdrew from the advanced position he had established. Some of these new harmonic events in the works of Reger, Strauss (in *Elektra* and *Salome*) and Mahler (particularly in the Seventh and Ninth Symphonies) met with very severe censure from the more conservative contemporary critics, and some novel management of chords which Schoenberg used in his early works was strongly criticised, e.g. the inversion of the chord of the ninth in *Verklärte Nacht* (1899) and the use of *Quartenharmonien* (chords built of fourths) in the first Chamber Symphony, Op. 9 (1906).

Schoenberg's use of the whole-tone scale can be compared to good advantage with the practice of Debussy. We find in Debussy's works passages that are almost entirely built, harmonically and melodically, on elements of the whole-tone scale. His predominantly vertical approach to harmony, which takes the actual character of the sound as a basis for the unity of the harmonic structure, led to impressive innovations and influenced many of Debussy's contemporaries (and even composers up to the present time). Schoenberg uses the whole-tone scale in a completely different way. In the Chamber Symphony, the fundamental structure is considerably influenced throughout the work by the partially whole-tone character of the first subject, but nevertheless all the appearances and developments of these whole-tone elements are strictly subordinated to the functional plan of harmony that binds together the whole work. Furthermore, Schoenberg uses many other methods of harmonic form-building (*Quartenharmonien*, varied sequences, etc.) which, although apparently complete innovations, are also assimilated into the plan of the overall harmonic layout in the manner of the German tradition of composition, and his ability to connect seemingly heterogeneous elements into one logical whole shows him clearly as a follower of Brahms and particularly of the later Beethoven. No such overall construction can be detected in composers of different traditions, such as, for example, Debussy.

The Chamber Symphony is of the greatest significance in showing Schoenberg's progress in the harmonic sphere. We cannot, within the scope of this article, describe in detail the complete freedom and mastery Schoenberg achieved in this idiom, using all the means available in expanded tonality to create a structure which was unprecedented in its variety and subtlety of harmonic form-building, but we want to mention his use of the free and more varied relationship of consonance and dissonance. Through his use of the widely leaping and internally varied melodic lines that were his heritage from Wagner and Wolf, he created a new and striking independence between horizontal melody and vertical chord. The result appears to approach in certain places some form of polytonality. Schoenberg in subsequent works made considerable use of this, even applying a technique of 'passing chord' anticipations and suspensions to whole complexes of chord movement instead of the usual single lines. This may be defined, in the terminology of Joseph Schillinger, as 'strata harmony'. If we compare harmonic movement to a succession of vertical straight lines, we see in Schoenberg's use of the technique that these lines become distended and, as it were, distorted. This led to a weakening in the effect of the functional harmonic structure. Thus the technique, grown from humble beginnings where composers ornamented and contrapuntally prolonged their cadences, now brought music to the point where these cadences had been decorated and disguised to such an extent that in many cases they disappeared completely from view (or rather from hearing). Schoenberg's use of roving harmonies, his contrapuntal prolongations and his all-important obscuring of the cadences led him imperceptibly to a position where he had to withdraw key signatures, which became obsolete and gave a false impression of the harmonic structure (starting with the last movement of the Second String Quartet, Op. 10 (1908)). This was a step towards the 'mythical' atonality that was attributed to Schoenberg, yet it was the logical, dialectical development of his technique.

It is, of course, an error to see the so-called 'atonal' works as representing some entirely new concept which fell from heaven. Schoenberg had stretched the harmonic structure to a point at which the fundamental harmonies and cadence points no longer had full functional significance either aurally or intellectually. For a time he was still prepared to use the technique of harmonic composition which became increasingly free, and relied more and more on his individual powers of imagination. It is indeed true to say that in works such as the Five Orchestral Pieces, Op. 16 (1909), or *Erwartung*, Op. 17 (1909), although the overall harmonies might still be analysed according to the principles of tonal structure, the overlapping and frequent use of neighbour-note technique, combined with the propensity of octave displacement, although completely coherent, make the works practically free of a felt tonality. Even as early as the Three Piano Pieces, Op. 11 (1909), we see, as it were in embryo, the kind of technique that he later brings to fruition. In the second half of the first piece, the subject is varied by a replacement of its smaller intervals with larger ones: the ninth replaces the second, the eleventh the third, etc. In observing this octave displacement, one can understand better the characteristic sound of this music. Whereas in music from Bach to Brahms the octave had played a most important part in the harmonic and melodic structure, the development of chromatic elaboration and the whole system of extended harmony show us these new intervallic progressions, as well as many fourths and a great insistence on the old bogy, the tritone, taking a preponderance of emphasis in the melody and harmony. The traditional functions of a harmonic structure could no longer be said to apply to Schoenberg's music. Sooner or later the composer had to face the problem of finding other form-giving elements with which to replace the weakened harmonic functions. From this time onwards, the analysis of his music in terms of functional harmony, which had generally provided a satisfactory method up to this time, must of necessity be insufficient, artificial and contrived. One need only examine Hindemith's attempt to analyse the third piano piece from Op. 11[7] to see how little it helps towards an understanding of the musical structure.

It will now be necessary for us to occupy ourselves with the analysis of those elements that Schoenberg began to introduce into his work as substitutes for functional harmonic structure, and all the topics discussed in the further part of our inquiry must be understood in that light. His development of counterpoint, his rhythmic practice, and the other new elements that he saw fit to introduce into his music will be assessed primarily according to the purpose with which they were introduced, namely, the substitution of form-giving elements for the faded ones of tonal harmony. Schoenberg's progress from *Pelleas und Melisande*, Op. 5 (1902–3), to the Serenade, Op. 24 (1923), the point at which he introduced the twelve-tone technique, can now be seen as the gradual introduction of such new elements, in their elaboration breaking more and more into the domain of the functional harmonic structure. Certainly the most significant among these elements is Schoenberg's reintroduction into his music, at the most fundamental level, of the principles of counterpoint.

During the nineteenth century the German composer's approach to counterpoint underwent a considerable change. Although Beethoven, especially towards the end of his life, and later, to a lesser degree, Reger and Mahler made considerable use of counterpoint and concerned themselves with the problem of integrating it with their basically homophonic styles, the Romantic followers of Beethoven (Weber, Mendelssohn, Schumann and also Brahms) tended to abandon the procedures of real counterpoint and to replace them with a harmonically inspired polyphony. With Wagner, who most clearly represented the spirit of the nineteenth century, the polyphonic texture developed still further away from the original contrapuntal methods, even remembering that the point of departure was not a strict modal style of counterpoint but the well-developed harmonic style of the seventeenth- and eighteenth-century German contrapuntalists. Strict counterpoint was the product of a musical age which thought not in the major-minor tonal system but in a system of authentic and transposed modes, the fundamental difference being that the modal form had a wider variety of possibilities for cadencing. Schoenberg realised that, with the disappearance of a valid tonal centre, the possibilities for introducing a freer approach to the cadence once again increased; in fact his adoption of the twelve-tone technique placed him under the obligation of regarding all twelve chromatic notes as equally valid for cadencing, i.e. a dodecaphonic system. But at the period in his work before the twelve-tone system had crystallised, we see him introducing the elements of a strict contrapuntal practice into the gradually dissolving tonal framework.

In treating the development of music of this period, Theodor Adorno observes that in harmonies composed of an unusual combination of intervals, the single note becomes less integral to the unity of the chord.[8] In a series of such chords, these comparatively loose notes lend themselves more easily to polyphonic treatment than they would do in simple diatonic progressions. Chord progressions of relatively constant and similar tension (according to Schoenberg's theory, dissonances are equal to heightened consonances) demand new means of counteracting the greyness and uniformity of harmonic texture. Schoenberg felt the need to reintroduce elements of strict counterpoint into his music. There are many examples of this in such works as the Five Orchestral Pieces, the opera *Die glückliche Hand* (1913) and *Pierrot lunaire* (1912). For example, at Fig. 10 in the first of the Five Orchestral Pieces, the trumpet plays a *cantus firmus*-like motif of ten bars in minims. This motif enters simultaneously in crotchets in the trombone part, while at the same time violins and violas play the motif as a canon at the octave in quavers. Eight bars later the strings bring a four-part canon of the motif at only a quaver's distance. Such adaptations of the principles of imitation to form the musical basis of the texture is one of the simpler examples of Schoenberg's contrapuntal practice. He took the devices known to contrapuntalists further than even Bach did in his strictest contrapuntal compositions. Besides making continuous use of augmentation and diminution, canon, fugato, passacaglia and other contrapuntal forms, he introduced inversion, cancrizans and quite a number of even more obscure contrapuntal practices which had not been in use since works such as the Musical Offering and the *Hammerklavier* Sonata. In the times of Bach and Beethoven, strict contrapuntal devices were modified according to the principles of tonality. While this was essential for the expressiveness and perfection of the harmonic style, the form-giving significance of real counterpoint was weakened. For example, in Beethoven's Op. 135 String Quartet, the interversions of the three-note motif are of only limited significance, the musical structure being achieved by other means. For Schoenberg such procedures had far more importance, in that he treated the contrapuntal devices as form-giving elements in themselves. In doing this, he made a major formal innovation within the principles of musical structure of his time, as such contrapuntal methods had hardly been used for three hundred years.

Schoenberg went very far in his emphasis on counterpoint. His music was impelled more and more by purely contrapuntal means, rather than by a fusion of harmony with counterpoint, so that in certain passages he actually endangered the primarily harmonic validity apparent in the post-Wagnerian musical language. In this, he went further than Mahler, who had also been working in this direction. Thus, comparing the Adagio of the latter's Tenth Symphony (1911), sketches of which were published after Mahler's death, with the first or last movements of his Ninth Symphony (1909), which in its finished state it would no doubt have resembled, we see that Mahler still conceived his work in the first instance vertically, only later dissolving it into its characteristically polyphonic texture. But even in a work as early as Schoenberg's Chamber Symphony, although it is still to a great extent conditioned by functional-harmonic considerations, many passages are no longer harmonically conceived, to such an extent are they primarily contrapuntal. The introduction of this rigid contrapuntal practice not only allowed the realisation of vertical combinations which were later to become the norm in Schoenberg's music, but also tended towards the even further liquidation of other traditional formal principles. In the final works of the early period the whole texture becomes so detailed, so attenuated and so fragmentary that harmonic development as it had been understood since the time of Bach virtually disappeared.

Among the younger generation, there is frequent criticism of Schoenberg's seeming lack of method in rhythmic construction. This criticism, made especially by non-German musicians, is based on a completely erroneous comparison of the characteristics of Schoenberg's German cultural tradition and those of other national schools. We do not wish to minimise the validity of Stravinsky's rhythmic methods or of other forms of rhythmic construction resulting from a strict attention to the combination of numerical values. On the contrary, one may well find a development of this long-neglected aspect of musical composition desirable. But it is valueless to criticise a composer from a viewpoint he did not share and consequently could not consider. The thinking that led Messiaen and his school to their adoption of rhythmic composition and eventually to serial forms of rhythmic construction could only have been alien to Schoenberg, even if known to him. It is important to remember that German music had always been rather simple in its rhythms; Luther's hymns had been a typically Protestant simplification of the subtle style of Gregorian chant. One need only look at the simple metres of German poetry of the Middle Ages, which always had a far more limited range of rhythmical interests than did that of other nations. The essence of German music can be found in rhythms of more or less regular patterns within binary and ternary forms. It was these, and not the more varied rhythms of the South or of the Slavs, that were in use in Germany throughout most of its musical history. The Germans wholeheartedly accepted the simple peasant dances of their own and neighbouring countries, and the march and *Ländler* form the main source of rhythmical inspiration in German music. (The other characteristic ingredient of German music, the sentimental song, is to be found at a very early date in the *Lochheimer Liederbuch*; its primitive rhythm and free layout became the main source of the characteristic singing melodies of the German slow movement.)

In the late eighteenth and early nineteenth centuries, the German composers developed a refined and subtle manner of using the few rhythmic elements which were known to them. The most astonishing examples are Haydn and above all Mozart, who brought to perfection a technique of composing with varied bar- and phrase-lengths. In doing this, they accorded with modern concepts concerning the nature of rhythm. Matila C. Ghyka, in his *Essai sur le rythme*,[9] quotes several remarkable definitions of rhythm, among them: 'Rhythm is in time what symmetry is in the Platonic sense, viz. the proportional arrangements of elements in space'. And, Professor Sonnenschein: 'Rhythm is that property of a sequence of events in time, which produces on the mind of the observer the impression of a proportion between the durations of the several events or groups of events of which the sequence is composed.'[10] If we agree with these definitions, or with the definition of James Joyce that rhythm is the relation of the parts to the whole, we find that in the music of the time of Mozart and

Haydn, many elements contributed to the expression of the rhythmic structure. In a deceptively simple manner, Mozart manages to create a form which is built of asymmetric quantities. We find examples of the diminutions and augmentations expressed not only in the juxtaposition of rhythmic elements, but also in the closely calculated interchanges of different types of musical texture (diatonic scales, chromatic scales, arpeggios etc.). Alban Berg in his article 'Why Is the Music of Schoenberg so Hard to Understand?' draws attention to this characteristic of Mozart's music. He quotes the nineteenth-century German theorist Bussler: 'The greatest masters of form cherish free and bold constructions and rebel against being squeezed into the confines of even-numbered bar groups.'[11] This method was further developed in the nineteenth century. The English writer C. F. Abdy Williams (in *The Rhythm of Modern Music*[12]) devotes a great deal of space to the analysis of the music of Brahms and others from this viewpoint. Wagner with the free declamatory style in his *Musikdrama* also contributed greatly to the freeing of the musical construction from the 'prison' of the regular bar groups.

Schoenberg was particularly interested in these rhythmic methods and created forms in which the music became almost totally free of metre. In this way he composed *Pierrot lunaire*, *Erwartung*, the Four Orchestral Songs, Op. 22, and *Die glückliche Hand*, among other works. It is a matter of great interest that later, with his adoption of twelve-tone technique, he tended to abandon this style of 'musical prose' and in such works as the Piano Suite, Op. 25 (1923), and the last two string quartets wrote phrases of varied lengths within a simple, almost static, rhythmical form. Here he is most closely allied to the eighteenth century. Whether this was a satisfactory development of the early twelve-tone technique could be disputed, and it is certainly a proof of the clearsightedness and the genius of Schoenberg that during the last years of his life he returned to the richer rhythmical structure of the works that he had written just before the adoption of the twelve-tone system.

These rhythmic developments went hand in hand with Schoenberg's development of the free-moving melody. Schubert, Schumann and Wagner had contributed towards a melody of great subjective expression. Schoenberg, after Wagner and Wolf, introduced the wide spans of series of compound intervals into his melodies. Although chromatic elements, variations of character and the creation of interval contrasts are already well developed by Wagner in the singing line of the parts of Brünnhilde and Isolde, Schoenberg's freeing of the octave led to a melos in which intervals appear as a result of melodic, as opposed to harmonic, elaborations and octave displacements. The abundance of passing notes and rhythmic decoration, in relation to the structural movement of harmony, which was a well-known characteristic of post-Wagnerian style, led Schoenberg to a form of melody which, for the sake of tension and variety, carefully avoids the notes sounding in the supporting harmony and gets more and more shy of repeating notes.

Schoenberg continued the endeavours of composers of the nineteenth century to expand and extend the existing forms of music. He went further than Mahler, who had considerably developed traditional forms. At the turn of the century, the discovery by Freud of the existence of free association and the consequent feeling for less logically and more subjectively connected association in art had the greatest significance for the development of Expressionism. They led Schoenberg to a greater degree of formal detail, an increasing amount of variation and a tendency to compress the single ideas of a piece into shorter spaces of time. In the first Chamber Symphony, although he is still working within a traditional form derived from the one-movement symphonic structure developed by Liszt, he liquidates many elements of this form and resorts frequently to a method which can be considered an equivalent to free association (Schoenberg liked to call these passages, which one can already find in Mahler, *Inselbildung*). Gradually, his habit of rarely repeating any subject, even in a varied form, led to the difficulty of understanding Schoenberg's music. This is certainly the underlying reason why the works of Schoenberg are, and probably will continue to be, more difficult for the ordinary listener to appreciate than the music of Webern, Berg and other composers of his time. Schoenberg himself seemed conscious of, and disturbed by, this fact, and he adopted many methods, some successful, some less so, in his efforts to overcome these difficulties. Many of the innovations he introduced, culminating in that of the twelve-tone technique, were designed to clarify and illuminate the highly individual development of his musical thinking. He dispenses with colour for its own sake and in his instrumentation uses the orchestra to bring the important lines of his musical argument into greater relief. At the same time he invented a new type of the application of orchestral colour, the *Klangfarbenmelodie* or melody of 'timbres', first to be found in a systematic application in the third of his Five Orchestral Pieces, 'Farben'. The musical argument of this piece is carried by changes of emphasis in instrumental groups, creating an entirely new kind of expression. In the fifth piece, 'Das obligate Rezitativ', the instrumentation is used to give the melody a constantly changing colour. (This technique is obviously an extension of the Wagnerian 'endless melody'.) The result of this experiment is that the natural connections and logical developments in his music can sometimes be more easily understood by the ear than by the eye.

As we have shown with the development of his harmony and counterpoint, when Schoenberg's works were no longer effectively bound by traditional structural forms, he was faced with the problem of finding suitable new forms. In his Six Little Piano Pieces, Op. 19, he attempted to restrict himself to the exposition and variation of one single idea. The best example is the last piece, allegedly inspired by Mahler's funeral, in which the alternation of chords and fragments of motifs, probably derived from the memory of bells, constitutes the piece. In these pieces, Schoenberg attempts something fundamentally different from the short pieces of Berg and Webern. Whereas Berg in his Clarinet Pieces tended to contract what had been large forms and Webern in many of his short pieces used traditional formal principles, which found here the utmost concentration imaginable, Schoenberg made his ideas suitable to the limitations of a completely integrated short form. Later, when he attempted larger forms again, we find a seemingly chaotic juxtaposition of such short forms, and it is in these works that the most daring and far-developed examples of Schoenberg's personal, essentially expressionistic, art are to be found. Yet they remain valid as a perfect development of the characteristic integration of form and content.

3

In order to conclude this part of the discussion, we shall examine a work which may be regarded as typical of the most advanced and most individual Schoenberg ever reached: the monodrama in one act *Erwartung*. Unfortunately it is not possible to go into sufficient detail to clarify all our opinions, but it is hoped that it will be sufficient to justify our argument.

The first reaction upon hearing *Erwartung* is the very antithesis of the experience when listening to the perfection and apparent Apollonian symmetry of the eighteenth-century classicists. That particular effect upon the listener of Classical music at its zenith was obtained by a skilful balance of asymmetries and variants which was so well realised that it resulted in the illusion of perfect symmetry. The style of Schoenberg's music tended to cover the well-calculated proportions in its texture which has, as has that of Wagner, an appearance of almost continuous unbroken movement. In *Erwartung* we experience a sense of being lost in a maze of variation and of being overwhelmed by a juxtaposition of elements which are hardly memorable and result in a seeming structural incoherence. But, as we get to know the composition better, we find that all these variants and 'free associations' are well moulded into an overall shape and can be understood in a similar way to the works in the style of the preceding, post-Wagnerian era. Though the chordal structure is complex, and the individual parts are heavily doubled in augmented fourths, sevenths etc. (which in this case tend to loosen the vertical coherence), an arc is circumscribed and the basic tonal principle of movement away from and towards a point or centre is retained. The technique of the work does not in itself seem to be a new departure. The basic idea for such immensely long and involved tonal structures had already been developed by Wagner, Mahler and Strauss. The novelty of the aural harmony results from the development described above. One feels that Schoenberg here already starts 'composing with notes': that is, that he tends to replace triads as the functional agents with the identity of individual tones.

The music of *Erwartung* falls into two parts. The overall 'top line' (Schenker might have called it the *Urlinie*), whether expressed by the voice or by the instruments, is clearly delineated, although it cannot everywhere be found in the apparent main themes and motifs of the music. The first section commences with a progression from G♯ via B♭ to C♯ at the beginning of the composition and closes in bar 270 at the words 'Nun küss ich mich an dir zum Tode'. The climax is reached in bars 190–93, at the cry 'Hilfe', with an accent and a leap down from the highest note of the voice part (B♭) to C♯ above middle C, a fall of well-nigh two octaves. The second part proceeds from bar 270 to the end. The general division is a dramatic one: the first half consisting of the woman's search and discovery of her lover's body and her subsequent dementia, the second part of a kind of 'Liebestod' which she sings in a fervid state of anguish and jealousy of the other 'she' (Death, who has taken her lover).

The orchestral introduction of three bars makes a clear movement from G♯ through B♭ to C♯ (quasi-dominant/tonic). It is repeated in a contracted form, this time moving to the leading note (C♮ = B♯ [harp, bar 3]); the soprano enters for the first time on C♯. The first scene, as it were in closed form, is clearly founded on a structure in which the notes C♯ and G♯ are predominant. To add to the illusion of a closed form, many of the chords are retained literally and appear throughout the scene. Practically all the important structural notes, the notes that begin and end all the phrases, are C♯ and its neighbour notes. There is a movement towards an emphasis on the semitone below at bars 29ff., but also a clear return to the quasi-tonic of C♯ in the codetta of the scene (bars 35ff.). In the following scenes there is a gradual heightening of tension. Twice high B♭s, in bars 153 and 179, lead to the cry 'Hilfe' in bar 190, on the high B♭ that falls back to C♯. This is the overall climax and the highest point of the melodic line. From here the melody falls, often in long leaps, back to the C♯ in bar 270. (It is interesting to observe the parallel of the falling minor sixth A–C♯ in bars 194 and 270, obviously characteristic as a cadential movement as well as a psychological weakening, a premonition of death.)

The second half commences from G♯ (the first note of bars 273 and 274) and moves up to the B♭ of bar 313, cadencing back to G♯ at bar 317, just before the extraordinary bars where the voice sings the words 'Oh, der Mond schwankt . . .' From here, the music falls again, with greatly augmenting note values, to the dramatic turning-point in bar 350, 'für mich ist kein Platz da . . .' The final section, which seems to act as a kind of spiritual resolution, lowers the tension by the introduction of chords of whole-tone triads, which move in a regular manner and, turning, reach another section in which C♯ seems to assume an important position, being introduced as a pedal in bar 416 and remaining prominent in the voice part, especially at the cadencing on 'dir entgegen . . .' in bars 422–3. The C♯ disappears completely in bar 424, allowing the bass to make a determined step towards B♭. The final solution comes in the third bassoon's C♯ in the middle of bar 425, introduced most characteristically by the last melodic phrase of the opera. The voice, which had again taken the G♯ (quasi-dominant) at bar 424, continues in bar 425 with its last utterance and moves by a tritone to G♯, just after the C♯ bass has been established by the bassoon. The oblique vertical resolution of the harmony is characteristic of Schoenberg's methods. It is also not without importance that the three trumpets enter on the triad A–C♯–F♮ at the point where the third bassoon reaches C♯ in the higher octave.

It might seem that an analysis made in the ways briefly indicated above must have but limited validity in this type of music. Yet we feel that the replacing of a harmonically valid form by an overall melodic one, though it could not have the significance of the old forms, nevertheless enabled the composer to differentiate between sections that return to their starting-point and those that move away from it. This is of the greatest importance towards an understanding of the subsequent revolution in the manner of composing music. The position may be compared to that reached by Joyce in *Finnegans Wake*. In this work, the author was able to hold a thread through the maze of images, diversions, etc. only by means of a continuous and relatively unvaried repetition of the so-called story (the cycle of death and rebirth). Evidently the method of free association could no longer in itself prove to be a satisfactory manner of creation. The artists concerned seem to have realised that in order to create larger and more variegated forms they needed a structural principle that would enable them to maintain some structural control over the perpetual variants that their expression demanded.

4

After the astonishing realisation of the last works described, it became apparent to Schoenberg that to continue his musical creation he had now constantly and intellectually to develop his method of composition with twelve tones. He saw clearly that for a time he would have to apply this method, which was entirely new, to forms much less elaborate than those he had used before. He made concessions in using older and simpler forms which he had formerly discarded. Even the regular sonata form and the form of the classical variations were used again and again, but now filled with the completely new content resulting from his initially strict use of the twelve-tone system. Although the last period of Schoenberg's musical creation (which does not come within the scope of this chapter) must be considered quite as important as the earlier periods, and he achieved works which can in every way stand comparison with his earlier ones, perhaps even in some cases surpassing them, the line of development in this last period is not as clearly definable as it had been earlier. While endeavouring to give older forms new content, Schoenberg creates intermittently works which might at first sight appear to continue directly the style of the great expressionist compositions like *Pierrot lunaire, Die glückliche Hand* and *Erwartung* – for example, *Ode to Napoleon, A Survivor from Warsaw* and especially parts of his opera *Moses und Aron.* But when observed and analysed in more detail, these works, although in effect and texture frequently reminiscent of those of an earlier period, speak in a completely new musical language and the use of the twelve-tone system is here, quite naturally and logically, freer and less strict than in those works based on older forms (which, for want of a better word, may be described as 'neo-classicist'). Schoenberg also, in some of the masterpieces of the last period (e.g. the Variations for Orchestra, Op. 31 (1928), and particularly *Moses und Aron*), combines new, free forms, which he went on creating in direct continuation of his expressionist period, with more stylised, 'classical' sections. The introduction and the extraordinary finale of the Variations for Orchestra are much nearer to this free expression than the variations themselves, which are kept to a large extent within the classical frame. And in *Moses und Aron*, for dramatic and other reasons – some of the material had been sketched many years earlier, during Schoenberg's expressionist period – free forms, with all the manifold applications of *Inselbildungen* and purely linear-based formulations (as explained in our analysis of *Erwartung*), alternate with the more consolidated and simplified forms of the dance movements.

Schoenberg's treatment of harmony and counterpoint certainly underwent a great simplification as soon as he had decided to compose in the strict twelve-tone system. Harmonically this system gave him security in its definite application, and in counterpoint he was no longer hampered by the unclear position in which the polyphonic style had been ever since the introduction of tonal and, later, functional harmony. In fact, only then did counterpoint regain the freedom and expression that it had had at the time of the early Flemish and Italian schools.

Schoenberg's rhythm (except in those few compositions in which he kept very close to traditional dance or *Lied* forms), together with his basic adherence to musical prose, was not developed much further in his last period. Here and there a simplification may be observed, but seldom a new refinement. The tonal works of the last period need not be discussed here, as they were written partly for teaching purposes or as commissions for certain American institutions. And Schoenberg has told us that several of these compositions, especially the very beautiful Second Chamber Symphony (1939), were based on material invented in his youth.

Schoenberg was a master of German music. Even the fact that he spent the later part of his life in America in no way changed his determination to follow to the end logically and methodically what he felt was the right way (although living in America had considerably changed the style and attitude of many composers, e.g. Hindemith and Bartók). We should like to see in Schoenberg's last achievement, *Moses und Aron*, on which he worked practically all his life, the climax of his musical creation.[13] Unfortunately he did not live to finish this work. The short experience we have of it gives us the impression that this is a work of supreme inspiration, perhaps Schoenberg's greatest. Quite new effects of sound, harmony and rhythm take us by surprise in the famous dances from Act II. The rhythm especially, as never before in Schoenberg's works, moves in an orbit not far from Stravinsky's, and the whole expression is far more striking than in any of Schoenberg's works since *Erwartung*.

We are not here concerned with the fact that Schoenberg's work will always be much more difficult for the listener and the student than the works of his pupils and other contemporary composers. We do not think that this fact has anything to do with the greatness of his inspiration and fulfilment. It will always be amazing to observe the particular intellectual quality of Schoenberg's compositions, their fast-moving sequence of thought and invention, their most imaginative colours of orchestration and the sometimes harsh and insistent reiteration of strong sounds and expressions. Just as we must recognise that Wagner's work, although prepared by many major innovators, was the culmination of nineteenth-century German music, we must surely recognise that Schoenberg's achievements – his compositions, his teachings and his writings – as well as his personal seriousness and his belief in his mission, make him the greatest and most important musician of the first half of the twentieth century.

(1957)

1. In *Das Meisterwerk in der Musik*, Vol. 3 (Munich: Drei Masken Verlag, 1930), p. 12. [This work has been translated into English as *The Masterwork in Music*, ed. William Drabkin (Cambridge: CUP, 1994–7). The translations used throughout this collection are AG's.]

2. [The characterisation of Brahms offered here is clearly influenced by Schoenberg's argument in 'Brahms the Progressive'. By 1983 AG had had second thoughts: cf. 'Brahms's *Aktualität*', pp. 175–88 below.]

3. Quoted by Dika Newlin in *Bruckner, Mahler, Schoenberg* (New York: Philosophical Library, 1947), p. 236.

4. [See *Style and Idea*, 2nd edn, ed. Leonard Stein (London: Faber, 1975), p. 414.]

5. [See *Theory of Harmony*, trans. Roy E. Carter (London: Faber, 1978); *Structural Functions of Harmony*, ed. Leonard Stein (London: Williams and Norgate, 1954).]

6. (Leipzig, 1853).

7. [AG is surely thinking of Hindemith's analysis of the Piano Piece Op. 33a, a twelve-tone rather than an atonal piece (but obviously the same reservations would apply). See Hindemith, *Craft of Musical Composition*, Vol. 1 (New York: Associated Music Publishers, 1942), pp. 217–18.]

8. [Source unidentified.]

9. (Paris: Gallimard, 1938).

10. *What Is Rhythm?* (Oxford, 1925).

11. [See Willi Reich, *Alban Berg*, trans. Cornelius Cardew (London: Thames and Hudson, 1965), p. 191.]

12. (London, 1909).

13. At the time of the writing of this article, Schoenberg's unfinished opera was posthumously performed for the first time. Hence the 'last'.

7

Schoenberg and Karl Kraus: The Idea behind the Music

In the last scene of Schoenberg's incomplete opera *Moses und Aron* Moses confronts his brother with the wrath of the true Old-Testament patriarch. Aron is barely able to defend himself: 'I have done only what was my task: when your idea (*Gedanke*) yielded no word for their ears, when my word yielded no image for their eyes, I created a miracle.' Moses has been away from his people for a long time, and they have believed him to be dead. Reproachfully, he asks Aron whether he has any understanding of the all-pervasiveness of the Idea in Word and Image; and Aron seems to avoid a direct reply. Instead he defends his actions, saying, 'I understand only this: this people is to be saved ... I love this people.' But Moses will not bend: 'I love my Idea and live for it ... The people *must* understand the Idea. It is only for the sake of it that they exist.' Taking courage, Aron reproaches Moses: 'You are bound to your Idea.' 'Yes,' answers Moses, 'to my Idea, as these tablets express it.' Aron: 'But they too are only an image, a part of the Idea.' Moses now seems to grasp the inconsistency of his position and angrily smashes the Tablets of the Law. He resigns from his self-appointed task; he stands defeated. 'Inconceivable God! Inexpressible, all-pervasive Idea! ... So have I too made an image – false as an image must be! So am I defeated. Everything I have thought has been madness and cannot and must not be said. O Word, you Word that I lack!'[1]

I want to discuss what Schoenberg was trying to convey with this Idea, which his Moses seems to equate even with God ('Inconceivable God, inexpressible, all-pervasive Idea'); and I should like to comment on the manner in which he chose to depict his Moses – one might say, his peculiar stance. Moses is absorbed by the integrity of his concept of the Idea. This sets him apart from his brother and his people. We know that he will not live to lead his people to the Promised Land, but will see it only from afar. He will disappear ('but no man knoweth of his sepulchre unto this day': Deut. 34,6). But his name will be a memory for his people; it will embody the Idea; his people will be called the people of Moses; and their law will be the Mosaic Law. They too, they will claim (as Schoenberg himself must have claimed, when, in the early 1930s in Paris, he was received back into the faith of his fathers), will be set apart from the peoples of the world by this legacy.

Schoenberg was not, in any conventional sense, a religious thinker. His work as composer, writer and theoretician is marked by a personal mode and style. Even where it is most obviously derivative of his models, as in his youthful compositions, or where he deals with theoretical and technical matters, it is very easy to recognise him. His expression is strident, sometimes laconic, elsewhere quite long-winded; and his argument and logic frequently reveal contradictory pressures and aspirations. In his music, the characteristic gesture is the rapidly rising voice, the forceful, sometimes foreshortened closure. This is partially the mark of his times and his tongue; but far more it is the voice of the man himself. Small wonder, then, if we think we can see some connection between his view of himself, as man and artist, and his portrait of Moses. It would be to accuse him of an overwhelming arrogance were we to suggest that in his Moses he had, in fact, attempted a self-portrait. But it is quite possible, indeed probable, that he should have given Moses words that expressed his own innermost beliefs about the nature of his work and his personal ethics; especially so, if we come to recognise that an ethical concern distinguishes him from run-of-the-mill composers, who do not want and are not able to think so intensely about the whys and wherefores of what they do. 'Everything I have written has a certain inner likeness to myself', he wrote.[2]

In the argument between Moses and Aron described above, Aron catches Moses in a contradiction. Moses seems to derive his concept of an inexpressible, all-pervasive Idea from the Jewish law 'Thou shalt not make thee any graven image' (Deut. 5,8). This in its turn, gives rise to the Word and the Law, and it is this law which is engraved on the two sides of the Tablets. But these words, in which the law is written and which convey the Idea *behind it* (as we would say), in themselves constitute an image and as such are false. Carrying the interpretation to such extremes makes Moses realise the impossibility of the whole undertaking. At the end of the opera, in complete gloom, he gives up; and so did Schoenberg. The opera remained incomplete, and despite sporadic attempts to continue there is little evidence to suppose that he was really able to imagine a concluding act. Certainly the text for the third act, printed in the score, gives one little idea of what a conclusion worthy of the venture might have been.

In an uncanny way, the motif of incompleteness connects with Schoenberg's continuing preoccupation with his concept of an inexpressible Idea. Unfinished projects abound in the life of this singularly impulsive and almost over-fertile man. A whole procession of such projects is bound together by this single preoccupation. First there was a plan for a five-movement choral symphony of Mahlerian scope and proportions, noted down from 1912 to 1914.[3] One section of this was called 'Death-Dance of Principles', and a text for it was published. The last part of the symphony became the basis for *Die Jakobsleiter*, the unfinished oratorio about the search of modern man for God. This is described in letters to the poet Richard Dehmel, who remarked of it: 'This is not an oratorio, but a heroic drama – Saul, Jonathan, David – but removed from the biblical realm into a mystical sphere.'[4]

At approximately the same period, and after the publication of his *Harmonielehre*, Schoenberg began to be concerned with the notion of a theoretical work to be called 'The Musical Idea, its Representation and Continuation' (*Der musikalische Gedanke, seine Darstellung und Durchführung*), or what is usually called the *Gedanke* Manuscript.[5] As far as I can ascertain, the first draft of this proposed theoretical work is dated 6 July 1925, although evidence suggests a much earlier beginning. Unfinished, it was put away in a folder marked 'Gedanke' and taken out from time to time, with a protracted spell of work on it between 1934 and 1936. Rufer quotes a revealing sentence on a pasted-on bit of paper, dated 7 April 1929: 'The question as to what a musical idea is has never been answered up till now – if indeed, it has ever been asked.' And in a postscript the composer adds: 'I thought that I would be able to state this clearly today, I had it so clearly in mind. But I must still wait. Perhaps, though, I shall come to it yet.'[6] In a letter of 6 June 1934 to Carl Engel of the publisher G. Schirmer, he refers to the project as a 'key book' (*Schlüsselbuch*), and says that he has worked on the subject for twenty years (which takes us back to 1914, the date of the projected symphony).[7] And in a letter to Edgar Prinzhorn of 1932, written in response for a request that he should write about the twelve-tone technique, he ripostes:

I have published nothing about 'composition with twelve tones related only to one another' and do not wish to do so until the principal part of my theory is ready: the 'Study of Musical Logic'. For I believe that meaningful advantage can be derived from this art of composition when it is based on knowledge and realization that comes from musical logic; and that is also the reason why I do not teach my students 'twelve-tone composition', but 'composition', in the sense of musical logic; the rest will then come, sooner or later, by itself.[8]

Later, of course, after Schoenberg's death, the keyword *Gedanke* was joined with 'Style' to become *Style and Idea*, the title given to his collected essays.

Schoenberg made various attempts to define what a musical idea is.[9] Apparently none of his definitions fully satisfied him. As early as 1922 he writes:

Science is concerned to present its ideas conclusively and in such a way that no question remains unanswered. Art on the other hand is satisfied with what is general [literally, many-sided], and the Idea rises up unambiguously from this, without having to be directly defined. A window remains open through which intuition may enter.

As I understand this passage, Schoenberg is saying that, while he is unable to state precisely what the Idea is, it may be divined in the complex texture of the music itself. He continues:

In counterpoint we are not concerned with combination for its own sake (it is not an end in itself), but rather with all-pervasive presentations of the Idea: the theme is composed in such a manner that all these many formulations [*Gestalten*] through which this all-pervasive presentation of the Idea becomes possible are already concealed within it.[10]

From this we learn, if not what the Idea is, at least what it is not. It is not a theme; nor is it anything like a twelve-tone row, which according to Schoenberg's later definition has the same properties that he here attributes to the theme. The theme conceals within itself the means of being varied and developed throughout an entire composition; and the many forms in which it is presented combine to bring about the 'all-pervasive presentation of the Idea'.

We are shown here a string of terms, one derived from another: theme leading to variations and developments, or *Grundgestalt* (basic form) leading to derived *Gestalten* (forms). But these *Gestalten* are not the same as *Gedanken* (ideas), which are continued by means of *musikalische Logik* (musical logic). For logical thought gives rise to new combinations of theme, variation and development. In their turn these may become the vehicle for a series of new ideas. All these ideas are the logical continuation of the original Idea. The conclusion we must draw is that the Idea is not of the tones themselves, in any particular order or combination, and yet the tones cannot exist meaningfully without the hidden presence of the Idea.

Schoenberg appears to have seen no substantial difficulty in translating such a concept of 'Idea' to music. He writes:

> If an idea may be defined as the establishing of relationships between things, concepts etc. (so also between ideas), so with a musical idea, such a relationship can only be established between tones and it can only be a musical relationship.

And just as an idea need not necessarily be thought in words, but rather in complexes or in representations, perhaps even in feelings, so a musical idea is not necessarily to be thought of in the pitch dimension alone, but may also be conceived in space and sound, in dynamic complexes, in rhythm and perhaps even in other dimensions. The implication is that, if an idea is embodied in language, its further development must observe the laws of language, as well as the general laws of thought; analogously, a musical idea must obey the laws of music. 'We may think in words and obey the rules for the combining of words, and equally we may think in tones and obey the rules for the combining of tones.'[11]

Most musicians will be puzzled by this concept of a musical idea. But it is clarified by the way in which Schoenberg deals with what he calls 'the logic, technique and art of its presentation'. In a curious way, however, this very process of clarification creates another difficulty, for whereas Schoenberg expends much energy in defining the usual elements of musical discourse – motif, theme, variation etc. – his very descriptions and prescriptions raise a suspicion that he is confusing his absolute, almost transcendental concept of the 'Idea' with his concepts of theme, *Grundgestalt* and twelve-tone row. Now, the concept of *Grundgestalt* in particular (a concept which has been discussed by David Epstein in *Beyond Orpheus*[12] and by Patricia Carpenter[13] among others) is a valuable and original tool for the analysing of some aspects of musical unity and continuity. All the fragmentary sections of the *Gedanke* Manuscript, in their translation of *Gedanke* into its derived forms, bring us back to the consideration of conventional musical techniques, such as development, theme shaping and techniques of variation. In the Schoenbergian conception these techniques obtain significance only insofar as they relate to the non-substantial Idea. But as this was never defined, many of the actual discussions appear disappointingly familiar, especially as they were extensively cannibalised by Schoenberg for his later harmony book[14] and the books on counterpoint and composition posthumously published by Stein and Strang.[15] As with the opera *Moses und Aron*, it is not unfair to surmise that here again the incompleteness of the manuscript indicates not only lack of time and energy, brought about by the hard conditions of Schoenberg's life in America, but also a real intellectual quandary. My own suspicion is that he believed that the concept of an Idea was central to his whole being as an artist and thinker, but at the same time could not satisfactorily define it in relation to the real world of composing.

He is quite clear about one thing, though: meaning in music arises from the manipulation of tones. Music is not to be considered as a vehicle for the expression of ideas or sensations derived from words. It is non-referential, born out of a meditation on the real world and presumably about things in the real world, but expressed according to the laws of music. He sums up:

> If the idea is expressed in language and follows its rules, as well as the general rules of thought, then the expression of the musical idea is possible in only one way, through tones; and the idea obeys the rules of tones as well as corresponding approximately to the rules of thought.[16]

Here, then, logical thought in music is not merely a transposition from logical thought in language (with its own significations), but a self-sufficient and independent system for describing the real world, where a musical idea, turning into a *Gestalt* and becoming in the act of composing a *Grundgestalt*, generates further *Gestalten* and thus expresses a musical logic.

3

Schoenberg repeatedly draws a parallel between the idea expressed in words and the idea expressed in tones. This suggests that his thought derives not so much from traditional musical thinking, or even from the philosophical aesthetics of music, as from the philosophy of language. It is well known that Schoenberg was extremely close to the writer Karl Kraus. He contributed early on to Kraus's periodical *Die Fackel* (The Torch). Later, in a questionnaire, he was to write: 'In the dedication of a copy of my *Harmonielehre* which I sent to Karl Kraus, I said, "I have perhaps learned more from you than one is permitted to learn if one wishes to remain independent." ' And he added: 'By this is meant not so much the scope as the level of regard that I hold for him.'[17]

Problems of subject-matter (which is often concerned with very local matters) and the difficulty of translation have ensured that Kraus's work remains comparatively unknown in the English-speaking world. From the second volume of Elias Canetti's recent autobiography, called, significantly, *Die Fackel im Ohr* (The Torch in My Ear),[18] we get some idea of Kraus's immense standing in Vienna in the years preceding, during and after the First World War, and the violent antipathies he aroused. His thought had a great effect not only on Canetti but also on Wittgenstein, Brecht, Walter Benjamin and probably Freud, as well as upon his immediate circle of friends, which included the architect Adolf Loos, the poet Peter Altenberg, the painter Kokoschka, Schoenberg and his pupils Webern, Berg and the pianist Eduard Steuermann. In his early days he had to do not only with the philosopher Otto Weininger but also with the playwrights Wedekind and Strindberg. Originally setting out to be an actor, he wrote poetry of great purity and translated some of Shakespeare's sonnets. He also wrote an enormous, rather Joycean and almost unperformable drama, *Die letzten Tage der Menschheit* (The Last Days of Mankind), set against the background of the Great War.[19] He financed his most ambitious and long-lasting activity, the periodical *Die Fackel*, which accepted no advertisements and few contributions from other writers, by a series of immensely fashionable public readings and performances of his own versions of plays and operettas by Shakespeare, Nestroy and Offenbach. (One of these performances is described by Canetti.)

In these performances Kraus played all the parts. He was not, apparently, a great singer in the usual sense of the word, and we read in a review by Schoenberg's pupil Paul A. Pisk that he had little sense of pitch. This review prompted an irate letter to *Die Fackel* from Steuermann, co-signed by Rudolf Kolisch and Alban Berg, interestingly, and for our purposes relevantly, suggesting that although Kraus was not in any sense a trained musician he could convey the meaning of the music, and to do this did not depend entirely on hitting the right notes.[20] If this letter is to be taken seriously, it would suggest that the meaning (or idea) of music can be conveyed by gestures approximating to the shape of the musical phrases.

Die Fackel is primarily concerned with language; not so much with theory or philosophy of any kind as with the exposure of meaning, especially where this derives from misuse. Fundamentally Kraus was a conservative, who regarded technical progress as a weapon of those who, for reasons of self-aggrandisement and in the search for power, exploited others, and, in so doing, distorted the naive and proper use of the written and spoken word. He saw this happening in the newspapers, and particularly in the propaganda surrounding the beginnings of the First World War; he also saw it in the 'false tone' of poets such as Stefan George, whose Shakespeare translations he disliked for that reason. Above all, he was a sceptic – and a fierce one: 'My beliefs about language cast doubt on all ways that lead to Rome.'[21] He expressed these beliefs in *Sprüche und Widersprüche* (Sayings and Countersayings/ Contradictions), published in 1909. Here he suggests: 'There are two kinds of writers, those who are and those who are not. In the first category, form and content belong together as body and soul; in the second, form and content match as body and dress.' From this arise further aphorisms about the functions of literature, the ethical imperatives upon writers and the betrayal of such imperatives:

> The written word is the natural, essential embodiment of an idea, not the socially acceptable wrapping of an opinion ... The agitator takes hold of the word; the artist is taken by it ... The material of music is tone, the painter speaks in colours. No self-respecting layman whose language is the word makes judgments about music and painting. The writer uses a material available to all, the word. So every reader judges the art of the word. The tone-deaf and the colour-blind are modest. Sign language suffices to communicate the ideas which they have to communicate to each other. Are we entitled persistently to besmirch our clothes with oil-paint?[22]

According to his first biographer, Leopold Liegler, Kraus considered language not as a means of communication but as a means of revealing mental connections, since 'every idea is part of the real world. It is distributed into the parts of speech through a prism of quantitative perception.' Kraus sees the growth of the work of art as arising out of the organic build-up of the individual personality, and self-knowledge as arising out of the life of the community. This implies an ethical imperative, namely to express the Idea in the form of the written word. 'The writer has to know all the trains of thought that his work opens up ... the more the relationships, the greater the art. It is a matter of combining objectivity with background in a single stroke, so that the Idea is a precis of an essay.'[23]

If the determination of word by idea constitutes an ethical imperative, it follows that idea and word are not indissolubly linked. It thus becomes possible to misuse language, by deriving it from something other than the subjectively defined idea: for instance, it might arise out of the desire to manipulate, as in advertising and propaganda. There is a connection, then, between Kraus's beliefs about language and his fierce critical campaign against corruption in society. Just as banking and big business made use of the press, so journalists were drawn into the war effort: 'To have no idea and be able to express it, that's what journalists do.'[24] For Kraus the Idea is embedded within and realised in the constructs of language. A kind of organic growth is achieved which has its own independent existence and yet is related to the external world. The connection with music was first suggested by Ernst Krenek in his funeral address for Kraus in 1936. 'Music', he said, 'is the pre-historic, pre-logical existence of the idea, prior to its incarnation into the language process. The idea lives locked into its secret like a ladybird into a crystal.'[25] And in an article on Kraus and Schoenberg, first published in the periodical 23, Krenek suggests, rightly, that the two artists are connected primarily by the recognition of the ethical imperative inherent in Kraus's beliefs about language.[26] The ethical imperative is an important clue to the understanding, not only of Schoenberg's musical development, but also of his artistic stance ('I am a pupil of Mozart') and of the stance of his Moses. Both Schoenberg and Moses are men apart, servants of their ethical beliefs, 'aware', as Kant might have said, 'of their duty'.

Kraus's ideas may be traced back not only to Kant and Hegel, but more particularly to the German Romantics Schlegel, Brentano and Novalis. According to Friedrich Schlegel, 'An idea is a concept pushed to the extremes of irony, an absolute synthesis of absolute syntheses, the self-generating interchange of two conflicting ideas.' And Novalis writes: 'If only people would understand that, with language, it is as with mathematical formulae, they create a world of their own – they only play among themselves and express nothing but their marvellous nature, and just because of this they are expressive . . . Language is Delphi.'[27] The gap between language – as a freely developing system of words functioning according to its own rules – and the real world is bridged by the idea. The work of art is a synthesis in which a subjective perception of reality determines the structure of the language used. The similarity between Kraus's beliefs and Schoenbergian music theory consists primarily in the recognition that parts of speech are differentiated from ideas, yet this ingredient – the idea – determines the form of the speech (*Sprachgestalt*), which, however, is necessarily constructed according to the rules of speech. 'The surprising thing about this theory of language', remarks Krenek, 'is that it anticipates a theory of music which ought in fact to have anticipated it, insofar as music, which presupposes no extramusical material reality, ought never to have been conceived in any other way.'[28]

4

Echoes of Kraus's ideas ring through Schoenberg's writings. In the essay 'Problems in Teaching Art' he states: "The direction in which a true teacher of art would have to guide his pupils [is] towards that severe matter-of-factness which, more than anything else, is the distinguishing mark of everything truly personal.'[29]

Writing of his compatriot and the contemporary inventor of a twelve-tone technique, Josef Matthias Hauer, he suggests that Hauer 'looks for laws. Good. But he looks for them where he will not find them' – that is, not in Nature (Schoenberg here seems to identify the traditional musical language with nature itself). And writing of his friend David Bach he acknowledges the latter's influence on his character in 'furnishing it with the ethical and moral power needed to withstand vulgarity and commonplace popularity'.[30]

In popular image, Schoenberg is the inventor of the twelve-tone technique, and the difficulty of his music is put down to this. I am not concerned to deny that his music is difficult, but to suggest that the difficulty perhaps arises from his own definition of his task and from his particular stance. To clarify this, I should like to examine the way in which his Kraus-influenced beliefs affected some aspects of his work and contradicted his enthusiasm for the innovations of what we now call Expressionism.

Central to Schoenberg's compositional development is his use of motivic construction, which gives life to the otherwise still and inexpressive structures of harmony.[31] The motif is born directly out of the Idea and owes its significance to this fact. In an aesthetically successful piece, it recurs polyphonically in a continuous range of derived and varied forms, not only, as is commonly believed, to ensure unity, but also to carry on a logical and comprehensible argument in which Idea gives rise to related ideas through the agency of musical structures. This high aspiration lies at the heart of what has ignorantly been criticised in his work as a kind of retrogression into, if not a neo-classicism, at least a neo-academicism. However we rate his post-1918 compositions in relation to his earlier ones, it is important to avoid this mistaken interpretation of Schoenberg's reintroduction into his music of formal prototypes from earlier, tonal periods. Everything is there to create clarity; and this is the statement of a philosophical position, not the pious hope of a schoolmaster. The idea of clarity and restraint, the matter-of-factness (*Sachlichkeit*) referred to above, and the ideal of a composition proceeding from motifs which are developed as far as they can go – all this is common to the later works of Schoenberg and his principal pupils. It may be associated not only with the artistic beliefs but also with the actual literary style of Kraus. There is indeed an uncanny similarity of tone and method between a passage like the following (from an article by Kraus, written in 1914) and a movement from the Suite Op. 25 by Schoenberg or the Concerto Op. 24 by Webern:

In these great times, which I still knew when they were small, and which, if time remains, will become small again, and which, because in the domain of organic growth such transformation is impossible, we might well prefer to call fat times, or even weighty times; in these times, where precisely that happens which we cannot imagine and, were we able to imagine it, would not happen; in these serious times, which have laughed themselves to death, confronted with the possibility that they might be taken seriously; surprised by their own tragedy, they seek distraction, and, catching themselves in the very act, they seek words; in these noisy times, which drone with the appalling symphony of actions which are reported and reports which are belied by actions; in these times, you must expect from me no word of my own. None other than this: that silence protects against distortion . . . In the domain of impoverished imagination, where man dies of spiritual hunger without feeling a spiritual hunger, where pens are dipped in blood and swords in ink, what is not thought must be done, what is thought cannot be spoken. Expect from me no word of my own . . . Who exhorts actions, spoils word and deed and is doubly despicable. The urge has not died. Those who now have nothing to say, because actions have the last word, speak on. Let him who has something to say, stand up and be silent.[32]

Here the variations and developments, inversions and negations of words determine the flow of the ideas. The repeated keywords and their opposites give rise to a logical development of thought and lead inexorably to the final statement. The tone is matter-of-fact, the expression razor-sharp.

All this stands far removed from what we now call expressionism, but what at that time might more properly have been defined as the disruptive force of eroticism. This, Kokoschka's 'explosion in the garden'[33] and the subject-matter of Stefan George's *Buch der hängenden Gärten* (set by Schoenberg), was rightly regarded as a revolutionary force in a society of double standards. The use of erotic symbolism, dredged from the subconscious, increases the sensuous aspect of texture in art so as to alter the very nature of the subject-matter, making it seem revolutionary in content. It deals in detailed and 'decadent' ornament suggesting natural forms and so linking up with elements in Oriental and Medieval cultures, while at the same time referring to the sexual symbolism prevalent in the portrayal of plants, intertwining branches and long hair. The disruptive force of this eroticism (which manifested itself in Weininger's opposition of sex and character, in the typically Wagnerian conflict between duty and desire, in the male cult of the 'madonna', in the opposing images of prostitute and mother, and in many other forms) was recognised and feared by Kraus and his friends. They saw eroticism as an ultimate form of Romanticism in art, symptomatic of degradation and degeneracy. It was the flip side of power, which was associated with so-called technological innovation; it contributed to the very ills, the vulgarities and distortions against which it reacted. 'The man of our times, who besmirches walls with erotic symbols drawn from inner compulsion, is a criminal or a degenerate,' wrote Adolf Loos. 'One can judge the culture of a nation from the way its lavatory walls are defaced.'[34] Such highminded sentiments illustrate the gap that separates Kraus, Wittgenstein, Loos and Altenberg from their expressionist contemporaries.

This is only a contradiction, however, if we impose with hindsight some artificial division between expressionists and their opponents. In reality the division was less clear. But there is, nevertheless, some justification for considering that there was intense and productive conflict in Schoenberg's feelings and ideas at this crucial period, just before, during and after the First World War. He sets psychoanalytically inspired libretti (Kraus's aphorism about psychoanalysis – 'the disease of which it claims to be the cure' – is well known) and the poetry of George; he corresponds with Kandinsky; he composes pieces, like *Pierrot lunaire*, with a quite revolutionary intent. But if we look at these 'expressionist' works closely we see ample evidence, in the compositional sphere, of the same matter-of-factness, the same concern with clarity and directness, that characterise the later, 'post-expressionist' works. Intensity of emotion goes hand in hand with intensity of construction, in early and later works alike.

From a purely musical viewpoint it is usual to see Schoenberg's style as a synthesis of Brahmsian (Apollonian) and Wagnerian (Dionysian) elements, veering now to one side, now to the other. But I see also a progress away from the eroticism that characterises his work from *Verklärte Nacht* to *Erwartung*, away from the ornamentalism of *Herzgewächse*, towards a personal version of the Jewish God in *Moses und Aron* and towards the inexpressible, all-pervasive Idea. He describes this quest in the words of his Gabriel, in the unfinished *Jakobsleiter*: 'Right or left, backwards or forwards, up hill or down dale, one must go on, without asking what lies ahead or behind. It must be concealed; you may, nay must forget it, to realize the task.'[35] This task, as he saw it from the time of *Jakobsleiter* onwards, was to define his thoughts and to compose coherently out of them. He saw this as the correct stance for a conservative artist in the mould of Kraus. Looked at in hindsight, this may seem to be almost too stern a position for a creative artist to take. *Moses und Aron*, after all, 'works' as an expressionist opera rather than as an exemplification of Kraus's ideals; it is a work about ideas, in the traditional sense, rather than a discourse on the nature of Idea itself. Indeed, it is difficult to see how Kraus's ideals, with their tendency to abstraction, could have been realised effectively in an opera. Nevertheless, Schoenberg's preoccupation with them results in a quality of musical gesture which informs the whole work.

Moses the Lawgiver wishes to lead his people to the Promised Land. Schoenberg invents a method of composing with twelve tones related only to one another which will, he hopes, secure the 'hegemony of German music' into the foreseeable future. Uniting both achievements is the Kantian, ethical imperative which determines the progress of the artist as a mediator between idea and word, musical idea and tone, expressing only and nothing other than what the combinations of the tones mean, separated from the world by a sense of higher mission, and yet speaking only of the real world and to the real world.

'An individual can neither help nor save his own times, he can only testify to their decline,' wrote Kraus, quoting Kierkegaard, in 1928.[36] Kraus died in 1936, but Schoenberg survived to witness the full horrors of that decline. He did not, however, live long enough to see his own artistic formulations established worldwide and turned on their heads. Before too many years had passed, his methods had been freed both of the conditions in which they grew and of the ethical implications which they embodied. The method became a system of combining tones into structures, and that essential part of it determined by and expressive of the Idea came to be regarded as a romantic anachronism. Without Idea, in Schoenberg's view, compilations of tones must necessarily become arbitrary and therefore meaningless sequences of *Beigeräusche* (secondary noises), to borrow one of Kraus's happy formulations.

So, we might say, we are where they were, having neither returned to naiver times nor progressed to greater understanding. In his poem 'Rückkehr in die Zeit' (Reversal of Time), Kraus writes: 'My indicator turns backwards; for me, what has been is never complete, and I stand otherwise in time. In whatever future I roam, and whatever I take hold of, it always turns back to the past.'[37]

(1983)

1. Schoenberg, *Moses und Aron*, miniature score (Mainz: Schott, n.d.), pp. 499–540. I have slightly altered the translation given in the score. [AG]

2. Letter of 5 August 1930 to Alban Berg, in *Arnold Schoenberg Letters*, ed. Erwin Stein (London: Faber, 1964), p. 143.

3. Described in Josef Rufer, *The Works of Arnold Schoenberg: A Catalogue of His Compositions, Writings and Paintings*, trans. Dika Newlin (London: Faber, 1962), pp. 115–18.

4. Quoted in ibid., p. 118.

5. See Rufer, ibid., p. 137, and Alexander Goehr, 'Schoenberg's *Gedanke* Manuscript', *Journal of the Arnold Schoenberg Institute*, Vol. 2, No. 1 (October 1977), pp. 4–25. The manuscript is in the Arnold Schoenberg Institute, Los Angeles. Since some pages are unnumbered and (for the most part) undated, precise references cannot be given. [Since this essay was first published, the *Gedanke* Manuscript has been published in full: see Patricia Carpenter and Severine Neff, eds, *The Musical Idea and the Logic, Technique and Art of its Presentation* (New York: Columbia University Press, 1995).]

6. See Rufer, *Works of Arnold Schoenberg*, p. 137.

7. See Goehr, 'Schoenberg's *Gedanke* Manuscript', p. 4.

8. Quoted in Rufer, *Works of Arnold Schoenberg*, p. 140.

9. Following a tradition which is expressed in the title *Style and Idea*, I have translated the word *Gedanke* as 'idea'; but students of German philosophy from Kant onwards might prefer the word 'thought'. (All translations in this essay, unless otherwise attributed, are my own.)

10. *Gedanke* Manuscript, fragment dated 19 August 1922.

11. *Gedanke* Manuscript.

12. [David Epstein, *Beyond Orpheus: Studies in Musical Structure* (Cambridge, MA.: MIT, 1979).]

13. 'Grundgestalt as Tonal Function', *Music Theory Spectrum*, Vol. 5 (1983).

14. *Structural Functions of Harmony* (London: Williams and Norgate, 1954).

15. *Preliminary Exercises in Counterpoint*, ed. Leonard Stein (London: Faber, 1963), and *Fundamentals of Musical Composition*, ed. Gerald Strang and Leonard Stein (London: Faber, 1967).

16. *Gedanke* Manuscript.

17. 'Rundfrage über Karl Kraus', quoted in Werner Kraft, *Karl Kraus: Beiträge zum Verständnis seines Werkes* (Salzburg: Müller, 1956), p. 195.

18. Second edition (Munich: Hanser, 1980). Translated as *The Torch in My Ear* (New York: Farrar Straus Giroux, 1982). The relevant pages are 77–87 of the German edition, 65–74 of the English.

19. Elsewhere Kraus wrote: 'The dramatic work of art has nothing to do with the stage. The theatrical effect of a drama should last no further than the desire to see it performed: more than this would destroy its artistic effect. The best performance is the one that the reader makes for himself out of the world of the drama.' From *Sprüche und Widersprüche*, reprinted in *Werke*, ed. H. Fischer, Vol. 3: *Beim Wort genommen* (Munich: Kösel, 1955), p. 102. *Moses und Aron* has often been criticised, of course, for being 'undramatic'.

20. *Die Fackel*, No. 811 (1929), pp. 91ff. See Kraft, *Karl Kraus*, p. 198.

21. Quoted in Kraft, *Karl Kraus*, p. 189.

22. *Sprüche und Widersprüche*, pp. 111, 120, 113.

23. See Leopold Liegler, *Karl Kraus und sein Werk* (Vienna: Lányi, 1920), pp. 381ff.

24. Quoted in ibid., p. 347.

25. 'Ansprache bei der Trauerfeier für Karl Kraus im Wiener Konzerthaus am 30.11.1936' (Vienna, 1936), quoted in Kraft, *Karl Kraus*, p. 195.

26. Kant's conception of *Achtung für das Sittengesetz* (respect for the moral law) is discussed in S. Korner, *Kant* (Harmondsworth: Pelican, 1974), p. 163.

27. Both these quotations are from Liegler, *Karl Kraus und sein Werk*, pp. 287–9.

28. Quoted in Kraft, *Karl Kraus*, p. 197.

29. *Style and Idea*, 2nd edn, ed. Leonard Stein, trans. Leo Black, (London: Faber, 1975), p. 368.

30. 'My Evolution', in ibid., p. 80.

31. See *Theory of Harmony*, trans. Roy E. Carter (London: Faber, 1978), p. 34.

32. 'In dieser grossen Zeit' (December 1914), quoted in Liegler, *Karl Kraus und sein Werk*, pp. 293–4.

33. See Carl E. Schorske, *Fin-de-siècle Vienna* (New York: Knopf, 1980), Chapter 7.

34. Adolf Loos, *Sämtliche Schriften*, ed. F. Glück, Vol. 1 (Vienna: Herold, 1962).

35. *Die Jakobsleiter*, vocal score (Los Angeles: Belmont, n.d.), p. 12.

36. *Die Unüberwindlichen*, in *Werke*, Vol. 14: *Dramen* (Munich: Langen and Müller, 1967), p. 115.

37. *Werke*, Vol. 7: *Worte in Versen* (Munich: Kösel, 1959), p. 236.

8

Musical Ideas and Ideas about Music

I

In an article about the setting of poems to music ('The Relationship to the Text'), which Arnold Schoenberg wrote in 1912, he relates, rather disarmingly, that sometimes he was inspired by the actual sound of the first words of a poem he was reading and began composing – continuing straight through to the end without, as he says, 'troubling [himself] in the slightest about the continuation of the poetic events'.[1] So it is with me, in this chapter. I fear that I too have been inspired by the initial sounds and perhaps also by the musical form of the title I have chosen: it's almost a palindrome. And if one turns the second half, 'Ideas about Music', back to front, one gets 'Music about Ideas', which might well form a further title. But to talk about musical ideas and ideas about music will necessarily touch on considerations with which I am little qualified to deal, being neither philosopher nor sociologist, nor, for that matter, even a writer. And so I can only beg the reader's indulgence and hope that, like Schopenhauer's medium, who 'tells things of which she has no knowledge', I too may 'utter the most profound wisdom in a language which my reason does not understand'.[2]

It is almost a commonplace to speak of the vastly increased and unprecedented popularity that music of *all types* now enjoys. At no time has so much music been written, written about, played and heard (if not always listened to) as at the present. Furthermore, the mechanical reproduction of music has served to magnify the effect of this out of all proportion. Such reproduction has brought popularity and the problems of popularity to an art which, in its higher forms at least, was previously regarded as the preserve of the few. Now, in this changed environment, we must consider the nature and effect of many types of music which exist side by side in our lives. For although, in the past, serious men thought only about serious things, we ought now to consider also some of the seemingly less serious fruits of this mechanical revolution. The kind of sounding wallpaper which everywhere surrounds us and which probably represents the lowest, though not the least profitable, form of music generally available, is nevertheless closely related, in form and structure and in texture, to the higher forms of pure art music, and its effects are far-reaching in their implications.

The popularity of classical (I would prefer the term 'legitimate') music expresses itself not so much in the size of audiences at concerts as in the increased amount and scope of music-making of the conventional type, in the lives of a large number of people, especially children. Guitars and recorders lead to the more special-ized instruments of the classical symphony orchestra, and the obligatory middle-class piano lesson of our fathers has long been superseded by the school, town and county orchestra with its complex network of individual instrumental tuition, group coaching and public performance.

On the other hand, mechanised music, in the form of record and cassette, has contributed wider knowledge and higher standards to a huge audience of listeners. And this, in its turn, has an effect on more modest live music, as well as creating a music industry which can, not unfairly, be described as big business and which certainly shares the structure, and consequently the importance for our lives, of other organised means of production.

In the past, when the demand for art music was altogether more restricted, there was a direct relationship, if not always an untroubled one, between the beliefs and values of creative musicians and the tastes of their patrons and public. This is a norm, distorted, on the one hand, by the appearance in the nine-teenth century of avant-garde activity (which occurs when artists are no longer in tune with the sensibilities of their public); on the other, by intervention on the part of the patron to control the artist. There's a long history of such intervention, exemplified as far back as 1545 by the restrictions imposed on Catholic church music by the Council of Trent. The doctrinal and procedural deliberations of this body, calling for simplicity and the avoidance of complex musical device in the setting of the words of the Mass, had a quite immediate and direct effect on, for instance, the work of Palestrina. Generally, though, it was not impossible for composers to continue to work in their own way and yet in a close relationship to their societies. But in our new conditions there does seem to be a gap, and sometimes even a conflict, between the disciplines of composing music, which, in the most general terms, one might describe as the imagining of *musical ideas* and the composition of forms out of them, and the value-judgements and *ideas about music* embodied in what performers, listeners and businessmen think music should be and do. This is the opposition of musical ideas and ideas about music of my title.

The ideas and value-judgements of performers, especially of the amateurs who play for pleasure rather than for a living, are bound to be of a traditional and common-sense type. Easier forms of music-making such as that of the Baroque are, perhaps, more popular with children who play in an orchestra than with the concert public. So the first criterion of the player is practicability. And this will not be a value that changes significantly from age to age. With practicability come clarity, memorability and attractiveness of musical material, and all these are the ordinary values of music as they have existed in the past and, one hopes, may exist in the future.

Concert-goers probably hold similar views, although the more exciting manifestations of romantic and modern music will be more popular here. The visitor to the Royal Festival Hall will be drawn by *The Rite of Spring* as well as by the Tchaikovsky symphony. But both of these will be a closed book to all but the very best amateur performers. The public concert, which imposes a fairly conservative character on music-making and appreciation, applies to only a small class of people and almost pales into insignificance, statistically at least, when compared with the huge publics of the various forms of mechanised music-making. It is in this that the great names are broadcast and that the big money is made, and it would be unnatural if this huge activity and industry did not give rise to a superstructure of ideas and prescriptive values about music. Here, where massive popularity is a commercial issue, recipes abound. Whether in the strict controls imposed, say on the making of background music or on the choice of music for advertisement, film or soap-opera, or in the relatively freer and wider decisions of what to record and sell for popular consumption, we have a force which has ideas about music. I shall endeavour to show that these may, and usually do, conflict with the disciplines of the art itself. A distortion occurs which affects us all deeply. And such is the importance now attributed to music that in some cases the state even intervenes with judgements of its own. Artistic production is brought into line with other forms of production and is controlled by considerations which seem to have little to do with those that arise from the proper practice of the art itself. The study of such conflicts and interventions and their effects may become a legitimate way to study music today.

2

I talk about the *musical idea* as if it were absolutely self-evident what this means. In fact, the word *idea* crops up not at all in the classical textbooks about music. Students were long taught to write music in much the same way as they were taught to play an instrument. The books of the past, such as, for example, C. P. E. Bach's *Treatise on the True Art of Playing the Clavier,* do not particularly distinguish between performing and composing music. What there is of precise instruction on how to compose consists of rules of grammar and syntax: the availability and attributed character of modes and permitted intervals, together with instruction in the use of chords, cadences and forms of figuration. The elements of musical form are only described insofar as they suggest ways of performing, e.g. fantasias, recitatives. One learnt how to build up a musical form by imitating models, a method which depended closely on the relationship between teacher and pupil.

Today, in the West at least, this situation has considerably changed. We are more concerned than previously with the language and the constituents of form. So one might look to analytical philosophy for guidance, and there is no lack of definitions of *idea* here. If music is, as is commonly believed, a language, these should apply. Russell, for instance, says: 'When directly caused by a sensible occurrence, the word in the speaker applies to an impression; when heard or used in narrative, it does not apply to an impression, but it is still a word, not a mere noise; it still "means" something, and what it "means" may be called an "idea". The same distinction applies to sentences . . .' And he continues: 'Impression and idea must be closely related, since otherwise it would be impossible to give information.'[3] If we try to apply this formula – *word–means–idea* – to music, we might say that a group of tones distributed in time have a certain *meaning*, and this is a *musical idea*.

But the fact is, no such thing can be distinguished in music. The only analogy is a definition of 'correctness' or 'incorrectness' in terms of the specific style, or, better, the musical system of the historical period of the composition. One tries to explain this difficulty away by associating moods and descriptions of emotional states with specific intervals or groups of intervals. In recent years the most sensitive attempt to do this has been contained in *The Language of Music* by the late Deryck Cooke.[4] But although it is clear that certain moods have come to be associated with certain intervals, modes and *tempi* of music, that is still a very different thing from relating a specific piece or phrase of music with a precise 'idea' in the way Russell relates impression, word and idea.

One might do better to ignore the whole issue, going along with Wittgenstein when he says:

There could also be a language in whose use the impression made on us by the signs played no part; in which there was no such thing as understanding, in the sense of such an impression. The signs are, e.g., written and transmitted to us and we are able to *take notice of them*. (That is to say, the

only impression that comes in here is the pattern of the signs.)
If the sign is an order, we translate it into action by means
of rules, tables. It does not get as far as an impression like
that of a picture; nor are stories written in this language.

He continues, 'In this case one might say: "only in the system has
the sign any life".'[5]

I think musicians might be disappointed by this as a description
of what they feel when performing or listening. On the other
hand, it would certainly help when dealing with musics which are
unfamiliar. A Western listener to African drumming or Japanese
Gagaku, or, for that matter, a great deal of recent music by our
own contemporaries, would be quite ready to recognise individual
events as 'signs which only have a life within the system' and carry
on from there. But if this feeling is valid for us when we hear
exotic musics, might it not also be true for an Eskimo listening to
our music? 'Mightn't we imagine a man who never having had any
acquaintance with music, comes to us and hears someone playing
a reflective piece of Chopin and is convinced that this is a language
and people merely want to keep the meaning secret from him?'
asks Wittgenstein.

Turning away from this, we find Schopenhauer singling out
music as being essentially different from the other arts. 'We recognise no imitation or repetition of any idea of reality in the world.'[6]
The substance of music, with the exception of specific imitations
of natural sound, such as we find, for example, in seventeenth-
century pieces describing battles or the well-known natural imitations in Haydn's *Creation* and *The Seasons* (which are named
and criticised by Schopenhauer), cannot be related to impressions
in the way, say, that the material of the novel or of a painting
makes an impression on the writer or painter in the world around
him. However, says Schopenhauer, music is not a mere play of
numbers or proportions – *exercitium arithmeticae occultum
nescientis se numerare animae*, as Leibnitz called it. Were it so,
'The pleasure it gives would be like that to be had when perceiving
the working out of a mathematical problem.' But the philosopher

suggests a deeper meaning for music and proposes that, although the proportions of music do not themselves designate anything, they are themselves 'signs'. So music constitutes an alternative and independent system 'which could exist even if there was no world'. But music is understandable and is imbued with its own infallibility: 'It depends for its existence on precise rules which may be expressed quantitively and which must be respected if the result is to remain music.' So, unlike the other arts, it is 'in no way a representation of ideas' but, in Schopenhauer's system, an externalisation of the Will itself, and as such it is designated as a system parallel to that of ideas, for the 'idea' too is an externalisation of the Will. Schopenhauer believes that music never expresses phenomenal appearances, as do words, and that the association of words might be a trap for a musician. 'If music is closely associated with words and seeks to portray events, it is concerned with speaking a language not its own'. The philosopher singles out Rossini, of whom he says, 'His music speaks its own language and has no need at all of words. It would make its effect even if performed on instruments alone.' We, of course, would think of Wagner, and the popular way – successful too – of performing the 'Liebestod' from *Tristan und Isolde* without the voice, as a more appropriate example.

The only composer who has attempted to deal with these problems is Arnold Schoenberg, and it is not fanciful to think that the influence of Schopenhauer, or Schopenhauer via Wagner, looms over his music and his thinking. In his essay 'New Music, Outmoded Music, Style and Idea' [1946] he writes: 'In its most common meaning, the term idea is used as a synonym for theme, melody, phrase or motive. I myself consider the totality of a piece as the *idea*: the idea which its creator wanted to present.' He gives an example:

Every tone which is added to a beginning tone makes the meaning of that tone doubtful. If, for instance, G follows after C, the ear may not be sure whether this expresses C major or G major, or even F major or E minor; and the addition of other tones may or may not clarify this problem. In this manner there is produced a state of unrest, of imbalance which grows throughout most of the piece, and is enforced further by similar functions of the rhythm. The method by which balance is restored seems to me the real *idea* of the composition.'[7]

Schoenberg is either saying that 'idea' is a synonym for composition, or that, underlying the different manifestations of tone, rhythm, mood and character within a piece, there is a general *Ur-*'idea' of statement, destabilisation and re-establishing of balance – as it were, a kind of Aristotelian pattern, where order is perpetually reaffirmed. The great difference here is the attempt to define idea in terms of the stuff of music itself. Meaning *is* attributed to music; but it expresses an idea without reference to anything outside itself. At the same time it is not considered as an abstract system of signs. So this is more than a mere restatement of an aesthetic position, of the conventional *l'art pour l'art*.

John Cage echoes some of this when he says:

I believe that the use of noise to make music will continue and increase until we reach a music produced through the aid of electrical instruments which will make available for musical purposes any and all sounds that can be heard ... The present methods of writing music, principally those which employ harmony and its reference to particular steps in the field of sound, will be inadequate for the composer, who will be faced with the entire field of sound ... The principle of form will be our only constant connection with the past. Although the great form of the future will not be as it was in the past, at one time the fugue and at another the sonata, it will be related to these as they are to each other: through the principle of organization or man's common ability to think.[8]

For Cage, the musical idea is a 'great form'. This is an echo of Schoenberg. For my part, I feel one might go considerably further and also define a *little form*. A composer's partly subconsciously motivated gesture will stand apart and define the possible continuations of a composition. From the apparently limitless possibilities available at the beginning, we narrow down, as work proceeds, to something approaching automatic writing. The connecting of subconscious and objective elements creates little form. For me this is a musical idea; and it is not a synonym for phrase, motif or sentence, for all these can exist without this particular origin. The continuing of a composition in terms of such ideas constitutes what a creative artist calls truth in the Keatsian sense. The telling of this truth is the *raison d'être* of a creative art, and doing this kind of work implies an attitude to society which is often misinterpreted as an inability to compromise, snobbishness or elitism. Whether in the past, at the present or in the future, it leads the artist into temporary or permanent conflict with the world around him. For the world cannot understand why he, having received its patronage, should not be content to please.

3

The proper appreciation of a piece of music demands one's full attention, one's submission as well as one's critical faculties. Listening to real music may be compared to reading a novel or even to making a journey. One may be seduced by the beauty of the landscape, but one proceeds to one's destination according to plan. Such an experience is enough. But observations of the psychological effect made by rhythms and modes, and of the conventional characteristics attributed to these, have made possible the realisation of quite new functions based on new considerations of what music might do.

During the war there was a BBC programme regularly broadcast to factories, called 'Music While You Work'. It was given by light orchestras performing compositions in the traditional manner of entertainment music, and consisted of ballads and dance music without, if my memory serves me right, announcements. A paper sent out by Planned Music, the company marketing 'Muzak', explains the effect of such music on task performance. It suggests that:

> Studies in industry which have used entertainment type music, i.e. recorded vocal and non-vocal musical selections intended to be listened to, or classical musical selections similarly intended to be 'stage centre', have generally resulted in equivocal findings: sometimes the music helps, sometimes it hinders.

On the other hand:

> Studies of the influence of non-entertainment musical sound, in particular the programmed musical selections of Muzak, have indicated various positive effects in terms both of 'objective' performances, e.g. the speed and accuracy and the amount of task performance, and of 'subjective' performance, e.g. attitudes and preferences about the work, the organisation, co-worker, conditions of work.

The company quotes a laboratory study conducted by the US Army which finds that Muzak's musical stimulus programming related to 'Human vigilance, an aspect of perceptual and clerical performance especially in routine, boring situations.' That study indicated that 'Progressively increasing stimulation through the programming of musical selections progressively improved vigilance and that other experimental conditions, i.e. white noise and a no-sound did not have such an effect.'[9]

This means that what they helpfully call music-sound can achieve pre-calculable results if submitted to specific procedures and mechanically broadcast. Such procedures relate to the changing of the nature of the music from the entertainment to the non-entertainment category and to its arrangement into sequences and its framing by silence. One of the Muzak brochures describes a programme of music-sound as 'A selection of tunes designed to suit the time of day'. It states that: 'After recording, the master tapes are subjected to a process of limiting the dynamic range so that the contrasts between quieter and louder passages are not so marked as to cause distraction or irritation.' They find that music is most effective when interspersed with periods of silence; that once a form (they mean rhythmic type) has been established in two or three successive tunes, a subsequent switch has a positive effect; and that the families of instruments of the orchestra can be used to vary the emotional impact. One might go further and propose that the effect will be greatest when the music-sound is predictable and unvaried for measured durations and when it gives the impression (perhaps for copyright reasons) of being familiar while remaining slightly unfamiliar. In addition, different styles ranging from false Baroque to modern jazz, and the results of the use of synthesizer, will provoke stock associations. For the music to make its full effect it must be composed, as it were, in reverse. You have to start with the effect it is intended to make and then translate this into sound material. Any genuine musical ideas must be reduced and limited so as not to interrupt the regular pre-established framework. Such a procedure flies in the face of orthodox musical teaching and practice.

No doubt something of the same ethos lies behind our failure to understand pop music. I remember a confrontation between my composition students at Tanglewood and a visiting group who gave a much acclaimed concert to twenty thousand people. I asked some of the composers to comment on what they had heard, and a widespread complaint was a lack of any variety in the extremely long pieces played. The very intelligent leader of the group – I think he was an academic in his spare time – asked, in a kindly way, how much the students expected to earn from their work. When told that nothing was expected, he mentioned the very high sums he received. He wanted to point out that the criteria for this kind of music were simply other than those for legitimate music. He was making a positive use of technological means in order to achieve a kind of mass participation, a collective enthusiasm – perhaps even a hysteria – quite beyond the dreams of any but the Wagners among legitimate musicians. To this end, he was combining the heavy amplified sound quality of the technical age with the primitive repetitions of an archaic ritual which lies far behind legitimate music. If we, the legitimates, wish to produce a response which results from the harnessing of music-sound and its connected associations into intellectual form, his aims purposely avoided this. For us, technical manipulation impairs the response of the listener, as it impoverishes the quality of instrumental and vocal sound. It removes the unique nature of musical performance.

I do not think that we should criticise Muzak or pop music from a traditional, or what its practitioners would call an elitist, standpoint. We have to recognise that its forms and procedures are, to a much greater extent than our own, in accord with the technological possibilities themselves. Our objection to these things can only be related to their intentions and so must be political rather than aesthetic.

Acceptance of a definition of music as 'organised noise' (a definition popular in modern music circles) underlies the reduction of art music to music-sound. In a technical age music could be used, by politicians and others, to create a coherence of viewpoint based on the shared experience of musical fashion. The idea of manipulating people in this way, to swift and gigantic effect, makes the band marches and patriotic songs of yesteryear look small beer indeed.

Until recently, legitimate composers have taken little account of the massive infiltrations of functional music and have been content to go their own way while their institutions remained intact. In the 1950s and 1960s, composers carried on the traditions of high art largely polarised into one side of an opposition of what the German critic Konrad Boehmer has called the alternatives of serialism and pop.[10] Only explicitly Marxist composers like Shostakovich and Eisler, or humanists like Britten and Copland, have avoided being pushed to extremes. Eisler put the object of art as being to 'Make people more intelligent; to purge men of sententious emotions, false grief, sentimentality and self-pity'. 'Music,' he said, 'should avoid the dependence on cheap effect. Music must create a place for great feelings.' He continued, 'For my part I am satisfied when a song concerned with sorrow is not composed sorrowfully. Better to know who is sorrowful and why. To ask this question is to adopt a Realist position.'[11] Such an attitude opposes both extremes, stressing the artist's need to fulfil a traditional purpose and at the same time deploring the emotionally cheapening mass qualities of mechanised pop. 'The uniqueness of a work of art is inseparable from its being embedded in the fabric of tradition,' writes Eisler's contemporary Walter Benjamin.[12]

But now, too, legitimate composers in the West are turning away from the Olympian positions adopted in the last two decades, having been directly affected by techniques and procedures developed in the commercial manipulations of music-sound. Particularly in Germany, they react against the subsidised plush of traditional opera and concert and envy the apparent freedom of pop and its link with young and unorthodox attitudes. This reaction takes the form of opposing the well-made piece, with its beginning, middle and end, and a turning away from traditional models to those composers like Weill and Eisler who tried to respond to a political situation by deliberately cultivating a prescribed [proscribed?] style. But it is not possible, now, to reproduce the political songs of the 1930s, which depended on a background of musical tradition. So these composers are trying to create a *collage* form in which different, mutually irreconcilable types of music are put together in order to make political comment. Stockhausen and Berio are the models for this. Berio, in his *Sinfonia* [1968], incorporates literary and musical quotations from many sources, including a movement from a Mahler symphony, upon which he imposes yet other music of his own. Stockhausen, in *Hymnen* [1966–7], bases a composition on national anthems (including the West but not the East German one) and manipulates these electronically into combinations that would defy the capabilities of traditional counterpoint. This kind of procedure has been defended on the grounds that it is less important to examine the material than to consider the way the material is combined and developed. But music with strong external associations, such as national anthems have, provokes a stock reaction which necessarily precludes organic development and fragments the continuity of musical ideas. The familiar element sticks out. It can only connect with other elements by juxtaposition, as in a surrealist work. Shock is the only way of conveying impressions in such music, and this presupposes some advance calculation of the effect. Here the composer follows the same sequence of activities as does the psychologically orientated purveyor of music-sound or the pop musician. But still he finds no greater audience. He cannot free himself from the ghost of art music.

We may today be seeing a most strange development. Prosperity passes and the subsidies are called in. Concert hall, opera house and even the radio become increasingly less available to composers who attract only minority audiences. They are forced away, and their concepts have ever less influence on the musical world. At the same time music-making based on the classical-romantic model has never been more popular. Music is one of the subjects that can gain from the comprehensivisation of education, and the demand to study music at places of higher education vastly exceeds the available vacancies.

I am not sure that I can fully explain to myself the reasons for the complex and seemingly contradictory situation that I have tried to describe. I have tried, by means of reference to philosophers, to formulate the inherent qualities of musical composition and have juxtaposed these with attacks upon them. Such attacks derive from social transformations and new possibilities, and the progressive mind somehow expects to accept the new and be ready to bury the old. I can only hope that the present transformations of our environment might one day come to be seen as a kind of pollution. We will have to realise that the commercial exploitation of music is a political activity which must be controlled and that the traditional structures will have to be protected. Until that time there is a real danger that, although composers will not disappear, their voices will not be heard, and I think that isolation is one of the dread sicknesses of society. Only hope sustains the composer in his present isolation.

(1976)

1. *Style and Idea*, 2nd edn, ed. Leonard Stein, trans. Leo Black (London: Faber, 1975), p. 144.

2. [Quotation unidentified.]

3. Bertrand Russell, *An Inquiry into Meaning and Truth* (London: Allen and Unwin, 1951), p. 191.

4. Deryck Cooke, *The Language of Music* (Oxford: OUP, 1989).

5. Ludwig Wittgenstein, *Zettel*, trans. G.E.M. Anscombe (Oxford: Blackwell, 1967), p. 26e.

6. Arthur Schopenhauer, *Die Welt als Wille und Vorstellung*, 2 Vols, Book III (Frankfurt a. M.: Cotta: Insel, 1960), pp. 166ff. [AG's translations.]

7. *Style and Idea*, pp. 122–3.

8. John Cage, *Silence* (Middletown, CT: Wesleyan University Press, 1961), pp. 3–6. Cage capitalises these sentences, setting them off from the rest of the text to form a 'Credo'.

9. James J. Keenan, *Study of Clerical Task Performance under Different Conditions of Programmed Music (Muzak)* (Planned Music Ltd).

10. Konrad Boehmer, *Zwischen Reihe und Pop* (Vienna: Jugend und Volk, 1970).

11. Hanns Eisler, quoted by H. A. Brockhaus in *Sammelbände zur Musikgeschichte der DDR*, Vol. 2 (Berlin: Verlag Neue Musik, 1971), p. 61.

12. Walter Benjamin, *Illuminations*, trans. Harry Zohn (London: Jonathan Cape, 1970), p. 225.

9

Traditional Art and Modern Music

There was a time, not so long ago, when it was widely believed that the fundamental disorder of what was then called the 'savage mind' was demonstrated by the irrationality of its music. It was believed that Western music was rational precisely because it was in accord with the laws of nature, a relationship expressed most simply in the derivation of its thought modes from the overtone system. Then there was a time when composers and public could be charmed by the 'otherness' of exotic cultures. So perhaps was Debussy charmed when he heard a gamelan orchestra at the Paris Exhibition; and when he imitated what he had heard he was doing something not unlike Picasso, when he imitated African masks. 'Returning from the great Exhibition to his own village in Africa, the Negro, in deadly earnest and amid the wails of his fellow villagers, performs the rituals which so charmed the European audiences,' comments Kafka with a very human accuracy, although he wasn't there, but perhaps believing that he was the Negro in question.[1]

But today, standing where we do, our concerns with traditional arts, and especially with traditional music, may be different. Today we may share something of the excitement of the researchers in the field, who now bring us some glimmerings of musical institutions, not only in the 'high cultures' but also in the least familiar areas, where no direct analogies with our own cultures obviously appear. From this improved knowledge we are more likely than were our predecessors to ask whether the apparent strangeness could be some underlying unity in diversity, whether apparent strangeness masks an underlying similarity of nature or purpose. Whether in fact there exists something that I might call 'the spirit of music', as I once saw and heard it invoked in a ceremony I attended in 1986 in Bangkok.

The place was a Teachers' Training College; the end of the academic year was in sight. After the ceremony invoking the spirit of music, which was conducted by a senior teacher before an altar built up and decorated with flowers, food and musical instruments, and which was interspersed with the performance of instrumental ensemble pieces by older students, came the initiation of the young students of music. A metallophone of some twelve gongs of various sizes was placed before the altar. One by one, the young students approach, placing themselves within the ring formed by the wooden frame holding the gongs. Each student formally greets the teacher. The teacher places two beaters in the hands of the student. Then the teacher strikes two pitch levels on the gongs. The student imitates, striking the same two pitch levels. This is repeated a number of times. Then the pupil repeats his formal greeting, withdraws and is replaced by his successor. A teacher explains to me: 'What the ceremony means is that nobody can learn to become a *good* musician without following what the teacher does. That is the only way to progress.'

No words have been spoken in the little initiation. The spirit of music is invoked by teacher and pupil. It is a tradition; the stones of which this tradition is built are made by imitating. The teacher shows, the pupil imitates; the teacher criticises, the pupil improves. But this spirit of music, this traditional institution which links teacher and pupil, is not unknown to us in the West. The Western child is instructed by his teacher in no fundamentally different way. Mozart, as we know from the Attwood studies, sets his Irish pupil to write simple pieces. Attwood carries out his tasks as well as he is able; Mozart returns and corrects what his pupil has written.

Underlying similarities of institution not only enable us to gain an insight into traditional cultures, geographically far from our own, but also enable us to make some *judgement* about our own ways of doing things. Perhaps we now have something to learn from precisely those musical cultures that have not had a history of rapid transformation of function and style.

In some ways, a study of the instruments, the modes of their performance and the surface characteristics of the music, sung or played, will necessarily and valuably illustrate oppositions and divergencies, not only of structure, but also in fundamental notions of what is aesthetically pleasing. A Western flautist will go for a pure, integrated sound, identical in character throughout the range of the instrument; the Japanese will employ a more restricted range of pitch levels, but the manner of articulation will involve surrounding the notes with breath sounds and all kinds of elaborations essential to the artistic expression. It is indeed the task of the musicologist to reveal these differences of surface and of underlying attitude in different cultures. But here I should like to ask a quite other kind of question. I am concerned with the criteria that constitute *excellence* or *mastery* in any particular musical culture, and I want to see whether, by comparing such criteria, insofar as it is possible to do so, I can say one of two things: *either* that there exist such and such conditions in which mastery or excellence is likely to be achieved, *or*, if this is not so, that mastery, artistic pre-eminence, presupposes only individual qualities which separate 'great men' (or masters) from the others. To say the latter would be to imply that however a 'great work' comes about, it is to be understood only in terms of itself.

2

If this latter alternative were to be the case, we would indeed be justified in studying only those works that have come to be considered masterpieces, as was always done in earlier times (and still is to some extent), and in thinking that any attempt to understand the phenomenon of musical activity in a wider context would have to be regarded as trivial. This then is the question that lies behind my title. Romantic and post-Romantic (modernist) thinking had it that the great masterpieces of Western music were somehow *sui generis*, and that being products of genius, of the superior mind, they might only be understood in terms of themselves. Even if this is not wholly an observation of fact, because such thinking, without necessarily mentioning them, certainly did assume the institutions of music-making in the background, it was and is nevertheless the aim and ideal of creative musicians to forge compositions that are as it were entirely new, in sensibility as well as in syntax. Even Eliot's 'What is entirely new is entirely bad' is said in a context which firmly places the individual creative innovators *against* a background of everyday mediocrity. In my essay called 'Schoenberg and Karl Kraus: The Idea Behind the Music', I tried to show how these great artists not only believed in what might be described as a kind of transcendental 'idea', housed in the mind and soul of the 'great man', but also held that this idea should, to the exclusion of all else, determine the detail as well as the form and overall continuity of the work of art. To be controlled by this idea they regarded, not as an aesthetic, but as an ethical, imperative. It may be said that the whole post-1945 ideal of modern music, as expressed by its most significant practitioners, and through the adoption of serialism, pays homage to this notion.

Such a notion attributes to 'great men' not only pre-eminence, i.e. the ability to do something better than others, but also qualities that are fundamentally different, separate: a quality of prophecy, an ability to determine what is 'relevant' to some mythical general good, or simply a superiority of stance. Schoenberg put it clearly as far back as 1911, in his article on Liszt, when he proposed that 'great men' have faith, while lesser men have convictions.[2] Fanatical faith impels genius to find truth only in himself, and to derive every detail of his product from some such quintessential 'idea'. This 'great man' is a believer (primarily in himself) and stands above comparison or even criticism. The implication of such a line of thought is that in the final analysis all great achievements of art are unique and, as I've suggested, to be understood only in terms of themselves. Perhaps I myself started life believing something like this. In these so-called post-modernist times, however, I can see only the implied superiority, even the ugliness, of such a view of creativity. For it implies that institutional values of taste, those criteria of *judgement* that accord with didactic and practical experience, have no meaning; that these laudable things apply only to lesser mortals, while geniuses may not only 'break the rules', as it used to be said, but can ignore the very existence of the structures of common language. With my academic hat I loathe such ways of thinking, and especially the political implications that seem to derive from them; and now, also as a creative artist, I prefer to make an image of myself which is something fundamentally different.

In a society in which music relates directly to the functions of that society, it might be more properly described as a craft than as an art. The music is intended to serve specific and predetermined ends; and the concern of the makers of that music is neither with its sophisticated elaboration nor with imaginative virtuosity in devising variations, but rather with the realisation of those ends. In certain musical cultures, Simha Arom reports, talking about the music of Central Africa, 'Each model corresponds to a cultural music-category. These are conceptualized and bear names. A traveller will know that a man has died in the village he approaches because he hears that the music is dying-music, i.e. symbolizing the presence of death.'[3] Here, instrumental virtuosity or improvised variations can only be taken into account insofar as they do not obscure or disturb the social connotations of the model. If they were to do so, the music would cease to be 'dying-music', and so lose, or at least complicate, its social function, becoming 'art' rather than 'craft'. Arom states that an African child, living in a collective milieu, will take a drum and, if he is intelligent, be able to perform the model of sounds-in-time that lies beneath the surface of the traditional music of his village. If this model is simple, it can be described quite easily as a set of language-statements. But, at the same time, the African child will not learn it as such; obviously he hears the model, separates it (as far as is possible) from its superstructure and reproduces it.

Music, in different cultures, exists without notations, or with notations as a system of mnemonics, or with notations that in themselves constitute models, the elements of which may be independently manipulated in such a way that a performance of the sound implies a translation of the notational signs, and must be seen as to some extent resulting from them. Where a music has no notation, it may genuinely be collective, for although not everyone can play it he can participate by swaying, dancing, clapping or making appreciative noises. In this case there is no rigorous dividing line between player and listener: each participates in a musical process. But the intervention of a notation implies a personalisation of the process. Some people are familiar with it, some not; and a system of training must be evolved in addition to that demanded by the music or the instrument itself. You learn 'how' to sing the song, or play it upon an instrument; but the rules of the notation and the manner in which it is read and translated may be conveyed by a language other than itself (as in the remark that a dot over a note halves its duration).

The existence of a notation separate from the sound of the music, be it based either on an instruction ('put your finger on the third string, second node') or on a symbol of actual sound, duration etc., opens up the possibility for the independent manipulation of the symbols for what we call 'writing music'. Clearly this requires special skills, most of which can be conveyed in the form of prescriptive rules to be learned and employed in a transformational way. At first glance, it would appear that this is a different order of activity from that of the performing musician, who obtains his skills in an imitative manner. If this were the case, the popular but by now discredited belief that traditional music is primitive and irrational – a forerunner of modern music which is nevertheless an essentially different animal – might well be true. But in one important respect the two activities are related: the writer of notation must be able to perform what he writes inwardly and imagine the result, to the extent that a symbol or combination of symbols is automatically heard (as in any written language). Such a skill can only be obtained by imitative practice, and is a function of 'musicality'. In at least this one respect, then, the composer of 'modern Western music', although its external apparatus may be very great, intuits his music in a way not fundamentally at variance with the practice of the traditional musician; and he too is judged by his musical intelligence, which is (to quote Ryle) 'not the knowledge or ignorance of this or that truth, but the ability or inability to do certain sorts of things'.[4]

In various types, and at various levels, of music-making, practical skills and personal experience, as well as the knowledge of a theory, have to be integrated. In unnotated musical cultures, a collectively understood model signifying this or that (and easily describable as a rule) may be elaborated, varied or decorated by means of personal skills – such as, for example, the ability to modify voice and instrument in a variety of ways – as well as by the fantasy and the taste involved in varying units of the model and combining them in different ways, e.g. by improvising upon the model. In notated musical cultures, on the other hand, a musician has special skills which enable him not only to alter the model itself (because the notational system makes this less fragile and at the same time more susceptible to change), but also to ornament and elaborate it more profoundly and systematically, until we reach the condition of 'compositional' virtuosity or mastery. And, in the final stages, where notation is manipulated, the model may by a process of gradual disintegration disappear as a separate thing. At this point a piece of music becomes almost entirely an expression of personal knowledge.

3

Let me try to exemplify some of these points. Here is a plainchant, a Gregorian Ave Maria, of singular beauty (Ex. 18). The music rises and falls, amplifying and enriching the words of the text; at the surface level, at least, there is an absence of any regular metre or pattern. Knowing a little of the history of such music, we might well say that the written version is a codification of improvisatory practice of some kind. Why so? Because an examination of the chant reveals (a) a simple and continuous pentatonic background (there is no alteration discernible in its scalic ordering) and (b) a simple note-to-syllable setting of the text. This constitutes what we have previously referred to as a model. Both of these aspects of

Ex. 18a: Ave Maria

Ex. 18b

the model are elaborated and decorated, so as almost to obscure any possibility of differentiation between structural notes or syllables and decoration (where the adjective 'structural' properly means 'part of the model'). When the chant is sung, the performance of durations within it will be such as to defy codification. So immediately we will say, 'This is music that can only have reached its final form, and may only be performed now, if a tradition exists, however tenuously. It would be impossible to formulate a rule which would enable us to learn how to sing this. Doubtless in the past, as now, monks learned to perform it by imitating their teachers. They learned "how", even if they could not define their practice as a general rule.'

How do we know that what we hear is a good example of its kind? In one of two ways: *either* by some inexplicable sense of 'significant form', whereby we feel instinctively that it's good, *or* by an implicit comparison with other examples of the genre. It will then be good (valuable) according to the amount of detail it contains, the number of deviations from an implicit model it displays, the manner in which it avoids formulae of a conventional nature (just as a salesman of traditional jewellery will point out the quality of filigree, the finesse of the workmanship, 'how long it took to make the object').

The same might be said, and with even greater justification, about my second example, a section of Orfeo's great aria 'Possente spirto', in Act III of Monteverdi's opera, in which he persuades Charon, the boatman of the Underworld, to convey him across to the Kingdom of the Dead (Ex. 19). Here perhaps the case is more complex. Monteverdi only provides *some* of the necessary information in his score, obeying a convention which allowed the performer a great deal of freedom to add decorative notes. Anyone

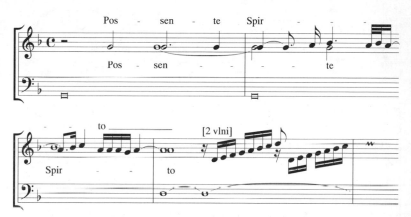

Ex. 19: 'Possente spirto' (Monteverdi, *Orfeo*. Act 3)

who can read the score, which is quite simple, could give a performance. But the essential expressive quality of the performance really depends on the particular singer's personal knowledge of and ability to perform a style of ornamentation. It's only in the last seventy years or so that this work has been revived. So in the first instance musicologists have had to reconstitute a practice of the past from descriptions of performances and old manuals of instruction. For the singer to sing it, however, he has to be able to perform the ornamentation intuitively. There may be a set of general rules, revamped from the seventeenth century, but it will only help up to

Ex. 20: Machaut, *Hoquetus David*

a certain point; from there on a tradition must be invoked or recreated, which enables the singer to apply an inventive performing skill.

Two conclusions may be drawn here: (1) that as soon as we become involved with a notion of better and worse, masterly or average, we invoke a concept of tradition; and (2) that this tradition exists in place and time. What was once a tradition may now no longer exist. And, conversely, things which we take for granted, which are now unspoken, or at least unformulated, common practices, were not necessarily so before. For example, there is a tradition of free accompaniment on the keyboard, which was common practice in the eighteenth century, or earlier, and which disappeared in the nineteenth, to be reconstituted in the twentieth. Conversely, there is a style of playing instruments today which we know (if only from the instruments themselves) bears only a very general relationship to what once was; compare only a fortepiano and a Steinway.

Now let us take what appears to be a pair of counter-examples. First, a three-part 'double hocquet' by Machaut (Ex. 20). Here we do not hear, or cannot separate, a free, unfixed component in the performance, and we might reasonably be tempted to believe that a fairly comprehensive rule or instruction might be formulated which would be sufficient for the creation of compositions of this type. We think this because we can either hear or read a proportional, abstract structure which determines the external events. Though we might imagine the melodic structure as resulting from improvisational practice, this has been submitted to a determined rhythmic structure which is both describable and quantifiable.

But if I now insert a comparatively modern example (Ex. 21), what do we find? A traditional texture, known in music and referred to in the title of the piece – Webern's Op. 16 No. 2 – as canon, is perceived as controlling the continuity (as the rhythmic structure of the Machaut example is perceived as controlling *its* continuity). But once having observed this fact, we can go no further. The notes follow each other, imitating the manner but not the substance of 'strict music'. These notes are the choice of the composer, the outward form of his 'idea', and cannot be reduced or altered in any way. Similarly, we admire the consistency and crystalline clarity of the network of *simultaneously* sounding pitch levels. But we can only hear them as themselves; we cannot relate them to any common harmonic origins, nor to any traditions or expectations of continuation. At best we can intuit that every element of this little piece has been placed where it stands by the personal decision of its maker. It is irreducible and cannot be varied without becoming something different. No conditions for its modification or analytic reduction exist. It approaches a condition of uniqueness, and is to be understood only in terms of itself. There is certainly no point in comparing it with, say, a canon in the *Goldberg Variations*. I wouldn't even know how to compare it with another canon by Webern himself.

Ex. 21: Webern, Op. 16, No. 2, clarinet and voice

Of my four examples, the first two clearly demonstrate, *in the sounds they make*, a duality of structure. We can actually hear a tradition at work. There is an implied common model in both cases. This has been modified, ornamented and expanded for expressive purposes, so that we can appreciate the personal skill of creator and performer. Another pair of examples might produce a lesser or greater example of mastery. In my third example, there is still a balance of traditional elements and speculative structure. Here the comparative function of the critic begins to complicate. But, in the final example, the composer sends out, as it were, radio beams – all may hear them, but only some peculiar affinity or sensibility will qualify a hearer to understand.

At the one extreme stands common practice based upon traditional knowledge; at the other stands personal gesture resulting from subjectivism, and according to common practice incomprehensible, except by an act of faith, of personal identification.

4

Different musical cultures consist of repertoires of pieces. A superficial glance at any of the collections of musical antiquarians and ethnomusicologists demonstrates groups of pieces identified according to function, mode and type; as indeed these are identified, in our own music repertoires, according to function (their use in religious worship, music education, amateur choral singing etc.). Theoretically, and probably in practice, there might be an endless supply of music satisfying the conditions of any one such category. But whether it is so or not, it is a fact that certain pieces survive, and that when they are grouped together they are called a *repertoire*.

Now, we must assume that the pieces that remain in a particular repertoire have some qualities which have ensured their survival. They are in some way 'favoured' by musicians and listeners. Their performance, sometimes in prescribed circumstances, such as weddings or funerals, or marking the time of year, rehearses and ornaments the collective history of a community. There is no way in which we can say that quantitative attributes of music, particular arrangements of rhythms or intervals, represent things in the real world. But as historians we can say that there are associations. So everyone in a given community will recognise the rhythm and mode of funeral, harvest or coronation. A qualified musician, in any culture, is one who not only knows how to manipulate voice or instrument, but also has learned a repertoire. If he is of average achievement, he fulfils these qualifications; but if he becomes known as a 'master', he not only fulfils them but adds certain other, exceptional, qualities which single him out from his fellows.

We recognise an absolute master by the uniqueness of his performance. He may first impress us with the quality of his playing:

his tone may be very sweet, his rhythms particularly snappy; he may seduce us by the personality or ethos he communicates. But, further on, he may please us (if we have sufficient experience and taste to judge) with the variations and substitutions he introduces on the common models. In traditional cultures, where the model is simple, this involves actual alterations in the common matrix. A master's general intention is combinational: he will combine the performance of the 'known' composition with variants which serve to remove, or postpone, the expected continuations, creating intensity by the suspension of common expectation. Even if by analytical activity we can catalogue and quantify the range of his variants, this will not mask the fact that we are dealing with a quality of synthesis, an aspiration of uniqueness. Individualism – the communication of personal knowledge expressed in superior practice – is an attribute of mastery, and as such is honoured in traditional societies. We admire the master precisely because he is able to perform something that his fellows cannot achieve. He 'knows something which his lesser fellows don't'. Here we understand something of the relationship of expertise, or mastery, to ordinary, run-of-the-mill activity. And in this sense it hardly affects the issue whether we talk of musician-performers or composers. The study of traditional musics has been and is now the study of repertoires and of the qualities that go to make an outstanding performer. By and large, the same is true of medieval music (except that we know little of its performance). But as we come to modern classical music, the situation radically alters. Josquin des Prez, Vittoria, Byrd, Monteverdi and Schütz usher in a period of music which in form, at least, persists to the present, and which has traditionally been seen as a collection of masterpieces by a string of geniuses. If today musicologists study the Classical, Romantic and modern periods as social histories with their typical repertoires, this is only as a mild corrective to the overwhelming feeling that the proper study of these periods is the study of their masterpieces: the B minor Mass, the Jupiter and Eroica Symphonies, the Haydn quartets, the music of Brahms, Wagner, Schoenberg and Stravinsky. We may be interested in the circumstances of Viennese Catholic ritual, but it's the Nelson Mass and the *Missa solemnis* we care about.

The greatest analytical historian of the classical period, Heinrich Schenker, grouped his studies together under the general title *Das Meisterwerk in der Musik* (1925–30); his purpose is defined *not* by the historical study of styles, but by an understanding of what a masterpiece is, and of the way in which it overshadows the lesser and more ordinary music of its contemporaries. In traditional musical thinking, genius has been imbued with almost divine origins. These have sometimes been deliberately and falsely shrouded in an aura of mystery, which in itself has profound psychological implications. Schoolboys have been taught maxims and rules, while at the same time they have been encouraged to worship the genius who is allowed to trample on these same maxims and rules. 'The rule exists in its exception', say the wise. 'Quod licet Jovis, non licet bovis', adds the schoolmaster.

Today we cannot be content with this, and the development of historical music analysis is informed by the intention to establish what genius is, as well as how it relates to its more conventional and ordinary background. Schenker, more than any other, assists us here. His work is limited to the study of masterpieces. For special (rather than general) reasons, he considers these as existing (in a state of becoming) in the pre-Classical period and declining as the nineteenth century gives way to the twentieth. Furthermore, with the exception of Scarlatti and Chopin, every creator of master pieces is of German, Aryan stock (which Schenker was not). We may (and do) ignore this, but we may not ignore the criteria of the masterpiece as he defines it. Many of Schenker's most ardent followers do ignore this, insofar as they like to forget or at least blur the crucial distinction that what Schenker describes in his mature writing is designed to cast light on the nature of masterpieces, and not to reformulate any general theories of harmony or counterpoint which are the traditional stuff of classical pedagogy and the preconditions of musical competence.

Traditional music analysis has tended to be descriptive. But in his mature work Schenker refines a method which has more in common with geology than with any traditional type of musical inquiry. Inevitably, he starts with the musical text (he was, in fact, a pioneer of the *Urtext*), but his early studies in ornamentation convinced him that this text did not come into being as a direct translation or notation of musical imagining, as is certainly the case with ordinary, run-of-the-mill music: dances, songs, hymns etc. So he came to consider that mastery was achieved by a kind of transformational activity. An ordinary, conventional (and for him, in the final analysis, out-of-Nature) sound formula was prolonged and transformed into something unique. 'Die Auskomponierung ist die Musik. Die Geschichte erweist es in den Werken der grossen Meister.' [The music is in the composing-out. History testifies to this in the works of the great masters.][5] *Auskomponierung*, literally 'composing out', can be defined, by a study of the different ways in which it is achieved, as resulting in the transformation of a rule-determined sequence of musical events (a sequence which is *ordinary*, in the real meaning of the word), or of a model which can very roughly be placed somewhere between Schenker's 'background' and 'middleground' analytical levels (too elaborate for the former, not 'extraordinary' enough for the latter), into the unique structure of a masterpiece. This is not the place to rehearse the means adopted by the great composers to transform the basic structures upon which, according to Schenker, their compositions rest. But I should like to make one remark on this subject.

In his final treatise, *Der freie Satz* (*Free Composition*, 1935), Schenker attempts to build upwards, from the common triad ('which exists in nature'), a theory for the composition of masterpieces, the elements of which comprise operations which transform simple harmonic relationships into more indirect and oblique ones. One can draw from this the conclusion – and this is supported by his other writings, notably those on sonata and fugue, as well as by his analyses of individual works – that Schenker believed that he was, as fairly as he was able, describing how the great Classical composers worked. Analysis moves from the text, by means of bracketing and reduction, to the background. This, Schenker implies, is a mirror image of the path pursued by the 'Meister', who moves from a simple background structure, or even a natural phenomenon, step by step towards his own unique and complex foreground. Somewhere (I don't have the exact quotation by me) Schenker says that the particular genius of the great masters consisted in their ability to create great and complex structures, while obeying the laws of nature (which for him boil down to the major triad – the *Urklang* – with its overtone structure).

I think that we can see an accord in our paradigms of a master in traditional music and of a masterpiece in European Classical music. Both depend, not only on the existence of, but also on a recognition and acceptance of, ordinary or common practice, identified as such technically and socially, be it the music of dance, worship or song. This may be learned and defined by a prescriptive rule. But, to avoid misunderstanding, let me add the further *caveat*: clearly this binary description of the creation of genius can only be understood as a model. In practice, sketches of composers show that sometimes they invent their music more or less as it exists in its final form (although Beethoven and Mahler are exceptions), and that the famous anecdote of Prokofiev's small son, who, when asked how his father composed, said, 'First he writes music and then he Prokofievizes it', need not be taken too literally. A more general observation suggests that in real life the re-invention of the familiar model, and its transformation, are from the outset intermingled. If this accord in the relationship of uniqueness and common practice were to be convincing, we would of course have to treat any model of traditional art in a far more sophisticated way than could have been attempted here. But the implications of such a thesis as this are intended to be polemical and include a specific criticism of the stance generally adopted by us, whether as makers or as students of music. The criticism is intended on the one hand to illuminate what ought to be the constants or invariants that lie behind the high aspirations of music, while on the other showing up the fundamental mysticism and irresponsibility of many current attitudes, especially towards new composition, for what they really are. One thing we might now usefully do is apply

the strict discipline of ethnomusicology to our own cultures. This
I am sure would be both helpful and illuminating.

(1985)

1. Franz Kafka, *Hochzeitsvorbereitungen auf dem Lande: und andere Prosa aus dem Nachlass* (Frankfurt a. M.: Fischer Verlag, 1953), p. 95. The English is my own.
2. 'Franz Liszt's Work and Being', in *Style and Idea*, 2nd edn, ed. Leonard Stein (London: Faber, 1975), p. 442.
3. Verbatim.
4. Gilbert Ryle, *The Concept of Mind* (London: Penguin, 1963), p. 28.
5. Heinrich Schenker, 'Fortsetzung der Urlinie-Betrachtungen', in *Das Meisterwerk in der Musik* (Munich: Drei Masken Verlag, 1926), Vol. 2, p. 40.

10

Brahms's *Aktualität*

I

I have borrowed my title from Theodor Adorno. Only he was talking about Wagner: his title was 'Wagner's *Aktualität*'.[1] And how good and natural it sounds – when concerned with Wagner! For, as a composer, dramatist and philosopher, Wagner is of very wide interest. His ideas are talked about, and his pieces are interpreted, in one way or another, as if they had been written yesterday. No doubt about their relevance!

But put Brahms in his place and the title seems a bit contrived, even slightly ironical. For how or why should we want to consider Brahms as relevant? And might one not feel that there is something rather suspect in the very notion of being relevant, anyway? I should say that by invoking the idea of 'relevance' I don't mean to discuss the popularity of a composer's work with performer or audience – that's self-evident enough! – but to consider whether his particular sensibility and the thought contained in his work have anything of special interest for the way we think about music today.

If the question is put like that, many will simply say no. Brahms's thinking has little (which is not to say it has nothing) to do with us. True, his reputation has recovered: he's no longer the object of the distaste he perhaps was for a generation who rebelled against their teachers' canon of the three Bs. Nor are people quite so critical of the 'heavy', nineteenth-century characteristics of his work (of which, incidentally, he might well have been expressing some awareness when in a letter to his friend Joachim, in 1856, he wrote: 'Polyphony means [music of] many voices, and today we must distinguish between many voices and filling-out'[2]). And yet reservations remain. The quality of his imagination is not that of

Schumann, let alone Chopin; nor is there the fervency of feeling that we associate with Liszt. Even his revival of Baroque forms seems, superficially at least, to lack the elegance we associate with Mendelssohn. And today it is the symphonic structure of Mahler that attracts public attention – where the heightening of subjective expression and the concept of form as a mirror of a world are preferred to the more austere and emotionally limited manner of the Brahmsian symphony.

2

By mentioning Brahms *and* Wagner, I suppose I can't help reminding you of the controversies about these great composers which took up so much of the thinking about music at the end of the previous and in the early part of this century. I shan't talk about that now; if anything, I shall talk about Brahms and Liszt. But I would like to mention one theme of the old dialogue which seems to have a good deal of life in it yet. Music, it was argued, exists not merely for our aesthetic pleasure, but also for our moral welfare. This notion reappeared frequently and is today almost taken for granted. Music, especially opera, conveys attitudes to life, and aims to alter individual consciousness. So modern music might perhaps be seen as continuing the traditions of religious music. In this respect, Wagner, Mahler and Schoenberg are the heirs of Bach and Beethoven, as opposed to the secular and bourgeois attitudes to be found in the works of Haydn, Mozart, Chopin and Brahms (who, if anything, evoke an image of 'religion of art'). Comic opera, string quartet, mazurka and intermezzo speak to an 'enlightened' audience who delight in the contemplation of beauty and form, and slightly recoil from the sense of higher aspiration contained in the *Missa solemnis*, *Parsifal* or Mahler's Eighth Symphony. In these, the very difficulties of the language, the indecent and inelegant demands of long durations, and the sense of unrealisable aims might be felt to indicate something higher and perhaps greater. Conversely, the well-balanced, organically satisfactory, succinct forms of chamber music represent the love of good craftsmanship, of the pleasing and tasteful object, that was and is an appurtenance of bourgeois culture.

So Thomas Mann (in 'Wagner and the Ring') writes:

> Wagner experienced modern culture, the culture of bourgeois society, through the medium and in the image of the operatic theatre activity of his day. The status of art – or of that art, at least, which appealed to his taste – in that contemporary world became the criterion by which he judged bourgeois culture as such: so it was hardly surprising that he should learn to despise and hate it. He saw art reduced to the level of an extravagant consumer product, the artist degraded to a slave of money; he saw superficiality and dull routine where he longed for holy earnest and beauteous solemnity; he watched with fury while vast resources were squandered, not for the attainment of high artistic purpose, but for that which he despised above all else as an artist: the easy, cheap effect. And because he saw that none of this offended anyone else as it offended him, he concluded that the political and social conditions that could bring forth such things, and to which they properly belonged, were utterly vile – and must be changed by revolutionary means.[5]

Inner values of classical and romantic art come under strain in a rapidly changing society, and so are transformed into fixed attitudes and forms. The denomination of the currency is retained, the actual value slips away. Art becomes ornament and is emptied of genuine force. Finally it is seen to be a despised simulation, a mere ghost of something which formerly had real content.

But already in the early years of this century this naive revolutionary posture was seen to be inadequate. As Karl Kraus sought to defend the formal properties of the spoken and written language against the attacks made upon it by the purveyors of propaganda (of one kind or another), so did Arnold Schoenberg modify the post-Wagnerian, expressionist inspiration of his work by retaining the 'progressive' elements (as he termed them) from the language of the composers of the past.[4] When, this year, we mark a Brahms anniversary, we also mark Schoenberg's own earlier celebration of the same anniversary in a lecture first given in 1933 and later published (in 1950) under the title 'Brahms the Progressive'. This article, which was and remains extremely influential, defined Brahms, along with Mozart and Mahler, as a 'progressive', insofar as he had contributed to a 'progress . . . toward an unrestricted musical language'.[5]

Even in his pre-First World War expressionist period, Schoenberg had diagnosed the problem of the nineteenth-century revolutionist ideal. Writing of Liszt in 1911, he says:

> Liszt replaced an old form by a new. What he thus did is certainly a worse formalism than that of the masters who had lived in the old forms. For they really had lived in them! They truly thought in that space, it was their home, they were almost born there, and therefore they moved in it with the most complete freedom.[6]

For Schoenberg, any continuing preoccupation with old form, or the replacement of it with a synthetic new form, represents an impoverishment of artistic content. His aim is a self-renewing and 'unrestricted' musical language which will serve to communicate fresh moods and images and which will have the inner coherence and strength to convey an unstereotyped and integral meaning. From old music he wishes to retain everything that is personal and felt, irregular and momentary, and to discard what is conventional, stock-in-trade and formalistic. Here he echoes Wagner, who complains of Mozart's 'stereotyped phrases', which give his movements 'the character of background music' and provide 'an attractive noise to accompany conversations between attractive melodies'.[7]

But this attitude has a longer provenance still. Liszt and his disciples, in what they liked to call the *Neudeutsche Schule*, distinguished between music 'in which traditional and conventional form contains and rules thought' and 'the other in which thought re-creates and fashions a form and style appropriate to its needs and inspiration'. And Liszt clearly sees the philosophical implication of his viewpoint. 'Undoubtedly, in proceeding thus,' he continues,

> 'we shall encounter head-on those perennial problems of *authority* and *freedom*. But why should that frighten us? In the liberal arts, fortunately, they entail none of the dangers and disasters which their fluctuations occasion in the political and social world, for, in the realm of the Beautiful, genius alone is the authority, dualism disappears, and the concepts of authority and liberty are restored to their original identity. Manzoni, in defining genius as "a greater borrowing from God," has eloquently expressed this truth.'[8]

Liszt admired (in Chopin) the primacy of inspiration and the freedom of form, and he believed that the artist 'should not do violence to his genius by subjecting it to rules and regulations which were not his own and did not accord with the demands of the spirit'.[9]

For all Schoenberg's concern for and love of the ideals of the Classical masters, Liszt's thought lives on in him. 'Form in music', he suggests, 'serves to bring about comprehensibility through memorability. Evenness, regularity, symmetry, subdivision, repetition, unity, relationship in rhythm and harmony and even logic – none of these elements produces or even contributes to beauty.'[10] He opposes his concept of 'idea' to form, so that everything that is 'striking, individual [and] self revealing is contained in the *idea*', in a way analogous to spoken language, 'where feelings and thoughts are expressed in words'. While *idea* is good, form is merely functional, expressively neutral. Indeed, at his most expressionist, Schoenberg wants to abolish the very concept of form. The musical idea, he suggests, is not a phrase, but 'the totality of a piece'.[11]

Liszt, Wagner, Schoenberg – all attacked the dualities of authority and freedom, form and content. They sought to replace these dualities with a unity, which would be characterised by an 'unrestricted musical language' (Schoenberg) in which 'thought re-creates and fashions form' (Liszt). But Brahms would certainly not have agreed to his recruitment into the lines of the freedom fighters. In the one public controversy of his life, he joined with others in a protest against what he wished ironically to call 'the productions of Dr Fr. Liszt and his followers'. The famous and ill-fated public letter of 1860, to which Brahms was a signatory along with Joachim and others, described 'aberrations' to be found in the works of Liszt and his followers, aberrations which were 'opposed to the innermost nature of music and of harmful influence to the future development of art'. Elsewhere Brahms writes of 'muddles' and 'fantastic new theories', implying that the work of Liszt and his followers 'ignores some of the fundamental principles (*Grundregeln*) of music'.

What were the 'muddles' and 'fantastic new theories' to which Brahms so vehemently objected? In 1860, they can hardly have been new harmonies or the use of unusual intervals, which in any case were not unknown in Chopin, who was admired both by Schumann (who ungratefully described the Liszt Sonata, dedicated to him, as 'noise') and by Brahms. Perhaps it was just Liszt's attitude to the relationship of imagination and form (derived origin-ally from Berlioz) that disturbed him. Brahms would surely have preferred the quotation from Schiller that Heinrich Schenker placed at the head of his essay on the *Handel Variations*: 'The Divine or Ideal only appears where *both* things combine: Where the Will freely follows the law of Necessity and the Understanding deter-mines the Rule amid the vicissitudes of the Imagination.'[12] In fact, Brahms had little time for Liszt's music, 'which gets worse and worse, e.g. the *Dante* Sonata'. *Christus* 'is so amazingly boring, stupid and silly that I can't understand how this swindle can be perpetrated'. He is even critical of Liszt's attitude towards Hun-garian folk sources, saying that he 'always wished he [Liszt] would just copy them out . . .'

But Wagner was a different thing. In a letter Brahms suggests that he, more than anyone else in Germany, knows what Wagner is trying to achieve, and elsewhere he writes: 'I could be called a Wagnerian, principally as the protest of any reasonable man against the frivolous way musicians here speak of him.' Nevertheless he is not all that enthusiastic. 'I don't rave about this composition' (he's writing about *Die Meistersinger*), 'or about Wagner in general. But I listen to him as attentively as possible and as frequently – as I can stand it. Granted one's tempted to babble on about it. But I'm glad I don't have to say anything loud and clear. One thing I do know: in all other respects in whatever I try to do, I'm embarrassed by the way I tread on the heels of my predecessors. But Wagner wouldn't inhibit me from attempting an opera – with great pleasure.'

Brahms did in fact consider composing an opera. A longstanding friend of his was a Swiss poet, Joseph Widman, and with him he discussed a number of operatic projects. It's worth mentioning these because they fit so badly with the popularly received impression of the composer. One can easily see what he had in mind when he said that Wagner's example would not get in his way. The subjects that he considered were a play by Calderon (*The Noisy Secret*) and Gozzi's *King Stag* (later made into an opera by Henze). These choices are startling enough, but more surprising still is the attitude towards opera composition that he expressed in letters to Widman. It seems clear that Brahms had a taste for a kind of *Singspiel* approach, a taste quite in keeping for someone who was so interested in folk music. In a letter of 1877, he suggests that he does not really mind how the dramatic text is treated, 'except at the moments of emotional intensification'. The rest should be dialogue or simply *recitativo secco*. Certainly an approach of this kind was intensely old-fashioned in 1870 (or else it was fifty years ahead of its time: think of *Oedipus Rex* or *Mahagonny*).

3

When Schoenberg characterises Brahms as 'progressive', he lists a number of qualities to be found in his music. They are: (1) increasing richness of harmony; (2) intervallic integration (such as that which connects the first and fourth movements of the Fourth Symphony); (3) asymmetry and the combination of phrases of different length; and (4) intensification of motivic integration. These, he suggests, demonstrate that Brahms, 'without renouncing beauty and emotion, proved to be a progressive in a field which had not been cultivated for half a century'.[13] In this way he clearly relates the inspiration for these innovations to Mozart and Beethoven.

Schoenberg gives examples taken from songs and chamber music. One of these is the setting of Heine's poem 'Meerfahrt'. He cites the first bars of the song, which 'consists exclusively of three-measure phrases, on account of the poem's metre of three metrical feet':

> Mein Liebchen, wir sassen beisammen
> traulich im leichten Kahn.[14]

Three-measure phrases do occur in the setting of the first verse (fifteen plus one bars in all). But surely the important point is contained in the setting of the second verse. When Brahms sets the words

> dort klangen liebe Töne
> und wogte der Nebeltanz.
> Dort klang es lieb und lieber
> und wogt es hin und her,

he expresses the rocking of the boat by replacing two three-bar phrases with two four-bar ones. In this way he points up Heine's repetition of words. Now he continues in four-bar phrases, only to return to three-bar phrases at the end. But this asymmetry is contained within an overall symmetry, the two verses being of about the same duration.

The intensification of the middle section is matched by a corresponding motivic and harmonic enrichment. The introduction contains a characteristic rising motif, which recurs at the end of the first verse (Ex. 22a). Now this is strikingly completed in the second verse (Ex. 22b). It is this ability to complete ideas that distinguishes Brahms from Liszt. The irregularities of phrase length do not exemplify a moving towards a free, prose-like continuity, as Schoenberg has it, but result from the conflict of formal and expressive forces within a fairly strict and predetermined framework.

Ex. 22a: 'Meerfahrt', introduction

Ex. 22b: 'Meerfahrt', second verse

From 'Verrat', Brahms's setting of a poem by Karl Lemcke, he gives an extract exemplifying 'looser construction'.[15] It is seven bars in length and contains phrase lengths of six, seven, seven and four beats' duration (Ex. 23). In fact, the example is only part of a verse and a setting of direct speech. Here the background structure is of four-bar phrases, lightly distorted by interpolations in the accompaniment to make them (with the exception of the last) seven-bar phrases. Our example is a recitative which, I suggest, makes its effect *not* because of its asymmetries, but because of its deviation from the established four-bar background expectation.

One of the most striking of Schoenberg's analyses is of the third of the *Four Serious Songs*. This was selected to exemplify the intensification of motivic integration. More than any other, this analysis changed our perception of the way in which Brahms worked, and the uncanny way it might be seen to anticipate Schoenberg's own methods. 'The most important capacity of a composer

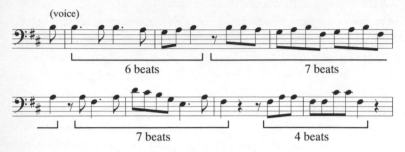

Ex. 23: 'Verrat' (after Schoenberg)

[Schoenberg writes] is to cast a glance into the most remote future of his themes or motives. He has to be able to know beforehand the consequences which derive from the problems existing in his material, and to organize everything accordingly.'[16] Schoenberg goes on to show how the whole song is evolved from a series of thirds: in a detailed examination of the first seven phrases, he demonstrates how each, in both voice part and accompaniment, derives from the series, by means of transposition, inversion and the filling-in of structurally positioned terms of the series.[17]

Ex. 24: 'O Tod', from *Vier ernste Gesänge* (after Schoenberg)

The thing that appeals here is the way the composer derives new and beautiful developments from a single intervallic series. 'The sense of logic [Schoenberg continues] . . . and the power of inventiveness which build melodies of so much natural fluency deserve the admiration of every music lover who expects more than sweetness and beauty from music.'[18] From Schoenberg's example it would be natural to deduce that Brahms's forward-looking method was indeed 'a progress towards an unrestricted musical language', comparable to the language of, say, Liszt's Piano Sonata, with its techniques of melodic transformation. But this would surely be to ignore the fact that, in this song, meaning in the detail of the continuity is only achieved within a very particular overall conception of the form.

The beautiful words, from the Apocrypha, contrast that Death which is bitter for the prosperous man, 'who liveth at rest in his possessions [and] hath nothing to vex him', with a Death which brings relief to him who is old and weak and has nothing to hope for. The contrast is expressed by the movement from the minor mode of the grim first part to the more open, consolatory major of the second. And the plan is worked so that the forty bars of the song are divided exactly in half. The opening words, 'O Tod' (in the minor first of all), recur at the exact middle inverted to a major sixth (in the major mode). The structural beauties that Schoenberg admires do, however, make their effect when heard in relation to their resolutions, in the first half of the song, on the repetition of the words 'O Tod, wie bitter, wie bitter bist du', where the vocal line falls through a seventh, and in the second half, where the seventh is most movingly reiterated, this time without any intermediate notes (Ex. 24).

Schoenberg's other examples should be carefully studied and related back to their sources. In all cases, it can be shown that the irregularities of phrase length (which are in fact frequently related to harmonic intensification) and the unusually intense motivic derivations are highly selective. When you look in detail, you tend to find that the effect of these apparent innovations relies on symmetrical forms and regular phrase-structures. If so, and it is so, it is false to see here a 'progressive' attitude, a tendency towards 'unrestricted' and prose-like construction – and truer to compare these striking effects to the kind of thing achieved, for example in poetry, by Gerard Manley Hopkins.

4

Today it's difficult, perhaps impossible, to imagine what the great masters of the past were really like: they are, in important respects, veiled by the very mystery of their genius. Who could transpose Bach or Mozart or even Wagner into this place and year and visualise him interacting with ourselves? But Brahms, who achieved an oeuvre at least to be compared with that of the greatest composers, is an amazingly modern, even familiar, figure. As we leaf through the volumes of his correspondence, we are struck by his particularly modern sensibility. His lower-middle-class Hamburg background does not feel like that mysterious nothingness which so often is described as the origin of the genius. It's a flesh-and-blood, mediocre environment; it and the people in it play a continuing role in Brahms's life – and like many who go on to greater things, Brahms never gets over the slights and rejections of his young years in his home town.

His friendships and activities are also not unfamiliar to us. He conducts amateur choirs and devises better programmes for them. And he has an eye for the better voices (and perhaps the better looks) among the sopranos. His letters to friends and professional bodies are generally regarded as being slightly mundane and laconic in comparison with the correspondence of other great artists. I can't agree with this judgement. Their very convincing reality may be the thing that shocks the reader who wishes for more mystery. In these letters the tragedy and misery of Schumann's last years, and the desperation of family and friends, come alive. Brahms emerges as generous, loving and, more than anything else, obsessed with the music of the past and the detail of his own work. Not here grandiose ideas and interpretations! Brahms's letters are full of the nuts and bolts of a musician's world: he finds wrong notes in the manuscripts of ancient composers, corrects bad part-writing, and tries to get his own pieces as right as possible. He has an agreement with Joachim to exchange and correct counterpoint exercises by post. The penalty for non-fulfilment is a fine to be spent on books. 'I'm sending you the earlier canons again,' he writes. 'Leaving aside technique, are they good music? Does the technique make them more beautiful or more valuable? Does anything occur to you? I've no idea.'

Brahms collected manuscripts of earlier composers and knew what to do with them. He revered Bach, Handel, Haydn and Scarlatti; loved Schubert, Schumann and Chopin. He edited their texts and may be regarded as one of the precursors of modern musicology, looking forward longingly to the complete editions which grace the shelves of our libraries and enrich our musical experience. Among his friends were Spitta, the Bach biographer, and Nottebohm, the first student of the Beethoven sketches.

I dwell on this modernity of outlook to draw attention to what seems to me to be something of a paradox. We can so easily empathise and even identify with Brahms, his feelings and his ideas. His tastes are our tastes, his attitudes, our attitudes. But the tendencies and deliberate limitations of his compositions are not generally reflected in the preoccupations of present-day composers; most would, if asked, consider him irrelevant to their own intentions.

Or is the contradiction in ourselves? Might it not be that contemporary values, veering as they do towards the expressionistic, if not the downright apocalyptic, and dramatising artists into something between scientists and explorers, are at odds with the realities of our lives? Could it not be that our daydreams, so successfully enlarged by advertisement, and the adolescent posturings that characterise so much of our cultural life are at odds with the reality of musical experience? Is the attack on the bourgeois canon of art perhaps not also an attack on art itself? And is it not then merely a high-class philistinism? From Brahms we can learn, or be reminded, that music is composed with notes, not with concepts, and on ruled manuscript paper.

Writing of the Bach Chaconne, Brahms wonders at 'a universe

of deepest insights and most powerful ideas, written on a single system and for a tiny instrument. If I thought I might have conceived and written this,' he adds, 'the sheer excitement and shock would have driven me quite crazy.'

(1983)

1. Theodor W. Adorno, *Versuch über Wagner* (Frankfurt a. M.: Suhrkamp, 1981), p. 7 note.

2. Quoted in Litterscheid, *Johannes Brahms in seinen Schriften und Briefen* (Berlin: Haline Feld Verlag, 1943). [All Brahms quotations in this chapter are taken from this volume; no page references are available. Translations are my own.]

3. Thomas Mann, 'Richard Wagner and Der Ring des Nibelungen', in Thomas Mann: *Pro and Contra Wagner*, trans. Allan Blunden (London: Faber, 1985), pp. 177–8.

4. [This line of thought was to be developed in the essay 'Schoenberg and Karl Kraus: The Idea behind the Music', written three years later: see above, pp. 124–41.]

5. 'Brahms the Progressive', in *Style and Idea*, 2nd edn, ed. Leonard Stein, trans Leo Black (London: Faber, 1975), p. 441.

6. 'Franz Liszt's Work and Being', in *Style and Idea*, p. 444.

7. Wagner, 'Music of the Future', in *Three Wagner Essays*, trans. Robert L. Jacobs (London: Eulenburg, 1979), p. 37.

8. In a letter to Wilhelm von Lenz (1852), quoted and translated in Sam Morgenstern, *Composers on Music: An Anthology of Composers' Writings* (London: Faber, 1958), pp. 168–9.

9. From 'Friedrich Chopin' (1850), quoted in ibid., p. 169. [The quotation reads: 'He [Chopin] must have had to do violence to his genius . . . every time he sought to subject it to rules and regulations which were not his own . . .']

10. 'Brahms the Progressive', p. 399.

11. 'New Music, Outmoded Music, Style and Idea', in *Style and Idea*, p. 123.

12. Heinrich Schenker, *Der Tonwille* nos 8/9 (April/September 1924), p. 3. It is not unreasonable to suppose that Brahms might also have accepted the premises implied by Wittgenstein (who frequently and favourably comments on Brahms), when he says of Shakespeare: 'I'm unable to understand Shakespeare, because I want to find the symmetry in the total asymmetry. It seems to me that his plays might be compared to huge sketches, not paintings: they are thrown down by one who you might say can allow himself everything. I can understand that one can admire it and call it the highest art, but I don't like it.' Ludwig Wittgenstein, *Vermischte Bemerkungen* (Frankfurt a. M.: Suhrkamp, 1977), p. 162.

13. 'Brahms the Progressive', p. 439.

14. Ibid.

15. Ibid., p. 422.

16. Ibid.

17. Ibid., pp. 431–5, 439.

18. Ibid., p. 435.

11

Franz Liszt

I

Of all the 'great composers' I can think of only four who, for a variety of reasons, incurred the criticism of incompetence from some of their contemporaries. They are Monteverdi, Musorgsky, Liszt and Wagner. All four have had a seminal influence on the composers who followed them – to such an extent that in the case of the latter three it would at least be arguable that they might be considered the real fathers of those early twentieth-century innovators Debussy, Scriabin and Schoenberg, as well as of Bartók and Busoni. The issues raised in the work of Musorgsky are to some extent local and specific; those raised by Wagner universal and too massive for any but the most dedicated and well-qualified enquiry. But although, as a musician, I would certainly push Liszt out of any lifeboat of survivors in which I could be accompanied by only three of these great masters (unless I was after agreeable company, in which case I would retain *only* Liszt), his oeuvre does raise genuinely interesting problems for the analyst, and perhaps not particularly those issues of taste which have been mentioned recently by Charles Rosen and Alfred Brendel.[1]

The problem as I see it is this. A number of Liszt's peers, who had every reason to like and admire him for his warmth and generosity, made quite specific and patronisingly negative obser-vations about his compositional endeavours. There is no doubt at all of his pianistic pre-eminence. But the compositions invoke a kind of slighting and ironical comment which might be understood as a legitimate reaction against the razzmatazz and showbiz per-formance of this larger-than-life Hungarian gentleman, but does also read as quite a specific charge of incompetence against him.

Schumann, who commented negatively on the parallel fifths and octaves in the score of *Tannhäuser*, said of the young Liszt:

> For protracted studies in composition he apparently did not have time; or perhaps, too, he was not able to find a suitable teacher . . . lively musical natures seem to prefer immediately expressive musical tones to dry paper. If he attained unbelievable heights as a player, the composer was left behind. And this results, inevitably, in an imbalance that has its effect even upon his most recent works . . . So we see him (for example in his *Apparitions*) indulging in murky fantasies, or in almost blasé indifference, while at other times he strives for reckless virtuosity, irreverent and half mad for its boldness.
>
> The sight of Chopin apparently first brought him to his senses. Chopin always has form. . . . Now dissatisfied, perhaps, with his own efforts he began to seek refuge in other composers, in Beethoven and Franz Schubert, and to decorate their music with his own art.[2]

Thinking back to the author's own early experience with the piano, there could well be an element of jealousy in this harsh judgement. Yet the tone persists. Of the B minor Sonata (which Liszt dedicated to Schumann), his wife Clara says it is 'merely a blind noise – no healthy ideas any more, everything confused, one cannot find a single, clear harmonic progression'.[3]

What a contrast between this and Schumann's own generous words reserved for Mendelssohn, Chopin and the young Brahms! But Brahms's own letters, culminating – if not concluding – with his ill-fated sortie against the *Neudeutsche Schule* in 1862, contain certain references to Liszt which reveal a deep dislike for him, as well as quite specific accusations of incompetence, of 'Verirrungen' (mistakes), in his pieces.

Now the point here is that one would not normally describe what one considered to be lapses of taste as compositional mistakes. Lapses of taste are generally diagnosed retrospectively and, at any other than a surface level, do not exist. For either the passage that contains the lapse of taste performs a function within the piece or it does not. If it does, and does so economically and sufficiently, then whatever the surface allusions may suggest there is no such lapse; if, on the other hand, a passage does not function within an organic form, or is reduplicative or unnecessarily protracted, a technical/compositional miscalculation has occurred of which the lapse of taste, diagnosed by our own tastes rather than by our ability to assess the functions of the parts within the whole, is merely the outward form. It may be considered that this viewpoint is that of a composer, and is even a bit prissy; but it does seem to me that Schumann and Brahms were actually accusing Liszt of making compositional mistakes and being, in a sense, incompetent, quite apart from any reservations they may have had about the psychological make-up of this extraordinary man, 'Mephistophelian and pious, sensitive and enthusiastic' (in the words of Busoni), whose work 'drew into its orbit all dialects, nations and epochs from Palestrina to *Parsifal*'.[4]

2

Looking back, we might well ask what the concept of an error, in art, and specifically in music, might mean. We live in a world in which certainty has evaporated. Few believe that there are universal rules which in any differentiable manner, other than in the realm of good intentions, work for *all* art or *all* music. At one extreme, at least in the field of high art, we might prefer the ambitious, if circular, proposition that each work of art suggests its own rules. Even if we need not go as far as this, few have any time for rules, and, consequently, for lapses from them, which can be directly and materially assessed. So if we talk of rules and their exceptions, we are surely not talking only of parallel fifths and octaves, and suchlike things, which are, at best, lapses in orthography and spelling, and can at worst be only a mild blemish on a composition.

There are well-established differences, but also relationships, between the rules of craftsmanship and those of fine art. Kant, in

The Critique of Judgement, distinguishes between the agreeable and the fine, concluding that 'Fine Art is an art, so far as it has at the same time the appearance of being nature'. He amplifies this in stating that:

> The finality in its form must appear just as free from the constraint of arbitrary rules as if it were a product of mere nature . . . The finality in the product of fine art, intentional though it be, must not have the appearance of being intentional; i.e. fine art must be clothed *with the aspect* of nature, although we recognise it to be art. But the way in which a product of art seems like nature is by the presence of perfect *exactness* in the agreement with rules prescribing how close the product can be to what it is intended to be, but with an absence of *laboured effect* (without academic form betraying itself), i.e. without a trace appearing of the artist having always had the rule present to him and of its having fettered his mental powers.

But 'fine art is the art of genius', and 'genius is the talent (natural endowment) which gives the rule to art'. 'Originality must be its primary property.' But, 'since there may also be original nonsense, its products must at the same time be models, i.e. be exemplary – and, consequently, though not themselves derived from imitation, they must serve that purpose for others, i.e. as a standard or rule of estimating.'[5]

In essence, Heinrich Schenker follows Kant here, as he follows Schumann and Brahms in his view of music. He also follows them in his ability to make extremely harsh judgements about those composers who do not earn a place in his canon of genius. He does not analyse the work of Wagner or Liszt, because he does not consider that it embodies true genius in his definition of the term. Probably rightly – though, from our point of view, regrettably – he is concerned, in all his work, with the positive determination of what is a masterpiece, rather than with a negative diagnosis of non-genius (except in his article about Reger). But odd observations are useful here. *If*, as he says, 'only genius is blessed with a sense of tonal space' (which is his *a priori* exactly as 'the projection of his own corporeality, and the process of growth and becoming, provide man with an inborn sense of space and time'), and 'only genius creates out of the background of tonal space', so that he 'harnesses freedom in the successive events at the foreground to the compulsion of the passing-note progressions in the background', then non-genius, though capable of 'creating and savouring successive events', inevitably runs aground.[6] And having echoed Kant's belief that genius has at its disposal an unlimited world, or a world limited only by Nature, which he calls the necessary guardian and ruler of freedom, Schenker adds that: 'Decay in music' – and in his own time he believed the art to be in a state of decay – 'is a decay in the sense of tonal space within the individual . . . [and in] the sum of individuals.'[7]

More specifically, but without naming names, he suggests that: 'The essence and flowering of the art of German genius lies in its latent repetitions. The technique of "motivic" repetitions in the German music drama, in programme music and also in the sonata forms of non-geniuses indicates a regression into a rudimentary stage and so a decay.' Elsewhere he amplifies this with the observation that:

Coherence in language does not arise from a single syllable, a single word, or even from a single sentence; despite the correspondence of words and things, every coherent relationship in language depends upon a meaning hidden in a background. Such meaning achieves no fulfilment with mere beginnings. Similarly, music finds no coherence in a 'motive' in the usual sense . . . Thus, I reject those definitions of song form which take the motive as their starting point and emphasize manipulation of the motive by means of repetition, variation, extension, fragmentation, or dissolution. I also reject those explanations which are based upon phrases, phrase-groups, periods, double periods, themes, antecedents, and consequents. My theory replaces all of these with specific concepts of form which, from the outset, are based upon the content of the whole and of the individual parts; that is, the differences in prolongations lead to differences in form.[8]

Here he emphasises the way in which the fundamental meaning of a prolongation determines the function of every individual bit in advance and in this way saves the composer from the 'agony of aimlessness, of decay, and of the perpetual search for a continuation'.[9]

3

In a certain sense, and on the evidence of his own words, one might believe that Liszt's juxtaposition of freedom and the authority of rule and form, clearly expressed in his famous letter to Wilhelm von Lenz, gives support to a similar view of things. Insofar as the mature work of, say, Brahms is a progress from the hegemony of material form such as it is found in the sonatas and symphonies of post-Beethovenian composers to a more organic development of the material, there does appear to be a similarity. Perhaps even Liszt's own question, 'How much does the traditional, conventional form necessarily determine the organisation of thought?' could be put in the mouth of Brahms. But I think the similarity is quite superficial. Both composers in their work move away from conventional form, where form means formula, but in opposite directions. Brahms's own development, even if it does not wholly and circumstantially form the basis of Schenker's definition of genius, certainly accords with it. Liszt's does not. He replaces, in Schoenberg's just words, 'an old visionary form by a new. A new expressive form had to arise from this.'[10] Here we come to the centre of our argument: what to Schumann, Chopin and Brahms seemed erroneous, mistaken or, as I would prefer to put it, arbitrary, but in any case a lapse from their own beliefs about the nature of music, could, in the eyes of Wagner, possibly of Debussy, and certainly of Busoni and Schoenberg, be considered to be a substantial, even if flawed, *Vorgefühl* (premonition) of what they

themselves would do, and of the way in which their achievement
would become exemplary for all that has come since.

4

Just as Monteverdi in his day defended his own innovations in
terms of an aesthetic intention, an increased realism in the depiction
of emotion, so also did Liszt defend the new in terms of his own
aesthetic intention. But if Monteverdi, and later Musorgsky, talked
of realism in the portrayal of the emotions of others in the world,
Liszt was concerned primarily with the portrayal of his own feelings, as well as with the subjective emotions aroused by the
landscapes in which he moved and by the literary figures who
served to delineate the area of his inspiration. In such a way he
was already irked by what he considered, in his own words about
Chopin, the violence done to genius 'every time he sought to subject
it to rules and regulations which were not his own and did not
accord with the demands of his spirit'.[11] It is precisely this desire,
that the work of art should accord with the demands of the spirit,
which determines the posture of this composer, and which is taken
up by Schoenberg in his insufficiently read article on Liszt of 1911.
He attributes to Liszt what he considers the essential quality of the
great man, which is 'fanatical faith'. The convictions of *normal* (as
opposed to *great*) men 'get farthest away from the primal source,
while faith remains closest to it . . . the work [of art] stands roughly
in the middle'. This explains both what he calls the 'undissolved
residue', that is, 'the difference between [the artist's] expressive
urge and his powers of depiction', and the formal urge 'which uses
unification of the outward phenomenon to disguise the gaps and
deficiencies of the inner'.[12] I understand this to mean that the inner
inspiration of the artist expresses itself in a partial and deficient
manner – i.e. he cannot simply spit out complete works – and that
the formal urge, the means of unification, are employed to complete
that part of the work which results directly from an inner urge.

The closer this 'fanatical faith' remains to the self, we might conclude, the more is the resultant work one of 'pure genius', lacking the distancing and objectification that come from any recourse to form-giving and unifying elements. In this sense the 'formal urge' is equated with the unification of phenomena, which are the outward forms of the musical 'idea' dredged up directly from the self. It follows that an artist of genius creates not in accordance with nature or tradition, but in accordance with the self: the submission of self to rule and regulation, or form, taken as Liszt took it, must lead to conflict.[13] The 'real' form of a piece should approximate as closely as possible to the inner idea.

5

We can illustrate this idea quite specifically, I think. Take the introduction to the piece called *Funérailles* (Ex. 25). A pedal of C evoking sombre bells; a D♭ chord with added sixth, a motive or snatch of melody F–E♮–F–G–A♭–G–F♯–F♮–E♮ over three bars with heavy dotted rhythms; two sequences of this motive, each a tone higher than the previous; an elimination of the motive into a chromatic scalic passage, leading to a return to the opening, this time in a higher position with dramatic *sf* tremolos; a repetition and elimination, altered and leading now to an *fff* restatement of the D♭ heard already at the opening. At the climax, this D♭ is reharmonised with a fourth chord, D♭–A♮–E♭, on four accented crotchets; a final, extended repetition of the opening motive closes on the diminished seventh chord E–G–B♭–D♭. This will be a piece in F minor. Dynamically there is an intrinsic and dramatic development within it, sufficient to make the immediate effect it seeks. The whole is a prolongation of a single gesture, a single motivic idea. The idea literally becomes form. Looking forward, we can see this as a prototype of many introductions of similar character, for example, the beginning of *Prometheus* by Scriabin. There is expression but no genuine structure here: 'Musical sound acts directly on the soul and finds echo because, though to varying extents, music is innate in man' (Kandinsky).[14] We could be deeply stirred by such

Ex. 25: Liszt, *Funérailles*

music, or we could find it a lapse not of taste but of content.

Compare it to the introduction of Beethoven's Piano Sonata Op. 111, with which it shares certain characteristics (Ex. 26). The proportions are quite similar, as well as the dotting, the full and sombre chords and the final simplification to a bar of four crotchets. But here the similarities end. Beethoven's opening music, like Liszt's, is a threefold statement of a turning motive, Eb–C–B–C–D, treated sequentially and eliminated into a scalic descent to a dominant and a varied reprise of the motive Ab–F–G–Ab–Bb–C–Bb with an exchange of voices and a pattern of repeated seconds (this pattern is later found in the Liszt Sonata). These seconds are repeated in the acceleration which leads to the very Lisztian first

Ex. 26: Beethoven, Piano Sonata in C minor, Op. 111, opening

subject. But in no sense can the rich harmonic structure be directly equated with the motivic idea. The first bass movement, F♯ to G and B♮, is simply answered by B♮, A♭ and E♮ – but in what a way! The simple diminished seventh B♮-D-F-A♭ is redirected so as to avoid a resolution on the bare tonic, through a further passing diminished seventh and a subdominant ⁶₃, finally closing on the tonic in first inversion. And what a continuation! By an unexpected movement a ⁶₄ of ♭III leads to a series of 'passing' chords, barely related to I, before finally homing in on the dominant.

The difference in effect of the two fragments is startling. Liszt operates in real time: the effect lasts just as long as the notes sound. Beethoven's foreground is heard as a manipulation of a simple and conventional background: his unique effect is realised in terms of the distance he has travelled from it. The effect is profound, though in purely material terms his chords and positions are less spectacular than those of Liszt. Prolongation achieves a suspension of clock time. The effect does not date.

6

Schoenberg correctly identifies the importance of Liszt's innovation, and it is not without far-reaching significance that his essay was written in 1911 at a moment which might be regarded as the highwater mark of a tendency where, in his own words, 'the discovery made by . . . intuition' would be 'transformed directly and purely into an artistic deed'. Liszt's 'true insight' was his recognition of the primacy of 'poetic feelings', the things 'behind' craftsmanly qualities.[15] But an act of transference is required to turn these 'poetic feelings' into the language of music. Speaking from 1911, the year before *Pierrot lunaire*, Schoenberg criticises Liszt on two counts: on the one hand, he feels that Liszt's recourse to programmes or texts drawn from literature introduces a 'third party' which in some way contradicts the urgency and directness of the process; and on the other he suggests that by substituting a new form for an old form *consciously*, he 'prevented the discovery made by his intuition from being transformed directly and purely into an artistic deed'. Thus he produced 'second-hand poetry instead of exclusively allowing his own visionary form, the poet in himself, direct musical expression'. And his new form is in reality 'a mathematical and mechanical further development of the old formal components'. This is:

> a worse formalism than that of the masters who had lived in the old forms. For they really had lived in them! They truly thought in that space, it was their home, they were almost born there, and therefore they moved in it with the most complete freedom. There, form is not felt as a boundary [here the word *Grenze* echoes Kant and Schenker] that hems them in, but as a framework [Schenker's *Gerüste*], a brace, the support for the construction.[16]

With a rapid flanking movement, Schoenberg thus criticises Liszt on the one hand for not going far enough in deriving outward form *directly* from inner experience, an expressionist viewpoint appropriate to a friend of Kandinsky, on the other (and here Schoenberg is influenced by Kraus) for committing the error of conscious formalism in replacing the old and the well-worn with the arbitrary and the new.

7

This is very harsh and not always justified. At times less white hot than 1911, artists are, as Schoenberg later was, concerned with synthesis, rather than with the systematic pushing of formulated ideology to extreme positions. I think that some of Liszt's successes, successes even in terms of Schoenberg's ideas, can be exemplified quickly by looking at some brief examples.

First, the song 'Blume und Duft' to a poem by Hebbel.[17] The poem consists of two four-line verses with conventional rhyme in which the poet moves towards the expression of an opposition of immortality and mortality. In Liszt's setting the two verses are separated by a pause; two further pauses underline the expression of immortality before a 'sotto voce', throwaway setting of the final lines, recapitulating the opening but involving a break in the texture. What is remarkable here is the way in which the harmony sweeps through the implied divisions of the text establishing first a harmonisation of E♭–C♭, then D♮–C♭ and finally E♭–C♭ again. The comparatively long paragraph (nineteen bars) which climaxes and ends on a chord of C♭ major with seventh is in the real sense of the term a *Klangfarbenmelodie* – a colour melody – the colours of the changing harmonies related by notes in common and an overall rising feeling. This progression, with its subsequent resolution, goes against the verse structure but with the sense of the poem, creating its effect by the tension between the dynamic structure of the music and the static division of the verses (Ex. 27).

Ex. 27: Liszt, 'Blume und Duft'

Secondly, 'Wer nie sein Brot mit Tränen ass'. Liszt's setting of Goethe's famous poem is introduced by a rising unison passage establishing no key. A chord of F-A-B-D (marked with an asterisk in Ex. 28), with D rising to D♯ (a kind of French sixth?), moves through a passing ⁶₄ chord to its inversion (on D♯). This represents the only real harmonic movement in the first section. The central part of the song, *un poco più mosso* and characterised by a regular accompaniment figure, is a rising and falling chromatic progression, constructed with what Schoenberg calls roving harmonies, really improvised reharmonisations. The original 'chord'

Ex. 28: Liszt, 'Wer nie sein Brot mit Tränen ass'

F-A-B-D-A becomes D♯-A-D♯-F♯-B, moving to an A♭ $\frac{6}{4}$ and leading enharmonically to a sequential repetition a tone higher and then one a further semitone higher, before ultimately returning to itself. Clearly an 'error' in terms of Schumann and Brahms, but prophetic of similar procedures in later composers, such as Schoenberg in his early songs, in its failure to 'close' and in its 'front-derived' development (Ex. 28).

Further examples demonstrate how, within the conventions of what one might call the *Lied à la* Schumann, Liszt was able to construct his pieces in such a way as to appear as significant fragments (as in 'Gebet'). Such fragments take as their point of departure the underlying sense rather than the conventional strophic forms of the text. One can see this at its most developed in a longer song such as 'Ich möchte hingehn', to a text by the anarchist friend of Wagner and Liszt, Georg Herwegh.

This is a setting of a seven-verse poem, telling of the poet's desire to die as the sun sets and night approaches. The identification with nature is elaborated for five verses, each beginning with the identical phrase 'I want to die as . . .' But then suddenly the poet contradicts this aspiration; his spirit will be broken by suffering, here, in this world; his heart will crumble before he dies! In some ways this is a traditional song in the mould of Schumann, as the beautiful opening motive suggests. This motive, in fact, pervades the setting, coming before each verse and undergoing variation and expansion. The striking 'modern' element of the setting is its defiant conclusion: the *mf* Phrygian unison on the words 'You *will* perish, perish without trace', leading to a protest close (E major turning finally to minor).

It would be possible to analyse the harmonic progression step by step, and I have done so. But perhaps here it is enough to draw only the conclusions of such an analysis. If one were to imagine a setting of this poem by Brahms (say in the manner of the *Four Serious Songs*), one could assert that quite a lot of what we hear in the Liszt would be possible. What would *not* be possible, as the song progresses, would be the roving harmonies, heightening certain moments and developing them by chords linked chromatically, but not establishing any clear-cut modulations. There is here an expansiveness and an open-endedness which I cannot believe Brahms would have achieved. The point is that this corresponds exactly to an artistic intention. The setting moves in a series of harmonic upbeats, so that cadences do not have and are not felt to have the inevitability they would have in a composer like Brahms. Brahms is certainly as innovatory, technically, as Liszt – perhaps even more so – but he contains these innovations in a cadentially controlled framework: the innovation harmonically prolongs what must ultimately be the cadential resolution. But here in Liszt there is no feeling of an anticipated close. One must, I think, hear the music as a step-by-step renewal, one felicitous, short-term invention after another. Either the connections are motivic in the modern sense, or they work by the extension of tones and sequences of tones, progressively, step by step. In this sense, as with the example of *Funérailles*, this is composing in real time – one moment follows another – the repetition dramatised by the subjectivism, the 'inner faith' of the artist. There is no prolongation and consequently no mutation of time into artistic suspension.

8

Imaginatively it is not a long step from here to the notion of a music which exists either as a fragment or as a static structure in time and space, the freedom from that sense of gravity implicit in the tendency of a tonal composition to cadence. The issue is not one of the material presence of triads but of their behaviour. Taking a 'late' piece, like the *Trauergondel* of 1882 (Ex. 29), we have a further example of a non-form in the traditional tonal sense. The lapping of the water on the Venetian canals provides the entire material, expressed not only by the 6/8 rocking movement, but also by the melodic fragment drawn from it and circling around it: C–Ab, then C–A♮–Ab, falling through a Db minor scale (giving Gb and Fb) which twists like lapping water around the Eb–Db. This is extended into a recitative modally indistinct (G–F–E♮), falling towards a B (Cb) major triad in first inversion and downwards to the augmented triad D–F♯–A♯. The whole thing is now repeated to an A and again down to the augmented triad C–E–G♯. The whole undynamic structure is based on a whole-tone relationship:

Ab–F♯–E (bars 4, 42, 80)
C–A♯–G♯ (*et seq.*)
E–D–C (*et seq.*)

– light years away from Mendelssohn's 'Cheery Gondolier', relating to it as Whistler might to Canaletto.

The importance here is not the level of the composition (which is a bit simplistic) but the composer's conception of musical space and time. This piece is a precise illustration of Schenker's observation about music being organised out of its very first tones.

Ex. 29: Liszt, 'Trauergondel'

9

The tendencies isolated here, and identified not only as innovatory but also as prophetic of what was to come, are not unknown to traditional formal music. The opening of Beethoven's Fourth Symphony, in the way the tonic note is continually reinterpreted, might be regarded as an example. But in the world ending perhaps with Brahms such ideas are conceived as prolongations or post-ponements of an inexorable movement towards the cadence. My thesis has been, though I could hardly demonstrate it in other than small-scale examples, that Liszt's failure (or inability, in the eyes of his contemporaries) to do this is directly linked to his inventive-ness and innovatory aspiration. I purposely draw a veil over the vexed and insoluble but nevertheless fascinating question as to whether there is a causal link between such inability to do what is considered proper and the achievement of newness. It raises the further question as to whether innovators choose to innovate or, as Schoenberg once implied, innovate because they've got to do something (!). This is a question of great importance to me person-ally. I can only ask it; I cannot answer it.

(1984)

1. See *New York Review of Books*, 1983–4.

2. L. B. Plantinga, *Schumann as Critic* (New Haven: Yale University Press, 1967), p. 216.

3. Quoted by Alan Walker in *Liszt* (London: Faber, 1989), vol. 2, p. 157.

4. Ferruccio Busoni, 'Vorbemerkungen zu den Etuden von F. Liszt' (Berlin, September 1909), in *Von der Einheit der Musik* (Berlin: Max Hesses Verlag, 1922), p. 108 [AG's translation].

5. Kant, *The Critique of Judgement*, trans. J. C. Meredith (Oxford: Clarendon Press, 1957), pp. 166–9.

6. 'Erläuterungen', in *Das Meisterwerk in der Musik* (Munich: Drei Masken Verlag, 1930), Vol. 2, pp. 196–7.

7. Ibid., p. 197.

8. *Free Composition (Der freie Satz)*, trans. and ed. Ernst Oster (New York: Longman, 1979), p. 131.

9. Ibid., p. 132.

10. 'Franz Liszt's Work and Being', in *Style and Idea*, 2nd edn, ed. Leonard Stein, trans. Leo Black (London: Faber, 1975), p. 443.

11. 'Friedrich Chopin' (1850), quoted by Sam Morgenstern in *Composers on Music: An Anthology of Composers' Writings* (London: Faber, 1958), p. 169.

12. 'Franz Liszt's Work and Being', p. 442.

13. It is in this way that we can understand Wagner's remarks about Mozart: 'Time and again, one might almost say as a general rule, he falls back upon stereotyped phrases giving his movements the character of background music providing an attractive noise to accompany conversations between attractive melodies – at least, that is how those perpetually recurring, pompously fussy half-closes in Mozart's symphonies strike me.' *Music of the Future*, in Wagner, *Three Wagner Essays*, trans. R. L. Jacobs (London: Eulenburg, 1979), p. 38.

14. Wassily Kandinsky, *Concerning the Spiritual in Art*, trans. M. T. H. Sadler (New York: Dover, 1977), p. 27.

15. 'Franz Liszt's Work and Being', p. 443.

16. Ibid., pp. 443–4.

17. 'If you smell the scent of the flower, don't look for the flower itself. In the scent you sense eternity – the flower can only remind you of its mortality, how soon it will wither.' [My translation.]

12

Some Thoughts about Stravinsky

Throughout his long life Stravinsky caught people's imagination like no other. But his works haven't been accepted in anything approaching their entirety by the musical public. Only a handful have won unqualified appreciation in concert programmes: these are the early ballets up to and including the *Rite of Spring*, the *Symphony of Psalms*, *The Soldier's Tale*, the Mass, *Pulcinella* and perhaps the Violin Concerto. Recently *The Rake's Progress* has begun to take its rightful place in the opera repertoire. But since his death, there haven't been opportunities to hear many of his other works as frequently as one would like: revivals of *Les noces* and *Persephone* are special events (but then they always would be!).

Yet mention his name and you get an instant response. For Stravinsky, as in their different ways Schoenberg, Picasso, Eliot and Le Corbusier, is rightly or wrongly regarded as representing the spirit of the first half of the twentieth century. This is a modernist inviting us (or our fathers) to alter the manner in which we see the world. It implies a change of consciousness on our parts. Such a view is borne out by his many laconic, frequently partisan and sometimes a trifle snobbish utterances. Even in his most impromptu replies to silly questions, the persona comes across. From the foyers of Europe and New York's most expensive hotels, and from the milieu of the finest people, he comes over as the representative of a particular combination of high artistic sensibility and reactionary anti-contemporary views which is the hallmark of modernism and the reverse image of bourgeois values in Europe. He is the Man of his Age (rather than the child of his time).

Critical writings reveal a quite extraordinary tangle of contradictory and complicated attitudes. His fellow composers were and I suspect are very much divided in their assessments of him: Varèse, Copland, Falla and Shostakovich on one side, Schoenberg, Dallapiccola and Nono on the other. Messiaen didn't consider that anything after *Les noces* was of great interest. Stravinsky himself, in his later years, seems to have been influenced by some of his younger colleagues into regarding the neoclassical works as a mild aberration. Music critics after the war regrettably considered him as insincere and a bit tongue-in-cheek. Perhaps he didn't express enough concern for nature or the ocean: we all know that these things are of crucial importance in defining artistic sincerity. Worse still, he kept changing his style and offensively contradicting his own critical image, which once delineated must be retained for life (ugh!).

Of course it's true that the man covered an enormous stylistic and emotional distance in his oeuvre. Was *Petrushka*-Stravinsky really *Threni*-Stravinsky? And was *Abraham and Isaac* by the author of *Pribaoutki*? Can we really predict the serial compositions of his old age from the Rimsky-Korsakov-inspired *ballets russes*?

Recent writers have indeed attempted to see the unity, or at least the continuity, underlying his work. This has led to valuable insights into his musical philosophy (Robert Craft, Eric Walter White, Lawrence Morton) and discoveries about his technical procedures (Edward T. Cone). Further, this reconsideration has traced the emergence of a set of musical preferences – spacing of chords, isolation of intervals, instrumental colours in wind and brass, a unique way of writing for the violin – which seems to have survived through all the apparent technical and stylistic changes. It's the same rather awkward and stiff counterpoint that makes the *Berceuses du chat* and the trombone canons of the Dylan Thomas piece. The notes change; the hand holding the pen is the same.

It's generally supposed that the great genius emerges as a child prodigy with a superlative natural ability. Mozart is the most common example of this. It seems, however, that the majority of child-prodigy composers were originally performers who composed, as it were, out of their performing experience. Stravinsky does not seem to have been one of these. It is not at all clear from his student pieces that he is destined to be a great composer. One could look at this from another point of view. Most artists, when they are young, are bound to have certain exceptional urges for artistic expression and also some special abilities. But then, on the other hand, they may well have certain weak points. I think one can often see that it's precisely an artist's own recognition of what he is least able to do well that leads him to his most striking achievements. Turner's extraordinary sky and water paintings are not presaged by a great talent for sky painting in his early work; the early songs of Berg do not anticipate the great formal achievements of *Wozzeck* and *Lulu* in any direct manner; Wagner's and Brahms's transformations of musical form are directly relatable to their ability to overcome what is weakest in their early works. It may be going too far to attempt any grand generalisations, but there is some truth in the notion that the great innovators of music came to their most remarkable ideas through the realisation of their weak points. Certainly, at a lower level, it's the function of a composition teacher to confront his pupil with the achievement of the past almost in order to divert him from what he naturally does well to the consideration of those weaknesses which he might otherwise be tempted to sweep under the carpet.

Stravinsky seems to me to be a particularly good example of a composer who achieved a really big thing by overcoming his own less obviously talented sides. If one compares his ear for harmony both in the immediate and in the long-range sense with that of, say, Strauss or Ravel, one cannot resist the conclusion that it operated in a most particular and, by ordinary standards, unsatisfactory way. Compare some of those typical harmonisations of simple tunes consisting of a few notes, such as in the *Rite*[1] or *Les noces*, with something analogous, *Ma mère l'oye*. In the Ravel, the vocabulary is simple, but the integration of melody and harmony is such that one cannot visualise them apart. Yet this integration is totally original and appeals directly to our taste for the individual and the unconventional. We are constantly amazed by the unexpected colourings of the notes. This kind of originality results from traditional musicality, and it gives immediate satisfaction to performer and listener.

Now Stravinsky too achieves a recognisable originality in the detail of his harmonic-melodic language. But it's done quite differently. He sets up his material in the way that every child or amateur salon composer imagines music is made: tune in the right hand, block triad up and down in the left. One sees this clearly in the fascinating sketchbooks for the *Rite* and other sketches reproduced in *Stravinsky in Pictures and Documents* by Vera Stravinsky and Robert Craft. These harmonisations are not good or even adequate by any normally accepted standards. But the wonder is – and I believe this tells us a great deal about the composer – in the way he homes in on the irregularities of the harmonisation (the kinds of irregularities that are easily tested by running a hand in parallel triads along the piano) and makes these the point of departure for a compositional elaboration. This technique has been variously described as 'wrong-note harmonisation' or bitonality. But no systematic categorisation or imitation obtains an analogous effect. Rather the procedure illustrates an ancient rule-of-thumb: 'either get it right or make it seem that the mistake is intentional'. Generally it is believed that good music is characterised by a suppleness in the voice leading and an expressiveness in the individual part. Stravinsky does not attempt these, and the very stiffness, the almost mechanical character of his writing is turned into an advantage by the idiosyncrasy and certainty of his ear. His pre-eminence as an artist is assured by the way he sticks to the minutiae of his inventions: not 'too much rummaging around with the theme' (as Brahms said). He even believed that a composer should always retain the notation of musical ideas as he originally wrote them.

I think this very precise attitude is a clue to the understanding of Stravinsky's artistic nature. In the sketches one can observe the way he picks up or invents a little melodic tag and simply 'sets' it. The striking thing is not that these tags are rather ordinary and inexpressive, but that one is not able *a priori* to see their potential. Stravinsky borrowed folksongs, bits of Bach, Pergolesi and Tchaikovsky. But when I examine these original sources, I wonder at the way in which Stravinsky hears them. He seizes upon characteristics which we others do not even notice.

For each little idea he rules an appropriate number of systems on blank paper: the sketched setting is often instrumentated but not orchestrated (the differentiation is his). The resulting 'bit' is in sound and on paper only as long as the idea itself demands. The music at this point is static and doesn't carry any clues for its own continuation; it is quite unsuitable for constructing through-composed symphonic movements. It took Stravinsky some time to realise this and to make the decision, some time before the First World War, to break totally with the world of inherited musical forms. This break, and the abandoning of the Russian exotic style, freed him from the contradiction between his own imagination and what was demanded by traditional form, and enabled him to achieve his great revolution in musical sensibility.

The break came finally between the two versions of *Les noces*. Of course there may have been other reasons for it too: a change in artistic climate, the Russian revolution which separated him from his homeland, or personal developments resulting from these. But it isn't hard to see that the episodic nature of his invention – which may be regarded as a fault in a piece like *Petrushka* – becomes a virtue in the *Rite of Spring*. Here the forms result directly from the character of the original ideas; the composer frees himself from received notions.

We observe now a gradual emergence of a new way of organising musical time. If Schoenberg's innovations (at roughly the same date) may be related to the 'psychological' ideas of Expressionists like Kandinsky, those of Stravinsky interestingly parallel Cézanne and his followers' experiments with space. The little 'bit' of melody and accompaniment is now defined as a sounding object or 'block': it is limited by duration, speed, pitch span and instrumental colour, and is generally stable if not static in harmony. Stiffness of relationship of voices, repetitiveness and inexpressive tags of melody – disadvantages in traditional music – come into their own now as virtues. Continuity is achieved by the literal or varied repetition of these little bits and by stark juxtapositions with contrasted but similarly constructed bits. Each is defined by an absolute duration; the manner of development is 'real' (by addition) rather than 'psychological' (by division). This procedure results in an almost crude conception of time-form. Gisèle Brelet describes it as a 'mélodie du rythme', characterising this. She describes this as the 'very essence of Russian music'. She says: 'Et si la forme chez Stravinsky revêt un aspect avant tout rythmique, c'est que dans le rythme s'affirme avec une particulière netteté le pouvoir du temps pur de construire a soi seule le forme musicale.'[2] There is a (perhaps superficial) similarity between Stravinsky's newly achieved formal conception and the concerto grosso principle of the eighteenth century. This too is based on the repetition and alternation of static blocks. So perhaps the move from the 'Russian', *Les noces* style to the European neoclassicism of *Pulcinella* is not, after all, so arbitrary a step. The outward forms may change and the fashions replace one another, but beneath this glittering and amazing surface we can see the artist working out his own problems. The changing surface styles are nothing less than the stations of a journey into the self.

His historic decision to abandon the luxuriant style of the early ballets – or the realisation that he had to abandon it – opened the way for Stravinsky to realise a very new conception of musical time. This central but rather abstract concept is filled out and coloured by the self-knowing precision of his aural imagination. The turns of style, the models, whether new or old, are of secondary importance, although they seduced a philosopher-critic as remarkable as Theodor Adorno (in his *Philosophy of New Music*) into a quite erroneous description of Stravinsky's musical character. But the uniqueness and greatness of his artistic achievement is incontestable. This he owed, in part at least, to the way in which he was able to turn limitations into advantages. It arouses our wonder and admiration. His is a message of hope for the continued possibilities of artistic excellence.

(1981)

---

1. See the harmonisation sketch of 'Uncle Armand' in Vera Stravinsky and Robert

Craft, *Stravinsky in Pictures and Documents* (New York: Simon and Schuster, 1978), p. 127, and the sketch for *The Rite* on p. 78. The sketchbooks for *The Rite* have been published in facsimile: *The Rite of Spring; Sketches 1911–1913*, ed. Robert Craft (London: Boosey and Hawkes, 1969).
2. Gisèle Brelet, 'Essence de la musique russe', in *Musique russe*, 2 vols, ed. P. Souvchinsky (Paris: Presses universitaires de France, 1953), Vol. 1, p. 75.

13

Music as Communication

Topography and Politics

As soon as we talk about music as communication, we imply a topography, and arising from it a politics. Imagine musical progress as space. The topography is determined by the way the various participants associated with it relate to each other: at one edge the original sender of the music, he who made it or composed it, at the other its recipient, the listener; and between these two are the musicians, the singers and players who manufacture sound, and nowadays even the recording engineers who effect its electronic transmission. Arising from this, the politics is played out between the sometimes complementary and sometimes conflicting concerns of these three (or four) groups. Each has its own values. Which is to predominate? Should the entire musical process be regarded as the re-creation of the composer's original intention? Or should we bear in mind that he is quite a recent phenomenon, that music existed for centuries without any observable separation between composer and performer? Then again, is music really a performing art? Compositions, if they have a separate identity, can be regarded as of no greater importance than a set of instructions: to be followed, but adapted to circumstances. Fidelity to the composer's intention is then less important than the performer's own feeling, as expressed in the way he plays his instrument. Yet again, should not everything be evaluated from the point of view of the recipient? After all, it is he who pays! Never mind who makes it, or how it's played: let us consider it to be no more and no less than what it is heard to be.

The relative weight to be attached to these considerations does not remain constant at all times. No one hierarchy can be assumed as valid for the whole history of music.

This is because music fulfils different functions at different times and in different places. Although it is tempting to consider it as no more than a system of perceptible sounding structures, an understanding of the psychological process does not of itself explain why people actually cultivate music, or what they see in it. Nor does it account for the fact that some kinds of music are simply not understood and will be rejected out of hand, and not merely because they are judged to be aesthetically poor. In fact, as much confusion is generated by regarding music as a system of sounding structures as by the sentimental old notion that music is a universal language (which inevitably presupposes that one's own musical language is universal, because, were it not, music could not be considered in this way at all). The physical sounds made by blowing, singing, plucking, bowing and banging are more or less the same wherever they occur; there are after all only a limited number of ways of creating them. But everything that might be considered to make up the way music is understood (could I even say, loved?) – the being moved by it, the being aroused by it or the admiring of skill – depends on specific ways of ordering such sounds into specific and familiar contexts. As with food, the raw materials are the same everywhere; but this does not make us like everybody's cooking, even if it's as nutritious as our own.

Music is as bound to context as is language. Whereas we don't take seriously the person who, without a knowledge of a particular language, supposes that he can extrapolate meaning from phonemes, we do tend to assume that music of whose rules and practices we know little or nothing will somehow succeed in evoking images of a purely sensuous and vaguely associative kind. But where the context is established (and we are part of it) and where social function is predetermined, real communion can be taken for granted.[1] Here and now, in our society, different kinds of music emanating from different periods of history and different contexts all coexist; and communication has to be effected largely without reference to the original function of the music. Without knowing whether a piece of music is intended to celebrate a funeral or a marriage, we nevertheless suppose that we are able to understand it. Inevitably this unleashes a process of continual rejigging and adapting of such different kinds of music to fit into the way in which music functions in *our* society and is understood by us. For we should not delude ourselves into supposing that, even in what is clearly a complex society and one in which simple communal values have been submerged, there would not now be unspoken conventions and customs which determine functions. Inevitably, the fact that music is extracted from its original context to make it fit into our own distorts it and changes its identity.

Function and Affect/Lack of Function, Failure of Affect

Wer Gefühle als Wirkungen der Musik davonträgt, hat an ihren gleichsam ein symbolisches Zwischenreich, das ihm ein Vorge-schmack von der Musik geben kann, doch ihn zugleich aus ihrem innersten Heiligtum ausschliesst!

(Whoever derives feelings from music as its effects has in them, as it were, an intermediate realm of symbol, which while providing a foretaste of music at the same time denies entry to its innermost sanctuary!)

Nietzsche, 'Über Musik und Wort'[2]

Comparison between music and language (or the belief that music is some kind of language) always falls on the issue of semantics. Is music a set of syntactic structures which constitutes a vehicle for transmitting affects or meanings? Or does music (in what was originally Stravinsky's pithy formulation) 'express nothing but itself': that is, refuse or fail to communicate things outside itself? The argument hinges on whether or not intervals between pitch levels, rhythms, melodies, modes and harmonies of themselves convey feelings and evoke images of place or time. Even if it is popularly believed that they do, it does not thereby follow that the capacity to do so is part of their nature. If there is a convention, established by whatever means, that an interval conveys a feeling, that feeling will be automatically aroused by the sounding of that interval. Such conventions are part and parcel of the very functions which the music originally served. But when the music outlives these original functions its conventions are only half (if at all) remembered, and only a vague penumbra of affect and emotional meaning survives.

The discussion of the origins of musical affect, whether they are to be found in nature or convention, is of course an old chestnut, and I doubt that there is much to be gained from turning it over. Most performers and listeners still do consider music in terms of its affects, even if academic attention is principally focused upon problems of structure. Crude as it may sound, it hardly matters whether a piece expresses joy or sadness, is religious or witty, because its intervals, harmony and rhythm genuinely evoke such emotions, or whether the convention of these emotions is merely a convenient tag for describing the effect of music in words. Insofar as such characterisations of musical affect do actually survive and are judged useful, I am happy to leave it at that.

But how explicit and precise can such individual musical affects be? A musician aspires to total exactitude: to play a wrong note, or to play the right note at the wrong moment, or to play loudly what is marked quietly, either renders the passage grammatically incorrect or changes its identity. But if such a discipline were deemed to hold true for the listener, most of what is normally assumed to be an understanding of music would be thrown into question. Few are those who, with hands on heart, can claim to absorb each and every musical event with equal and undivided attention. In reality, music transmits different kinds of information, and each requires a differing degree of concentration. Intervals and motifs need to be precisely registered, whereas long-term continuity is often perceived in a dreamy state. If one asks for a street direction, there is no point in listening to only a small part of the answer. But aesthetic pleasure and consequently some meaning can be obtained from the semi-attentive reading of a complex poem. There what is actually called 'its music' is communicated, even when many of its specific allusions are missed. This suggests that music is sometimes more appropriately perceived *grosso modo*, from its passing flow towards its detail, rather than from its detail towards its totality. Paradoxically, as is the case with much of the music of this century, the more differentiated and the more complex the structure of a piece is, the more one tends to be satisfied with only a small amount of precise information. Though music teachers train the aural capacities and memories of their pupils (and test their work out of an imaginary 100 per cent), they well know that, in the real world, listeners' degrees of attention vary considerably from moment to moment, and that this reflects not only their powers of recognition and differentiation but also the span of their concentration and the amount of information which they can absorb at any particular moment. Whether or not an individual listener has absolute pitch or very good relative pitch, and whether he (or she) is capable of perceiving fine harmonic and rhythmic differentiations, may determine the quality of listening but not necessarily the amount or quality of either understanding or aesthetic pleasure obtained. Were it to be assumed that the ideal listener is the one who perceives each and every sound, not only would there be few of him, but there would be the implication that music all over the world had always fulfilled and did now fulfil an identical function; that it was to be listened to with total attention as if it conveyed a precise communication. Or it would resemble an abstract activity rather like playing chess. But, in reality, in music, as indeed more generally, the dimension of meaning is shaped by role. It makes no more sense to claim that a specific unit of meaning can be extrapolated from one event in a musical composition than to suppose that different pieces performing an identical social role – different marches, hymns or love songs – are sufficiently defined by that role and therefore convey an identical set of meanings to each and every listener. Arguments about affect and function have to be modestly conducted in terms of more or less, both quantitatively and qualitatively.

Despite everything that can be advanced in its defence, an 'argument in favour of imprecise hearing' (as one could term it) seems a bit complacent and even condescending. If a composition is in actual fact highly differentiated in its detail, and consequently charged with great intensity, we not only owe it, but are likely to give it, our full attention. Its very effect is determined by the degree of differentiation of its detail, and, if this is not to be precisely observed, of what else can the communication consist? How is the music to make its proper effect without it? Proper, I say; and 'proper' suggests that each and every isolated musical event is intended to have a specific effect, excluding all others, and that every sequence of such events has an equally specific effect, that every movement and every work therefore has a particular overall effect, and that there can be only one such. If a piece is not to be wholly perceived as the sum of its parts, it will be a partial failure on the part of either composer or listener, or both. Such failure leaves the listener with a sense of his own inadequacy. If this is so, dreamy, semi-attentive listening for the pleasure it gives might now become associated with mediocrity and guilt. It is cheap and easy, the line of least resistance, to be scorned as a feckless and ultimately frustrating hedonism and, as such, a debasement of proper artistic purpose:

> Pendant que des mortels la multitude vile,
> Sous le fouet du plaisir, ce bourreau sans merci,
> Va cueillir des remords dans la fête servile . . .

> (Baudelaire, 'Recueillement')

> Now while the common multitude strips bare,
> Feels pleasure's cat o' nine tails on its back
> And fights off anguish at the great bazaar . . .

> (translation: Robert Lowell[3])

(Or Karl Kraus, even more directly and aggressively: 'I detest the ugliness of a pleasure-savouring crowd who, after a suffocating day at the office, raises the lowered blinds over its soul to let in the air of culture.'[4])

Such high-minded expectations for art, and such aggressive reactions when they seem to be frustrated, lead the artist to despair of his audience and to seek out the commitment of the like-minded. Finally, when all else fails, he is left with his own imaginary double, his mirror image, the ideal listener made in the likeness of himself. Art can after all exist without the need to communicate anything at all to another, becoming entirely solipsistic.

Music without Listeners

Even without an exclusive retreat into the self, it is in fact viable to consider music as having a justifiable existence without listeners. In many communities to this day, music forms part of a ritual in which all present participate and no clear differentiation exists between performer and listener. Here the word 'communion' would most appropriately describe the way the participants relate to each other, each and every individual performing his allotted role. The gap in the original topography between sender and recipient is dissolved and no longer exists. But quite as much as with music specifically intended to communicate, the individual participant here too is provided with a range of different psycho-physical sensations.

Let me give a simple example: many years ago at a private party – in fact it was after the first performance of Olivier Messiaen's *Turangalîla-Symphonie* in London, and the first time I met my future teacher[5] – we played a clapping game. The idea, Messiaen explained, was that each person should clap in turn, contributing to what all together should come out as a regular and smooth sequence of claps. Of course this game could be endlessly complicated, but the point is that the participant not only perceives the chain of claps as a resultant but feels the rise and fall of tension as he prepares to make his own clap, matching it in sound to his neighbour's, placing it correctly and, as it were, preparing his successor's. To get it right, each participant not only has to 'know his part' but has inwardly to sing the implied resultant. This periodic repetition is the simplest form of the game, and is at one and the same time the mother of each individual clap and the final form of all the claps put together. It makes the world of difference whether one is to be a participant or an onlooker of the game. Though the identity of the claps is the same in either case, the feeling they convey is completely different. This has an ethical dimension too. Plato, observing the merits of musical activity, puts in Protagoras' mouth the notion that by 'making harmonies and rhythms quite familiar to the children's souls, they may learn to be more gentle and harmonious and rhythmical and so more fitted for speech and action; for the life of many has need of harmony and rhythm in every part'. Appropriately (for this discussion), Aristotle raises the question as to whether children are to learn by singing and playing themselves, or merely from listening to others. And Franz Kafka writes in his *Notebooks*: 'The law of the Quadrille is clear, all the dancers know it and it is valid for all times. But one or other of the hazards of life, which ought not to, but over and over does, occur, brings you alone out of step. But you do not know it, you know only your own bad luck.'[6] Here, he finely expresses what I have merely called a rise and fall in tension, the feeling of equanimity and harmoniousness when an action is carried out correctly and of 'bad luck' when it goes wrong.

I felt my own 'bad luck' when, many years after the party where I clapped with Messiaen – this time at a gathering of amateur Gagaku players in a temple in Tokyo one evening – I was assigned to play the Taiko (bass drum). I was told to repeat two strokes of the drum regularly: one masculine and one feminine (strong and weak). All I had to do was play one harder, more emphatically, than the other; but where to play them? I didn't know the composition or the idiom, and my strokes fell here, there and everywhere. Everyone laughed and my teacher tried to correct me. In my embarrassment, however, I knew I was out of the dance, and came to understand something which would never have come across to me had I been a mere listener: and that is, that music is understood in a particular and authentic manner when one plays it oneself (even wrongly). What can any of us possibly make of, say, the complex structures of Congolese pygmy polyphony? Even if we were accurately registering each and every event of the music, could we ever hope to feel it, as its performers feel it?

There is almost no point in even hoping to grasp what such music specifically conveys, assuming that the listener merely flies in and watches and listens (or most likely stays at home and casually listens to a recording). Any impression it leaves must be based on coincidental associations or preconceptions formed far away from the spiritual environment in which the music was actually played. At worst it will seem to be nothing but a deranged jumble, at best the equivalent of a picture postcard. To get anything authentic out of it, the listener must go and apprentice himself to African musicians who perform it in the full knowledge of its context, and so stop being a mere listener. But this is impractical.

Wherever music functions within ritual, its meaning and associations are self-evident. The basic tune and the words connected with it are familiar, so that individual and spontaneous variants occurring in performance can be observed and appreciated without difficulty. Within limits, complex modifications of a familiar structure may be effected in the interest of variety and sophistication, and appreciated without any of the attendant problems that would arise for us who stand apart. We cannot even guess at the network of tensions and relaxations brought about by such concerted variations. Hearing and re-hearing might enable us to measure and categorise, and ultimately even form a general view about, the practice of such music. But such understanding will be weightless and in no way equivalent to the sensations to be derived from being part of the music-making process.

Much the same in fact holds true for music made nearer home. Even where ritual-associated oral tradition gives way to a culture transmitted by written notation, where the taken-for-granted is replaced by an elaborate score, every performer participates in a communion, within which the whole is perceived through a network of individual tensions and subsequent relaxations. As in the clapping game, they are brought about by individual acts performed against an understood metrical background. The very textbook terms used in the training of musicians – consonance,

dissonance, suspension, syncopation, ornament, counterpoint, imitation, cadence, etc. – all express temporal and identity relationships, thereby evidencing a pursuit of harmony, not only in its
purely musical but also in its interpersonal sense. Such a concerted
sequence of tensions and relaxations is actually what music is.

Meaning conveyed to the participant in terms of tension and
relaxation can be further modified by the technical difficulty of
that which he is required to perform. A clap is easy; but if a pitch
level is difficult to produce – for example, if it is in the highest
register of the oboe – it will convey something other than the same
pitch level which may be obtained on a violin without special
difficulty. The different effect results from physical effort and concentration, not merely from the tone colour of the pitch level
produced on the different instruments. Analogously, a cross-rhythm
(where the strong beat is articulated on the metrical weak beat)
conveys a special effect which disappears when it is played on the
metrical strong beat, although the succession of its durations
remains the same (Ex. 30). The effect derives from the mental
effort required to perform the rhythm against the beat. Again,

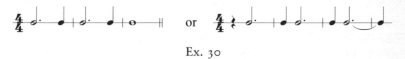

Ex. 30

quick passages are difficult on one instrument and straightforward
on another, are easy in some keys and hard in others. For example,
long leaps of pitch across the natural physical divisions of an
instrument or voice alter the effect of the sounds produced. It is
difficult to hit the right note on a piano when this requires a rapid
change of arm and hand position, and sometimes it would seem
logical to minimise risk of error in performance and rearrange the
hand positions to make performance safer. But to do this is not
only to cheat in a game, but subtly to alter the meaning conveyed
by the gesture. Here are three *loci classici* where difficulty conveys
a special effect.

First, at the opening of Beethoven's last piano sonata, Op. 111, the pianist is required to perform a long leap in octaves with his left hand. He could use both hands, thereby simplifying the execution. He will know what he did, but do we, if, for example, we listen to a recorded performance which we cannot see? (Ex. 31).

or

Ex. 31: Beethoven, Piano Sonata in C minor, Op. 111

Second, at the beginning of *The Rite of Spring*, the bassoonist is required to play in his highest register. When Stravinsky composed this, it was a dangerous and difficult passage (Ex. 32). Today any bassoonist can play it. 'It should sound like a strangled chicken,' said Messiaen. To convey that effect nowadays, the passage would have to be transposed up a third, or even higher, on the instrument to restore the effect of the original difficulty which has now gone. This can be tested by listening to early recordings of the passage and comparing them with current versions.

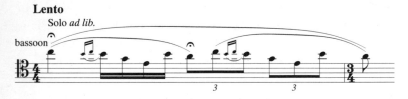

Ex. 32: Stravinsky, *The Rite of Spring*

Finally, in the second movement of Webern's Piano Variations, the pianist is required to play notes the length of the piano apart with one single hand moving across the keyboard, then with the other – at great speed. It's awkward and risky, but quite easy when divided between both hands (Ex. 33). The pianist knows what he is playing, but are we sure that we do?

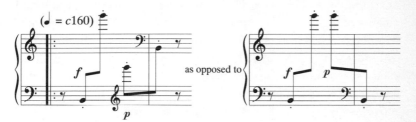

Ex. 33: Webern, Variations, Op. 27, 2nd movement

It may well be that such examples contribute only peripherally to the effect the music makes on the listener, and on a recording it is unlikely that such aspects could ever be fully appreciated. In a live concert the player's physical effort may be observed and might colour a perception of the actual sounds heard, in the way a hand gesture might qualify a meaning conveyed by the spoken word. The very fact that little of this physicality conveys itself to the listener must impoverish the effect of the music, making it more likely that extramusical or symbolic meanings will be invoked as ways of sorting out the flood of information transmitted by a piece. But there is little need of such if adequate meanings can be extrapolated from the psychological effects of physical effort in actual performance.

Communicating with the Listener

Even if much of the psycho-physical content of music inevitably remains hidden from the listener, he being presented with it, as it were, from the front of house, it would be pessimistic to think that nothing of it gets across. Possibly its tensions and relaxations, its sense of strain, effort and risk, do communicate something without necessarily being separately distinguished. Even without it, the bystanding listener can become an active, if minor, participant in the music-making process. Like the performer, he perceives the background metre of the music, expressing such awareness by beating time (either inwardly or, more irritatingly, outwardly) and singing along. If, for example, at the opening of Mozart's G minor Symphony, he is able to relate what he hears to its implied background, he is doing exactly what the performer does and thus establishes a kind of bridge between himself and the performer, feeling the tensions and relaxations of each momentary event as it moves away from and coincides again with the beats of the metre (Ex. 34). This provides a physical perception of the music exactly mirroring that of the performer. The same procedure can be applied to the perception of melody, mode and tonality: if the listener is aware of the common elements or mode of a song, he will perceive a melody unfolding against its background. To be able to do this requires skill and experience (sometimes simply called musicality), and this constitutes an entry ticket into the musical community.

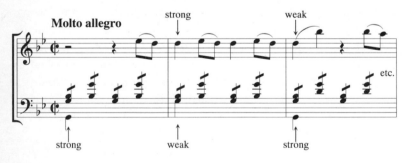

Ex. 34: Mozart, Symphony in G minor, K. 550, 1st movement

The listener might thus regard himself as a legitimate extension of the performer; and in this way abolish the gap that separates him from the sender of the music. This inevitably happens in popular music, which is monodic in form and easy to follow and memorise. But although Western art music is an outgrowth of such monodic structure, it has become so complex that only the gifted can be relied upon to perceive a background and remain conscious of it while listening. Most of us are content to form impressions from more partial and transient perceptions.

Perhaps it is for this reason that people like to hear the same piece rehearsed over and over again. Even if one thinks one knows the *Eroica* very well and has studied it carefully in all its details, somehow its full complexity inevitably escapes one at any single hearing. Possibly what is called a 'classic' is, in fact, a composition of such multi-dimensionality that it can never be fully perceived at a single go. Inevitably one wants to hear it again. (But this cannot be the only explanation, because the public also wants to re-hear popular songs of very little complexity, until they come out of their ears!)

The effect of Western polyphonic music of the Classical and Romantic periods can be traced back to two specific inventions. The first is the distribution of information, formerly transmitted by a single voice, between several individual voices, each in turn coming to the fore as the carrier of the main melody, and sometimes retreating to the background and contributing accompanimental or complementary material. This represents a considerable development of the simpler kind of polyphony, in which the information to be conveyed by each voice is established at the outset and remains constant. The second is the idea of the independent bass voice which supports all the voices above it and exists in a state of continual tension and cadential relaxation with them, qualifying and even entirely altering their effect.

Classical string quartet writing perfectly exemplifies the first of these developments, as, for example, at the beginning of the final Allegro of Beethoven's first 'Razumovsky' quartet, with its 'Thème russe' (Ex. 35). The tune is stated twice, first by the cello and immediately afterwards by the first violin. The texture now complicates: the viola begins a third statement of the tune, but Beethoven throws the listener off by altering bits of it and adding imitations of it in the violin parts. The texture continues to complicate itself, with a corresponding rise of tension between the parts which communicates itself to the listener, who may now perceive only swirling movement in place of clear-cut tune. This may result in a sense of being momentarily lost, with a consequent rise of anxiety. But all is well again when the four voices come together at the cadence, the tune reappearing. The extract may be interpreted as a sequence of tensions and relaxations, expressed in terms of precise and individually identifiable events as well as more complex accretions of instrumental voices into swirling masses, which perhaps are not, or are not even meant to be, totally graspable in each and every detail. The exceptional listener will be able to give them back *in toto*; but this might prevent him feeling the appropriate rise and fall of tension.

Ex. 35: Beethoven, String Quartet in F major, Op. 59 No. 1, 4th movement

Such transitions between simple and compound effect are not in the final analysis confusing, because the proficient composer leads the ear and prepares it for each successive situation by what we call musical logic. The listener is not excluded. Gestural signposts prepare him for what comes next, providing just enough for him to hold on to and not so much as to allow his mind to wander off into reveries. Regular phrase lengths and a regular rate of textural alteration secure him, giving him the necessary confidence to remain a participant, holding on to the background metre and, at one and the same time, perceiving foregound and relating it to background. The process has been variously described, by psychologists and critics such as Hans Keller and Leonard B. Meyer,[7] in terms of the frustrations and resolutions of aroused expectations.

An analogous (as it were) double perception is evoked where an independently moving bass line is added to a melody. As an example, here is a simple chorale melody, easy to sing and remember, as set for voices and instrumental accompaniment in four parts in the St John Passion (Ex. 36). Bach's bass alters the effect of the chorale melody by stressing and colouring particular notes of it. The gaps or intervals between it and the chorale melody are filled in by middle voices, softening the tensions created between the two. There is nothing natural or automatic about the relationship of the bass, and consequently of the harmony, to the chorale melody. No one particular bass is implicit in the melody. Our example is only one solution, and it is significantly altered when the chorale is sung again later in the work. In the second version, the first four and last lines are identical with the first version, but the fifth, sixth and seventh lines are altered. The need for this alteration probably arises out of the change of text (a different stanza of the same poem).

In his well-known dispute with Rameau, Rousseau observed that for the common man a melody does not of itself suggest an independent bass, and surmised that if required to provide a descant to a melody this common man would merely double it at the unison or an octave lower, whichever suited his voice better. If this is in fact what goes on naturally, this common man will inevitably compare the composer's independent bass line with his own, 'natural' doubling – another activity implying a foreground–background relationship. Musical meaning might just as well then not be something that is transmitted *by organised sound* but rather something that arises directly from (or even *by*) the changing tensions and recolourings of background brought about by foreground elaboration.

First version, lines 5, 6, 7

Second version, lines 5, 6, 7

Ex. 36: Bach, *St John's Passion*, 'Christus der uns selig macht'

'Avant Garde Music'

Not to understand, not to perceive, meaningful continuity might then be no more than a failure to relate passing foregound events to background, with a resulting inability to identify tempo, harmonic tension and textural logic. In this sense, a great deal of music written in the last seventy years cannot be regarded as a straight-forward continuation of Classical and Romantic music, either in the way it is conceived or in the way it is meant to be listened to. Background–foreground perception is inapplicable here because, in reality, insufficient background is implied. Continuity is frag-

231

mented or constructed of events unrelated to each other, pitch succession too complex to be memorable, and constructional procedures too difficult to be perceived as aural logic. Composers are said to re-invent their musical language anew for each composition they write.

In such circumstances a sense of expectation, or a feeling for good continuation and satisfactory closure, previously considered the necessary conditions for musical reception, can hardly be aroused. Easiest would be to assert (and there is no shortage of those who have done so) that such music has simply gone off the rails: there are plenty who believe in a kind of Spenglerite version of history, where great civilisations are in a continual process of becoming, flourishing and declining. Measured against the certainties of the not-so-distant past, the present with all its inherent difficulties (they might conclude) testifies to a decline of potency. At this late stage, I shall not consider such apocalyptic views, preferring to restrict myself to a few simple observations.

Avant-garde music ought not to be dismissed out of hand merely because it cannot be understood as an obvious continuation or extension of past music. Certainly some vestiges of past music are retained in it: for example, most of it is (more or less conventionally) notated and is performed in a modified but recognisably traditional manner. Consequently, it looks as if it might be understandable in more or less the same way as the music of the past has been understood. Observation of the way audiences react and what is said about avant-garde music suggests that listeners perceive it as a proposed continuation of the manner of earlier music, but, failing to obtain similar pleasure from it, feel they have been cheated. Underlying coherence is presupposed to exist and is then not perceived; unresolved anxiety ensues. The difficulty arises from the frustration of a conventional expectation. The gap between sender and recipient is at its widest here.

Faced with this, composers have two alternative courses of action available to them. They can try to fight for a foothold in the traditional musical world, matching up their imaginative flights with the observable and presumably learnable realities of past musical practice. But in fact the vast majority of them see this as a pointless, nostalgic and debilitating course of action, preferring in its place an experimental, exploratory activity. There is no way forward, they believe, but to start again from scratch: which would seem to mean abandoning the criteria of conventional logic or appropriate continuation in favour of the presentation of momentary, unrestricted and unrestricting sound-events. Uncombined signs and gestures, kaleidoscopic alterations of timbre and texture, aperiodic rhythms and freely hanging, quasi-expressive phrases, are densely presented so as to engulf the willing listener. Where earlier composers intended to communicate a particular aesthetic impression, and to do so aimed at clarity, subjugation of detail to broadly moving melody and rhythm, and a carefully graded relationship of certainties and ambiguities, avant gardists prefer saturation and prolixity of musical phenomena, aiming so to kick over their traces and thereby create what might be described as a magical effect. This music is to be instantaneously perceived either in a state of shock created by rapid alterations, or in dreamy states brought about by an apparently endless extension of constantly repeating and more or less identical patterns. It is to physically surround the listener, and in this way remove the conventional gap between sender and receiver. Some believe it works best with the high loudness levels and high-quality speakers of recorded music, which extend (and sometimes transform) the location and distribution of sound-events. The listener is then materially immersed in sound. Exclusive attention is not even demanded; the composer hopes to create a new community, even a world, rather than convey specific information.

Gruppen by Stockhausen (1957), *Répons* by Boulez (1981) and much of Cage's music are the most radical attempts once again to alter the conventional relationship of sender and receiver by physically enclosing them in a single continuous context. The majority of composers have neither the material possibility nor the will to go so far (it means rebuilding concert halls, hiring expensive equipment or involving a regrouping of players), but even where they restrict themselves to more conventional locations, and have their works performed alongside works of the past, they subscribe to the spirit if not to the letter of such ideals, adopting the new criteria and the new values of avant-garde music and trying to make them work within the old forms of transmission in the concert hall.

Conclusion

Underlying what I have said has been an assumption that regardless of cultural considerations, the rules of perception, insofar as they are known to us, are invariants. But the degree to which they apply to each and every listener might vary, and the reasons why they vary might affect the quality of the listener's perception of the music. Categories of differentiation continually alter, even within a single society which (like our own) is subject to rapid and simultaneous changes and accretions. Effective communication might seem to presuppose an identity of attention, and a body of common expectations, the possession of which puts the communicants in context and ensures some authenticity of personal experience. Because, of course, we believe that there are authentic and inauthentic ways of understanding, and that different communities imply different authenticities.

As far as is possible, we now make a point of defending such authenticity as remains to us. Yet the intention to preserve it seems to run counter to that very openness to new experience which appears to be the only way of coming to terms with the variety of currently available cultural manifestations. So extensive is this variety that it might almost seem preferable to try to destroy what remains of any feeling for authenticity and context. To do so would be, as it were, to deregulate musical experience: all musics – Mozart and Machaut, Stockhausen and Stravinsky, Gregorian chant and the music of the Gambias – would be no more and no less than potentially evocative noise to be turned on and off as and when required . . .

There seems something rather threatening in such an invitation to clear the mind and leave it blank, so that new characters might be drawn upon it.

(1989)

1. I am indebted to Sir John Lyons for drawing my attention to Sir Henry Maine's differentiation between 'communion' and 'communication', reflecting as it does the difference between community and society.

2. *Werke* (Leipzig: Insel Verlag, 1930), Vol. 1.

3. Robert Lowell, *Imitations* (New York: The Noonday Press, 1958), p. 54.

4. Quoted by Walter Obermaier in *Arnold Schönberg Gedenkausstellung* (Vienna: Universal Edition, 1974), p. 26.

5. See above, pp. 42 and 56, note 1.

6. *Hochzeitsvorbereitungen auf dem Lande: und andere Prosa aus dem Nachlass* (Frankfurt a. M.: Fischer Verlag, 1953), p. 100.

7. See Meyer's book *Emotion and Meaning in Music* (Chicago: University of Chicago Press, 1956).

The Composer and his Idea of Theory: A Dialogue

Christopher Wintle writes:

Some time late in 1990, I invited Sandy Goehr to give a talk in the Faculty of Music at King's College, London. To the Faculty's delight, he agreed at once, and a date was fixed for 23 October 1991. But before then he and I met, first in Cambridge and later in London, to discuss what might be said. At our first meeting, Sandy offered to revise a paper he had given ten years earlier to the theory seminar at Goldsmith's College, London, on 'Composers and their Idea of Theory'. My reaction was one of only qualified enthusiasm. It was not that there had been anything unsatisfactory with his original talk; on the contrary, the issues it addressed had revealed very clearly his sense of involvement with the traditions of composition teaching: harmony manuals (Schoenberg's and Schenker's especially), the Mozart–Attwood papers, figured bass, strict counterpoint, basse fondamentale *and, more generally, writings by composers on their creative intentions (sometimes, as in the case of Wagner, a voluminous subject in its own right). Rather, I had been puzzled by the talk's ending. There he had appeared to turn away sharply from (mainly) eighteenth-century theory to the contemporary situation, closing with the remark that as a working principle the modern composer should have 'no idea of theory'. In view of what went before, this had struck me as odd. Of course, I could understand that the cultural position had changed – Romantic defiance of institutionalised theory has left its legacy – and that composers do not, and probably should not, set out to demonstrate theory through their music, except perhaps by way of a technical exercise. Yet I had still wondered whether it was really true that contemporary composers, who are often so articulate in*

*both word and print, worked in an entirely unprincipled fashion:
did they never formulate the challenges and problems of their
pieces in ways recognisable to theory? And where did that leave
the composer–teachers, those figures found so often today in British
universities and colleges, of whom Sandy Goehr was, and is, one?
I sensed that the problem lay much more with the word 'theory'.
In some quarters this has come to assume a certain opprobrium
– and not perhaps without good reason: 'theory' can imply a
conservatism and limitation in the choice of musical repertory, as
Joseph Kerman pointed out in his* Musicology *(1984); it can represent a tendency towards social exclusivity – the modern theorist
works mainly through journals, conferences and closed societies;
it can imply a narrowing of interest to just what suits its purpose,
whereas, in the eighteenth century, Matheson's* Der vollkommene
Capellmeister *(1739) addressed a 'completeness' hardly known
today; and, at its worst, it can enjoy a damaging remoteness not
only from musical composition and performance, but from history
and criticism as well. Therefore I made a tentative suggestion that
the new talk might adopt a different and more empirical approach,
by addressing 'This Composer and his Idea of Theory'. Because of
our own historical circumstances, moreover, it occurred to me that
the enquiry would have to go beyond the relatively straightforward
issues of working procedures to more personal questions of influence and psychology; and by doing this it could align itself with
some of the broader critical issues of our day as they have
developed outside music. The aim would not just be to uncover
theoretical autobiography, but rather to offer some model against
which other composers could set their own experience, and also
something to which analysts could turn when they considered what
the legitimate scope of their own work might be. This suggestion,
as it turned out, formed a reasonable basis for development; and
in the following months the material for the dialogue was generated, partly through an exchange of cards (questions) and letters
(answers), partly through the talk itself, and partly through the
need to form a coherent and publishable text. Some of my questions
were quickly answered, one or two received no reply; but with*

others – notably the question on Flaubert and 'models' – it took several months, and a number of attempts, before a satisfactory conclusion was reached. (In the 'Flaubert' case, the challenge was for us both to understand the ramifications of a question that seemed at first sight perfectly straightforward.) Neither of us felt by the end that the issues were exhausted; and indeed the exchanges could have continued far longer had they taken the issues further into the chapter and verse of musical composition, or into areas that belong more on the side of analysis than composition. Of the examples included here, the first was originally intended as a sketch for part of a work-in-progress on the Death of Moses (to original Hebrew poems, translated and edited by John Hollander), though it was not in fact evolved into a section of the score, at least not in the form presented here.

cw: *I haven't failed to notice that Hans Keller often cited you as a composer who subscribed to his 'theory of music'. The theory, at least in Britain, is fairly well known, and argues that a musical foreground is projected against a background of expectations, and that these expectations arise either from the internal procedures of a piece, or from procedures established by earlier pieces, whether by the same composer or not. From this Keller concludes that form itself is 'the sum total of our expectations', the norms that a piece establishes or presupposes. When we have talked about your Sonata for Cello and Piano, Op. 45 (1984), you have referred to the disparate sources of your material: first, there is a twelve-tone row, then something 'a bit like Fauré', and so on. Is it true that you think of these backgrounds in a way that HK would have recognised, and is this what you mean by the term 'synthesis', a term to which you clearly attach some importance?*

AG: I am flattered that HK considered that I subscribed to his 'theory of music', and it is true that I do. Internal procedures and examples of other pieces come together in an inspiration, or general idea, of what is to be done. I can and have proceeded in different ways at different times; but all the ways have in common the aspiration to write down (preferably at a single sitting) a complete thing (schematic or gestural (or both?)) which has, in embryo at least, a beginning, middle and end, and achieves some 'synthesis' – in the case of a constructed row piece between melody, harmony and rhythm, in tonal structures the same, although more specifically bass-orientated.

In slightly greater detail, this must produce a set of hierarchies – specific, predominating pitch levels placed on specific beats of the bar, and, if tonal, relating to a bass (for instance, as an implied dissonance suspension requiring resolution) and repeating (often in an altered relationship either to the row matrix from which they derive or, in tonal composition again, to the bass).

My ideal achievement, at this stage of a compositional process, is to make something in itself complete which at the same time indicates its own ways of further development or elaboration: where rows are involved, generally from left to right as it were, e.g. in variation-type structures, where the model is reworked. Here I find it crucial to stick to the hierarchies of the original as much as I can; in tonal structures I proceed by 'splitting' the model (into binary – for instance, antecedent–consequent – structures where the model contains none), melodic extension, 'developing' (tonicalisation) and by extending the movement between two elements of the original, placing 'new music' in between them. But in tonal as opposed to row structure, I generally try to leave my original beginning and end intact, and expand in the middle.

What may be achieved in the subsequent stages of my elaboration might indeed be regarded as relating to my original model in a way that HK might have recognised. But he of course was describing what he heard in the music of the past, and not necessarily asserting that there existed a preformed theory according to which the composer worked (or was he?). Naively, I believe (or do I?) that the 'great masters' needed no other theory than that of figured bass, which may not indeed be a theory, as they 'spoke their own language'. I suppose I incorporate viewpoints about composition derived from analysts (or from my own study of works of the past) into a 'strategy' of some kind. I suspect this makes me a 'different kind of animal'. It is not just a matter of being less good than the 'great masters'; it makes me feel that there is a 'historical situation' relating to the past by a bridge of theory, where the nature of compositional activity has significantly altered from what it is perceived once to have been. Or, to put it another way, I do (methodologically) what analysis reveals composers of the past did, but which historians would have to modify from actual knowledge of what composers might have done. (A difficult sentence, but it contains, I think, the point I am trying to make.)

cw: *I should like to dwell on the term 'synthesis', which is also well known to Schenkerians for describing the second stage of a musical investigation: first a piece is resolved into its parts through analysis, and then it is reassembled through synthesis or 'rational reconstruction' (to use Milton Babbitt's term). All analysts know that this 'synthesis' is only an artificial way of ordering the different dimensions of music which during composition may well be worked out concurrently: composers would not normally write a Schenkerian background, prolong it with a dozen or so 'middle-ground' transforming techniques, and in due course arrive at a foreground. Yet your description of how you work with a musical 'embryo' does seem indebted to your knowledge of just this kind of step-by-step generative process, and from that point of view would indeed make your work seem 'theory-bridged'. On the other hand, I hesitate to place you in the Schenkerian camp. Of course, you have explained that the importance of Schenker's work for your generation lay in its having forced you to consider pieces as wholes: your principal objection to Schoenberg's* Fundamentals of Musical Composition *is that it pays too much attention to beginnings, and not enough to middles or – especially – ends ('closure'). On the other hand, you have always insisted that Schenker's principles apply only to the precise (Bach–Brahms) canon he specified: you would be rather disconcerted, I suspect, if someone produced 'synthetic' graphs of your music à la Schenker! (I find your Bach–Brahms 'exclusion zone', incidentally, slightly controversial: for example, Schenkerian diminution could already be heard in Rome by 1681 at the latest in the music of Corelli.) So could I ask you to give an example of one of your 'embryos' and explain the senses in which it should be understood as forming a 'synthesis'?*

AG: First let me answer your points about Schoenberg and Schenker. In my mind, theory-building represents an attack on the unknowable: attempting to describe what makes a satisfactory whole. So a constructional theory (the 'categories' within which I work) has to do with criteria of satisfactory continuation and closure. Thereto, I would add good proportion and the possibility of memorability as subjects of concern. I know a good piece or a good tune when I hear one, but what makes it good? I learn from an analyst (and that doesn't mean all of them) when he is able to demonstrate convincingly, or at least partially so, how a piece functions as a whole, how the continuation continues and how the closure closes. 'What' I know, 'how' I want to know.

When I began, we only used to look at the beginnings of pieces, and odd striking bits thereafter. That changed because of Schenker. Not that I wanted to apply his 'method' to all kinds of pieces, and thereby 'extend' it, as has been attempted; I admire all he has to say of music 'between Bach and Brahms', where diminution plays a crucial part. I have generally thought that it would be sensible to view Schenker as a kind of historian of ideas, even if not an accurate one. It is at the other end from Bach (or Corelli) that there is a genuine division of views. I do not believe you can find similar forms of growth in the work of, for example, Debussy and thereby absorb him too into the Schenker canon. But when I try to see how Debussy works, it is not that I am simply satisfied with the idea of *Harmonielehre*-type surface chord connections, but, inspired by the example of Schenker, I search for a model, theoretical, of course, from which the whole has been elaborated (or can be elaborated). The methods I employ are clearly derived from Schenker, but are quite other, depending as they do on traditional French theory presumably unknown to him: for instance, the principle of harmonic *litanie*, continually reharmonising a single or a pair of pitch levels.

I have always wanted to refind, hopefully in a new form, *that* particular property of music (i.e. diminution). I take everything

Fig. 2. 'Synthesis model', adapted and annotated by Christopher Wintle from my sketch for the way the opening idea of Schönberg's *Moses and Aron* is introduced to and then made to pervade the structure of the fifth and sixth movements of 'The Death of Moses'.

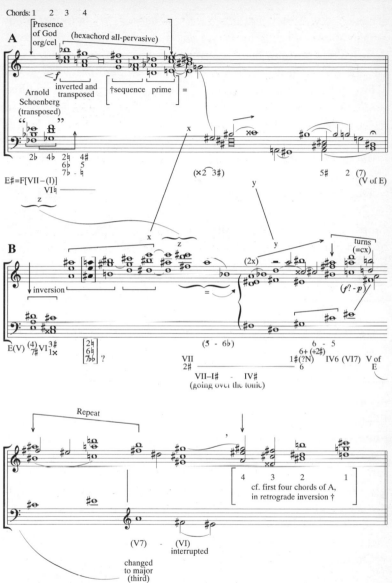

Ex. 37: Annotated synthesis-model

Schenker says about that *absolutely to heart*. That is in fact what I mean about refinding tonality. (As opposed to some to me incomprehensible – and even if comprehensible, quite inapplicable – stylistic theory of post-Modernism or neo-Romanticism.)

Fine talk indeed, but perhaps it could be clarified by an illustration (Ex. 37) of what I could call my *synthesis-model* (I had never done this before: writing as I composed!!). Situation: Moses (on the mountain top) protests to God his objection to dying. This is the first appearance of God in the piece. And, also, it is the first appearance of Moses' (or my) musical genealogy (Schoenberg).

This is an improvised model on the Aron versus Moses 'pair of chords' (hexachord), transposed for local reasons. The pair of chords is heard in its proposed new context in a kind of ♯I (♭II) of E major/minor. This determines the level of transposition of the subsequent pair, prolonged sequentially (in F: B♭–A♭–G♭–(E–D♭)–E♭ (top line)). Reinterpreted in E, it is now (gradually) bass-rooted to cadence on V of E.

The second, and larger, 'B' section begins on B (V of E) with a variant (positions) of the 'A' material. The arrangement of the triads is varied so that the relationship of 'B' to 'A' is strengthened (e.g. high A♯ = B♭), with upward movement for downward movement, and so forth. At one point where it becomes 'rooted' tonally, the harmonic movement 'crosses' the key centre, i.e. D–E♯ (avoiding E) (an idea at the root of my opera *Behold the Sun*): 'going over the tonic – too far – destined to fail'; and this gesture is strengthened by the bass rising in fourths D♯–G♯–C♯ then E♯. At the end of the second system it 'turns back' to V (with a natural 3) of E – then V (with a sharp 3) in the third system. An interrupted cadence to the first inversion C♯ chord allows the G♯ to refer back to the fourth triad of the model (in the 'A' section), and the first four chords there are now repeated in retrograde inversion.

The idea is that the hexachord is all-pervasive (symbolising God). The tonal push against it is both realised and frustrated. God himself, as he appears in the original text, isn't quite in charge. He answers Moses' question with the words 'You have to die, because it is ordained', not 'I have ordained it'.

'On the real meaning of repetition'

Ex. 38a

A contrasting and different kind of example of the way I try to
write down a 'whole piece in embryo' is taken out of the sketches
of the second movement of my Piano Trio, Op. 20 (1966). (The
sketch and part of the finished composition are shown as Ex. 38a
and b.) Here I have a twelve-tone row arranged as two related

245

hexachords. In the sketch the 'chords' are constructed by redundant repetitions of the same hexachord, starting at a later point in each form and superimposed upon the original: i.e.

3 4 5 6 1 2
5 6 1 2 3 4
1 2 3 4 5 6

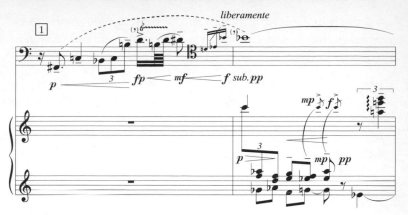

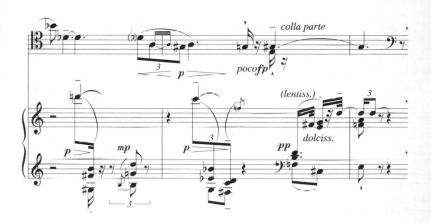

Ex. 38b: Goehr, Piano Trio, Op. 20

giving a triad upon the 'root' tone within the hexachord. (This is a procedure I picked up from Richard Hall and possibly more remotely from Krenek or Messiaen.) Now the melody, with a fragmentary sketch of an accompaniment, is made of segments of different transpositions of the row; first D, E♭ leading to C, then to G♭, F and thirdly, with an upbeat to B♭ and the next note will be D♭. This is a way of proceeding fairly familiar to twelve-tone composers, although most do not draw the segments together in quite this way. The point is that this 'melody' or 'structure' has a beginning, middle and end which remain in the worked version of the piece.

cw: *As an analyst, I react to your sketch by trying to 'translate' it into terms familiar to conventional theory, setting out my findings*

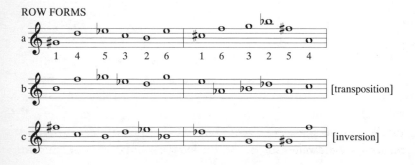

ROW-PERMUTATIONS with (new) permutations:

Ex. 38c

(in Ex. 38c) as I go. The sketch shows that you make two arrange-
ments of the twelve tones: at the top on the right, you lay out

a pair of hexachords in a 'bare-bones' form, as compositionally unordered 'sets'; here the second hexachord can be derived (only) by inversion and transposition of the first. Your sketches show that you are well aware of the 'secondary set' implications of this property (to borrow Milton Babbitt's terminology): the 'inversion' of these hexachords produces, in effect, a reordering of the hexachords of the original (cf. the Prime and Inversion in my example). Using your permutation formula, it is then easy to generate the 'triads' that accompany these hexachords.

At the top of your sketch on the left, you order these sets into a 'row', which (as my example shows) appear as a prime (a), a transposition (b) and an inversion (c). To the first hexachord of (a) you have applied the same permutation formula as before. As you indicate, it is the shared motifs within segments of these sets, and their relation to the construction of the cello melody, that determine the selection of the row forms: the pivotal notes are D/E♭, C/B and G♭/F. However, perhaps the most striking feature of the sketch as far as our discussion is concerned comes at the bottom of the page, where you write a note to yourself: 'on the real meaning of repetition'. This suggests that you are intensely conscious of transmuting a banal form of melodic structuring (i.e. a line which returns constantly to its starting-point in order to vault ever higher) into something original: the D/E♭ may be a motivic constant (hence a 'starting-point') but it is also constantly under serial review (and hence ever changing). In other words, your compositional foreground is projected against a Keller-like background of a recognisable norm. (The other serial manipulations, whereby you transmute row-forms (a), (b) and (c) into (d), (e) and (f) respectively, do not appear to be so immediately relevant to this discussion.) I am less sure, though, how you derive the material for the piano accompaniment, and exactly how, in both sketch and score, it interacts with the cello melody. But, in general, your examples are indeed strikingly different.

AG: There is certainly an important difference in the modes of continuation of the two sketches. The first, 'aiming' as it does at a tonic resolution, implies that the original sounds are to be heard as dissonances requiring resolution. They are, in my terminology, *back-orientated* ideas, and they can be 'prolonged' (with all that that term implies) by adding excursions, further suspensions and contrasting sections, even 'islands' in Schoenberg's terminology (as found in the *Gedanke* manuscript), but nothing can be added (unless a coda) at the end of the idea, as presented in the sketch, and nothing put before it.

(a)

(b)

(c)

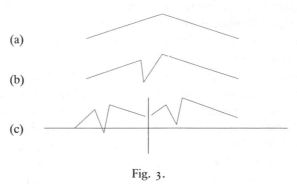

Fig. 3.

Incidentally, in Japan I took lessons from a Noh-singer. If I did not misunderstand him, he suggested that Noh-melos was constructed by placing an identical formula (rising and descending scalic arch) under each sentence of the text. The formula would then be varied by the introduction of caesuras which altered the shape of the formula, even resulting in a change of final note, and then the next version of the formula would have a new incipit. In this way a continuous expressive and free melos could be achieved (see Fig. 3). In this example of Japanese formula, (a) shows the original formula, (b) shows it altered by caesura, and (c) alters the final and leads to a new incipit. I never found out whether this was a true analysis, but, whether or no, it had a great effect on the way I thought of musical form (although the practice described in my Trio sketch predated my time in Japan). I like the idea of artistic creation moving from repetition of the identical formula towards seamless and continuous variation achieved by alteration, and by composing over the cadential break.

CW: *In the first example, I am immediately struck by the fact that you have created some kind of harmonic ambiguity out of Schoenberg's orthography, which in itself may have contained little or no implication for tonality. The* Moses und Aron *'hexachord' that begins the example is notated, in Schoenberg's opera, entirely in flats. You preserve this 'flat' notation as you make a 'local' transposition of this hexachord. Yet, in system 'A', in order to make a half-close in E, you re-spell the 'flat-side' eighth chord as the 'sharp-side' ninth chord. Is this kind of harmonic ambiguity, so important for nineteenth-century practice, also central to yours?*

AG: Harmonic ambiguity, the possibility of reading a tone, or pair of tones, or a chord, in more than one way, the *litanie* I mentioned earlier, is the most important artistic means available to any composer, and it is the way to discover aspects of and implications inherent in both spontaneously improvised and formally deduced material. It is a matter of changing the emphasis, the relative weight and the character of an idea. My obsession with this particular aspect of composition goes so far as wanting a particular musical constellation to be heard as referring to a tonality and then to a dodecaphonic structure. For instance, the opening of my Cello Sonata fulfils these requirements, and the development proceeds accordingly. This is not at all the same thing as when Berg and Schoenberg constructed deliberately tonal-orientated rows. My examples are 'objects' to be shown, as it were, in various lights.

CW: *I should like to take you back to another of your remarks. You look to analysts to show you 'how a closure closes', and by 'closure' you mean some harmonic process which recalls Schenker, without necessarily being equivalent to the kind of closure (tonal cadence) which most concerned him. Yet there is also another aspect to closure, the rhetorical one. In his lecture 'The Main Stream of Music' (1938), Tovey claimed that he could only 'teach composition as musical rhetoric'; and literary critics, if I am not mistaken, have identified at least a dozen 'archetypal' endings for narratives. In music, classical variations obviously show different modes of ending; Wagner made closure (cadence) an element in,*

rather than a condition of, music drama; and Strauss, Stravinsky
and the school of Messiaen have all made us think afresh about
conclusions. So how have you thought, not only about the rhetoric
of endings, but about rhetoric in general? Would you, do you,
'teach composition as musical rhetoric'? Is there a modern rhetoric
which we understand, but haven't yet codified? And can composers
write operas today without clarifying just these issues?

AG: I find such questions genuinely difficult to cope with: the reason
being that (a) I cannot easily equate music with language, and (b)
if rhetoric is the art of persuading (a listener) of something (a
meaning, a feeling?), I am afraid that my lack of awareness of
what I am persuading might serve to reveal my limitations as an
artist. Leaving aside 'abstract structures' of instrumental music,
where it might be argued that rhetoric is either non-existent or will
'look after itself', let us focus on opera and works with text, where
it could reasonably be assumed that the practices of rhetoric are
in action.

I will study a chosen text, trying to absorb its narrative and the
particular character of individual moments; but then there has to
be a jump. I am never aware of responding directly to the text, i.e.
by choosing mode, metre or motif for a 'suitable' setting, but 'say
the words' over and over until a 'beat' materialises. This establishes the number of syllables per beat and consequentially the
tempo of the setting. More words per beat leads to recitative, slow
tempi; a word, or two syllables per beat, to faster tempi – and this
too suggests the character of the accompaniment (number of chords
per bar) as well as the type (polyphonic, homophonic). In something like this way, the words and their characteristic *gestos*
(Brecht) are absorbed into a purely musical context where purely
musical criteria operate as in instrumental composition.

As a young composer, I subscribed to the exclusive belief of
Schoenberg, Webern and Boulez in the primacy of 'structure' and
'musical logic' – and would never now be able to shake these off.
Such beliefs are embedded at the very roots of the way I set about
composing. As far as 'rhetoric' is concerned, I basically believe(d)
it to be unethical: I heard Stockhausen answer a question of

Krenek's about climaxes in his music, saying sardonically, 'I'm not a writer of cheap dramas.' But I do believe in the rhetoric of non-intentional gesture. By this I mean that while busy constructing the continuity of my music, I seem to be constantly confronted by 'gestures' (from the unconscious, by chance?) – unrelated harmonies, melodic fragments, rhythmic personages – which I will not censor, and which consequently change the scope of my piece, possibly making its effect multi-dimensional, rather than that of a straight working-out of a process.

I fear this is an inadequate answer; that more could only be revealed by a kind of musical psychoanalysis, and that I could only 'learn' to answer your questions by analysing my own work as I would the work of another.

CW: *Far from being inadequate, your reply seems to me to touch on one of the dominating concerns of post-war music: the embarrassment of what Stockhausen, describing a new form of 'dramatic form' for his* Kreuzspiel *(1951), called 'the burden of traditional emotional expression'. The word 'dramatic' here may be the crucial one, because the embarrassment discharged its aggression on the figure of the successful opera composer. In England, it was felt that Britten achieved his 'effects' through his allegedly opportunist exploitation of 'mode or metre' (amongst other things); and one thinks too of Boulez's castigation of 'pauvre Berg!' for his musical flirtations with Puccini. But this embarrassment (dare one say neurosis?) might also be understood as a kind of dramatisation of a conflict already established in the eighteenth century. After all, Mattheson did attack Heinichen for restricting the scope of rhetoric (the quest for the 'loci topici' was mainly concerned with the search for the extramusically suggestive figures), reminding him that the 'locus notationis' provided a rhetoric of intramusical differences of a kind by no means dissimilar to those you describe.*

May I go back though to your first example yet again? I am impressed by the fact that even at this early stage of development of the synthesis-model, you have drawn upon preformed musical material, the hexachord from the opening of Moses und Aron.

One could perhaps posit two kinds of musical idea: the purpose-built idea, freshly generated for each occasion; and the pre-existent material, which has to be adapted and treated anew. The organicist aesthetic of the nineteenth century, with its emphasis upon originality, militated against the second (there is nothing of this in Schoenberg's Fundamentals), though obviously every act of composition has to balance new and old in different proportion. You yourself, in talking on various occasions about 'recompositions' of earlier music, indicate that there is indeed a variety of practice within your own work. How do you go about these 'recompositions', and do you consider them to be essentially different from other kinds of piece?

AG: Perhaps I would have done better, as Schoenberg seemed to think when publishing details of the twelve-tone technique, not to have mentioned my imitations or recompositions of classical models! I am reminded of a story told me by the Hollywood composer Bronisław Kaper. In a speech accepting an Oscar, he referred to the way he had taken everything from Bach, Mozart, Chopin, Tchaikovsky and so on. He was reproached by a colleague (Dmitri Tiomkin, if I remember correctly): 'You should not have told them where we got it.' Kaper riposted: 'Would it have been better if I'd said I got nothing at all from Bach, Mozart, Chopin and Tchaikovsky?'

What interested me when I tried to imitate models was a very special thing. It had to do with the organisation of time in serial music. If you do not consider the problem of time, as it were from outside, from the viewpoint of performer and listener, you would be forced into the belief (and most significant serial composers believe it) that the external form and duration of music is directly related to the structural means employed. But this leads to the paradoxical situation where the listener cannot perceive the structural means, because they pass too quickly, and has to satisfy himself with the following of gesture, narrative (by analogy) and generally vague things. But I would like my listener to perceive the structural events, not vaguely as general intentions, but precisely as I think I sometimes can in the great masterpieces. This means

Ex. 39a: Goehr, Third String Quartet, Op. 37, 1st movement

that there has to be a second mode of compositional thinking which deals in the projection of material and structural device in time. I counted phrases and bar-lengths in pieces I admired to use as a measure. I have hardly ever tried to imitate the material or the nature of the development of older music, only the amount of time it took to get from point to point: as it were, lessons in the disposition of light and dark, placing of principal figures and perspective, to use the visual analogy. Example 39 shows the beginning of my Third String Quartet, Op. 37, set beside its 'model', the first movement of Beethoven's Piano Sonata in E minor, Op. 90. Here there is some imitation of the original material, disguised by my tied note, which as it were sets up a metric ambiguity.

Ex. 39b: Beethoven, Piano Sonata in E minor, Op. 90

CW: *These integrations, of aspects of older music in your 'recompo-*
sitions', and of analysis of older pieces in other pieces, have made
you wonder whether you aren't, in fact, 'a different kind of animal'
from other composers. But I in my turn wonder whether the
challenges you face aren't, in a different guise, the same as those
that all creators have to confront. After all, Nietzsche suggested
that everyone encounters two cultures in their lives, the first being
the culture of one's parents, the second the culture one forges for
oneself.

AG: I am reminded by your Nietzsche remark of my father once
saying that all beginners start by trying to write imitations of piano
pieces by Schumann. I didn't. I started by trying to set poems by
T. S. Eliot or Catullus in as advanced a style as I could visualise. (I
was learning Classics at school.) Then I had a period of constructive
games, either cricket and football with dice systems or compositions by numerical compilations. I don't know what this proves.
But I started 'far away' from any genuine first culture, perhaps
because of the idiosyncratic conditions of my home, where light
music rubbed shoulders with Schoenberg, Bartók and Stravinsky
to the exclusion of the middle. As a young composer, I was scorned
by Max Deutsch, my father and uncle, and later Hanns Eisler for
taking the 'easy option' – avant-garde, electronics and so on. They
did not consider that to do this, to follow Darmstadt, was being a
real composer. Maybe they were wrong; but they shamed me into
persisting in trying to do what they meant by being a real composer.
At the same time, I deeply resented the impression that they were
party to some traditional knowledge, which was inexplicable in
words, which was only referred to with knowing and mysterious
smiles (of self-satisfaction), which I could never acquire. The only
one who did not talk to me in this way was Michael Tippett. But
it was they, not he, who bugged me (and still do). That's why I'm
interested in theory (of past music).

CW: *In due course, I should like to come back to these questions*
of motivation. Just for the moment, though, can we stick with
your 'different kind of animal'? HK used to enjoy invoking Schil-

*ler's famous dichotomy between naive (*naiv*) and sentimental (*sentimentalisch*) artists (playing a trump card by demonstrating that Britten was both). In his famous essay on 'The "Naïveté" of Verdi' Isaiah Berlin offered a vivid characterisation of this dichotomy:*

> *The naive artist is happily married to his muse. He takes rules and conventions for granted, uses them freely and harmoniously, and the effect of his art is, in Schiller's words, 'tranquil, pure, joyous'. The sentimental artist is in a turbulent relationship to his muse: married to her unhappily. Conventions irk him, although he may defend them fanatically... Of him Schiller says: '... His soul suffers no impression without at once turning to contemplate its own play... In this manner we never receive the object itself, only what the reflective understanding of the poet made of the object...' Hence the effect of the sentimental artist is not joy and peace, but tension, conflict with nature or society, insatiable craving, the notorious neuroses of the modern age...*

In our exchanges, you have resisted my attempts to put you into one of these categories, telling me instead that 'for us, the relevant aspect (of this dichotomy) is contained in the subdivisions of the sentimental'. About this, Berlin writes:

> *The characteristic poetry of the 'sentimental' is satire, that is, negation, an attack on that which calls itself real life but is, in fact, a degradation of it (what is now called alienation from it), artificial, ugly and unnatural; or it is elegy – the affirmation of the lost world, the unrealisable ideal.*

But I wonder whether even this subdivision characterises your work in a way that might satisfy Berlin?

AG: Imagining a piece – a melodic/rhythmic tag, or a bit of song – to myself, visualising a 'colour' (by analogy for a piece), influenced by a determining force, some formal/chronometric 'event' within the piece (all quiet and smooth – suddenly a fright!), is naive:

spontaneous and emotional, and, in my case at least, quite direct. I try to continue as simply as possible, singing the continuation. But at this point I have gone as far as I can 'naively'. Now, all kinds of things – completion, criteria of appropriate continuation, categories (of musical thought) – come into it; and because of history, naivety inevitably is transformed by theory. Now 'sentimental' considerations predominate; the problem is to what extent the original conception is retained. So naive–sentimental is not merely an opposition, but an ordering/sequence.

As far as the categories are concerned, there is a further division of the sentimental beyond the one you mention (satiric/elegiac). Schiller says in the subdivision called 'Elegiac Poetry':

> Either nature and the Ideal are the object of mourning when the one is presented as lost and the other is unattainable. Or both are the object of joy, in that they are presented as real. The one results in elegy in the narrower, the other in idyll in the broadest sense.

This opposition is relevant to, say, the difference between Brahms (elegy) and Dvořák (idyll) or Schoenberg and neo-classic Stravinsky (even better Debussy?). It certainly applies to me, in that I am elegiac, now and again trying for the idyllic!

Incidentally, concerning the word 'synthesis': Walter Benjamin in a famous letter to Gershom Scholem about Kafka describes his style as being like an 'eclipse', where one set of preoccupations is momentarily masked by another. We don't *choose* (Marx, Adorno, Benjamin), history chooses for us!

CW: *Like so many of the dualities – one thinks of Schopenhauer's Will and Idea, Nietzsche's Apollo and Dionysus, or Berlin's Hedgehog and the Fox – Schiller's categories have a certain allure: everyone wants to know where they stand with them. But have they actually been useful to work with?*

AG: Although it's true that I have not had Schiller in mind all that often(!), I think his categories are useful in isolating a certain old–new feeling, probably emanating from Stravinsky and Dallapiccola. This connects serialism with an antiquarian, even pastoral ideal of medievalism. You find it in the Sappho and Alcaeus settings of Dallapiccola, and in the Monteverdi 'homages' of Stravinsky, as well as in his Shakespeare songs, the Cantata and other things too. I suspect it was even more important to Max (Davies) and Harry (Birtwistle) than to me (in, for example, Max's 'Stravinskyan' choral works, and Harry's *The World is Discovered* and *Entr'actes and Sappho Fragments*). But I touched this feeling – a rhetoric? – from time to time. It comes out particularly in the Psalm IV Triptych very strongly; elsewhere (and even in these pieces) it is only used as one element of a synthesis.

In Modern Music circles, this kind of musical imagery was associated with English 'middle-of-the-road', in that it was linked with pastoral. But in reality it might have been born in Webern. 'Country-dwellers' who pick medieval or pietist texts, or treat them with strict device, are the model.

CW: *So out of Schiller's categories, we may now form a further subdivision, the medieval-pastoral, which defines a position for a number of post-war composers including (if only to a limited extent) yourself, a position which is presumably different from that of earlier twentieth-century composers – English ones especially – who also drew on the pastoral and the medieval?*

AG: I suspect I do not really belong in this category. If it is one, it stands opposed to Varèse (futurist), Messiaen (religious surrealist) and Boulez (Mallarmist). But both sides of this opposition are 'aesthetic'; whereas I muddle up aesthetics with ethics, most of the time to my cost. If you are writing *Arden Must Die, The Deluge, Behold the Sun*, my new piece on Moses and so on, the categories get confused, I fear. I then retreat into exotic woodland music (*Metamorphosis/Dance, Eve Dreams in Paradise*, the Cello Sonata), which is written when I'm fed up with preaching.

CW: *So far, we have talked mainly about how you theorise, rather less about why you need background theory, and hardly at all about what stands in the background of your (or any artist's) theorising. So perhaps I can now turn to this last question of background. It was Flaubert, I think, who once advised a young writer to choose as models five writers he admired, and a sixth he didn't. When one listens to writers, or artists of any kind, especially established ones, one is often struck by how much they invoke their models. In your case you refer constantly to Schoenberg (with whom your father studied), Messiaen (with whom you studied) and Boulez (whose views you have obviously found challenging). In each instance, you speak both admiringly and critically. For example, you follow Messiaen in his admiration for Debussy; yet you reject his method of harmonic analysis in favour of principles of chord connection based on common notes, which are to a certain extent redolent of the Schoenberg of the* Harmonielehre. *It is as if you are creating space for yourself even as you celebrate their achievements; you theorise others in order, not to imitate, but to distance them. In terms of simple (Freudian) binary oppositions, you both love and hate them (if hate isn't too strong a word). If this is a theoretical operation of a kind – a way of coming to an understanding of your own position – then theory is an instrument for defining both the love and the 'hate'. Would you recognise this scenario as a necessary part of some modern idea of theory (after Flaubert, Goehr!)?*

AG: I am gratified again! First HK, then Flaubert! Let me try to reconstruct your thought – first, the *Desert Island Discs* aspect. To begin with my sixth composer: Mahler. I have reservations about the personality: his attitude to himself and his subject matter. Consequently I seek *not* to emulate his relationships to his models, his narrative forms, his symbolism. Even if his music is something else, today I dislike its self-indulgence, hyperbole and rodomontade, and it serves him right that performances of his symphonies are generally vulgarly exaggerated, and that he has become distorted, Hit No. l, advertiser of petrol and plastic objects. It could not have happened to Brahms.

Leaving aside the fifth choice, a composer from the past (Monteverdi, Bach, Chopin or Brahms perhaps), I find that there are composers to whom I feel related and others whom I admire but who are strangers.

Schoenberg's circle and pupils seem to be like a family around a parent whom they loved and feared. So Schoenberg is, as it were, a 'grandfather' for me. The fear, and Freudian (?) rejection, my father felt towards him have not been inherited by me; the love remains. Though I've 'gone on', am not emotionally tied to as a father, nor shadowed by him, he provides everything, including the way I look at other composers to whom I do not feel so special a relationship. But even with Schoenberg, I now dislike his slightly 'hairy-chested', 'aristocratic' refusal to compromise. Mrs Schoenberg wrote in a copy of *Die Jakobsleiter* she gave me, 'To Sandy Goehr, und so nimmt man's nicht wie's kommt! Nein, nein! Dafür herzlichsten Dank, Gertrud Schoenberg'. I politely agree and smile to myself: 'a bit silly'.

Related love No. 2: Webern. I love particularly the middle-period songs, and then again the Cantatas. But *in toto* he appears a bit dry and pedantic, and as with Schoenberg, the texts he sets are mainly not to my taste. Yet I do admire the way the word functions in his music, as a kind of object separated from its syntactic context by the technique (derived from his earlier work) of isolating sounds through rhythmic and dynamic articulation as well as octave displacement. I do not find that he always succeeds in sonata–fugue syntheses as well as in the variation forms. It is difficult for me to keep the material in mind when it is so minuscule. Consequently pieces like the Trio and Quartet, and the first movement of the Symphony, seem too long – longer than Schubert and Bruckner in psychological rather than real time! I have the same difficulty with some of Boulez's and Babbitt's work: there is simply too much of them. Schoenberg is easier.

I do not feel any sense of special relationship with the composers I would place third and fourth: they are Debussy and Janáček. Both are a bit self-consciously original (and I cannot admire Debussy's snobbish side – 'musicien français' – and humour); but both composers achieve non-explicit quivering forms, which Schoenberg only sometimes does. There is no didactic search here for clarity of expression. On the contrary, Debussy's figures rarely appear in more than half-light, unlike Mahler's which are too brightly lit, with too much pointing up in the presentation of ideas. (HK, reacting to one of my pieces, commented: 'I don't wish to be told how to compose when I listen to music.') I owe any understanding I may have of Debussy to Messiaen and Boulez, and I do not (as you have suggested) reject their method of analysing his works. On the contrary, such method as I have would be an extension of theirs.

CW: *Your reference to* Desert Island Discs *makes me think that my question, and perhaps even 'Flaubert's remark', was a bit glib, something that would be interesting for a mature artist to answer, but which in fact fails to address the psychological reality of a young composer struggling to find himself through his reaction to others. Perhaps the truth is less schematic?*

AG: Obviously I am not now a young writer, but I will try and put myself back to a time when I was, and reconstruct a moment or moments when I might have done what Flaubert suggested a young writer should do. Three images come to mind. The first, derived from popular musical biography, sees me, in the open air, writing down motifs in clear imitation of Beethoven's sketches – brief melodic and harmonic fragments which I would take home and try to develop. Beethoven again: I read Stanford's book about composition, and am particularly taken by his analysis of the Piano Sonata in E♭ major, Op. 31, No. 3. This struck (and sticks with) me, although it is not a piece I have used directly as a model. But from Stanford, I formed a particular image of composing in relation to models.

I can add to these two memories the strong impression made upon me by Stravinsky's Serenade in A for piano. (This time I did use it – or at least its first movement – quite specifically as a model.) At the same time I would have to mention Michael Tippett, in those days (mid-1940s) a frequent visitor at our house. I was allowed to overhear his conversations with my father, and he as a man, together with his music of that time (the first two string quartets, the Piano Sonata and *The Midsummer Marriage*, which was the subject of much of the conversation, as well as the First

Symphony and *A Child of Our Time*), had an overwhelming effect upon me. I surely modelled myself on him, writing quasi-T. S. Eliot poetry, polyphonic, free-madrigal-rhythm pieces, and planning a Yeats opera. Later, as a music student, my interests moved fairly rapidly towards Schoenberg on the one hand, and Bach on the other. In between there was a 'sentimental' time when I 'imitated' loneliness by setting poems by Trakl in a manner obviously modelled on Mahler. I remember showing (or even playing) them to a lady of some distinction in the Paris art world and explaining that they were, despite their newness, completely rule-determined. She was shocked that I should be concerned with obeying rather than destroying rules.

I must also mention Bartók: I struggled with the Suite Op. 14 and other piano works. In 1951 I was certainly trying to compose with short rhythmic motifs and irregular akzac-type metres. My first encounters with Messiaen altered all that and absorbed these efforts into a more ambitious experiment: the Liszt Piano Sonata, the Schoenberg Chamber Symphony, Bartók and Messiaen 'came together' in my Piano Sonata Op. 2, which also contained my first experiment in the combination of twelve-tone row and modal harmony.

cw: *The other side of learning about your attitude to 'models', it seems to me, is discovery about your own working methods and attitudes. And the instruction to 'know yourself', which, as Isaiah Berlin has pointed out recently (in* The Crooked Timber of Humanity *(1990)), became a touchstone for the Romantics, seems just as important now as it did a hundred years ago. (By contrast, in* Der vollkommene Capellmeister, *Mattheson offers a typically eighteenth-century ideal of a composer – someone so perfect in all his accomplishments, so morally upright and fastidious, that we would probably be rather nervous to meet him!) When I listen to you speak, both publicly and privately, I am aware of a constant and instinctive propensity to theorise about just the kind of everyday working issues that Mattheson, to give him his due, also addressed. Only now, I think the issues are not quite the same.*

Your own way of working might encourage composers not always to choose their own texts, but to let others choose for them, as with your Sing Ariel *(1989–90), where the very beautiful and striking poems were, as you have said, 'composed' into a text by Frank Kermode. You tell a comparable story about Benjamin Britten pressing a certain instrumentation upon you for your suite Op. 11 (1961) (since he specified the flute and harp, he may have thought the German backgrounds of your music needed something French added to them). You encourage composers not to mind if they don't want to hear other music when they are busy (you wrote recently that 'as a working composer' you avoided Wagner); or if they got stuck in a piece, to move to another part, and start again there (when Webern got stuck in the first movement of his Concerto Op. 24, he began a Hildegard Jone setting using the same row material). My question is probably rather hard to answer. But it goes something like this: what fundamental things have you come to know about yourself which affect the way you go about composing?*

AG: Much goes back to my parents. My father hated pretentiousness and 'arty' posing. As an adolescent, I wasn't allowed to own a corduroy jacket I fancied – because for him it signified bogus artist. Both my parents had great natural musical gifts, good ears and performing facility, which made me aware of my own modest abilities. I do think that overcoming one's own natural limitations, and finding particular ways of doing this, are not just pious intentions, but can act as quite specific inspirations. I originally became interested in dodecaphony as an aid to ear-training – using the mind to compensate for natural limitations. I want to rejig the mixture and at last break through to 'real music'. I'm always about to, but never do. I search in the lives of artists, in the detail of their work, with or without the assistance of theories or theorists, for a 'secret' of music. It is inevitably a matter of chasing clues – and the bits of advice of mine which you cite are no more than my own experience.

I have no style, nor any concern with one. John Cage once said to me, 'If someone likes anything you do, don't do it again.' In a way, I want to remove everything intentional and personal from the act of composition, in order to allow the material to take its own form of development. Such abnegation, paradoxically, is the only way I know of achieving a personal statement. But the experience of actually composing, day to day, is always different: sometimes I will submit myself to a structural discipline in some or various dimensions of a composition; at other times I will imitate a model; and at yet other times I will improvise. As far as my own self-image as an artist goes, I would like to contribute something, but not try to make my persona into my work, as some I could mention seem to want to do. If indeed I am in love with myself, I would prefer it to be my secret.

cw: *You speak about the 'assistance of theories or theorists', but I am also aware that you too have not only written about theory, but speak and write too in a directly theoretical way. Of course, in our tradition there have always been composers great and small who have lavished their energies on just this sort of activity – in our own time, Schoenberg, Hindemith, Messiaen, Boulez among others. I wonder, though, just why they do it. For example, this is what John Tyrrell says about Janáček in his very interesting article in* The New Grove Dictionary:

> *His activities as a theorist were no doubt prompted by his passionate interest in almost every subject; but they can also be explained by a defensive attitude that his piecemeal musical training and initial failure as a composer engendered: he needed a theoretical armour to protect him. This defensiveness is evident in his attitudes to composers and influences. He tended to reserve his greatest praise for petits maîtres from whom he could have learnt little, while being slightly disparaging about composers like Musorgsky, with whom he had most in common.*

Here Tyrrell really is talking about a composer's individual psychology; and it has been said before that the sheer scale of Schoenberg's theorising, and one aspect even of its quality, suggests over-compensation for some kind of inadequacy. Then there is also the question of resistance to theory. It strikes me as a paradox that, of your composing colleagues in Cambridge, the most vehement of the no-idea-of-theory partisans are, in fact, gifted with special powers of analytic insight (I'm thinking particularly of Hugh Wood and Robin Holloway). Why should there be this extraordinary range of attitudes? Is it because theory, consciously formulated or not, does stand at the heart of a composer's private working life, though by its empirically-testable nature it also stands very much in the public domain, open to scrutiny, general debate and so on? If I may ask so direct a question, what does your theorising tell us about you?

AG: This is the hardest of your questions to cope with! The key words in what you say are – inadequacy, defensive attitude, (initial) failure. I can go further: though it cannot be entirely true, I do believe that such feelings directly contributed to making me a composer. Composing is a way of compensating for the inability to achieve excellence as a performer. It is also a way of learning: compare the title of Schoenberg's article 'Eartraining through Composing'. In the field of composition, everyone to a greater or lesser extent has to find their own way of doing things. I remember Max Davies once saying about Harry Birtwistle that he 'had learned how to compose by avoiding composing'. What I think he meant was that Harry's very personal way of looking at things actually excluded him from the possibility of doing things as other people do them. Because Harry had the nerve to persist (many considered him very arrogant when he was a student) he became the out-standing composer he is.

You have suggested 'acknowledging debt and repaying' as a motive for my theoretical activities. Perhaps – but behind such apparent nobility there is surely a deeper, more damaging, motive: a feeling of being excluded. (Brahms once said that it was 'too late to write great music'.) Analytic activity and the power of abstraction hopefully prepare me to do what I always fear I am not going to be able to do, which is to invent a natural, elegant and free-flowing melody, and combine it, without effort and with a modicum of originality, with a suitable accompaniment and har-monisation. I suppose that to do this is the real (and essential) 'fundamental of musical composition', equivalent perhaps to drawing, and that all else is in the nature of elaboration. We have seen remarkable composers, apparently unable or unwilling to attempt such 'ordinary' tasks, nevertheless achieving 'extra-ordinary music' – but at what a risk!

I have a fear of 'cheating'. Cornelius Cardew once reproached me, saying, 'You should not have a guilty conscience about tech-nical means.' But I do sometimes mistrust all ways of generating material by systematic means, as opposed to imagining it. If taken too far, an abnegation of such means would be counter-productive and in itself become an artistic posture, thereby limiting my sponta-neity. Theory (history) mediates such apparently irrational but nevertheless genuine prejudices, by pointing out the hazard of allowing possible sentimentality to prevent me from finding the elusive balance between imagination and construction, fantasy and logic. To construct or borrow a theory of *what constitutes coher-ence and how spontaneity and calculation might connect to their mutual advantage,* if it does not correct, at least complements, the vagaries of daydreams.

CW: *May we return to the question of 'acknowledging and repaying debt'? You have already said that when you were young, you were fired by a book of Charles Stanford's (*Musical Composition: A Short Treatise for Students *(1911)), and in our discussions you have also told me that one day you would like to write something 'similar'. Can you say more about this analytic interest of yours in the music of others, and what a prospective student of your 'treatise' would expect to learn from it?*

AG: As far as an interest in others' music goes – how it's made and so forth – analysis exists to give me hints. I return continually to the classics, to Gregorian Chant, Monteverdi, Bach, Beethoven, Schubert, Chopin, Schumann, Brahms and Debussy, because they have all provided models to be imitated – not as a student who sits before a canvas in the National Gallery imitates, but *partially*;

which is to say right through certain movements in some aspects (I mentioned chronometrics above) – leaving others to other, possibly contradictory, types of creative activity. There is never a complete unity of parameters in a composition: I can consciously derive everything to do with pitch from row operations, while rhythmic, articulative, agogic and instrumental writing is determined by other forms of thought. Some areas of activity are conscious (front-of-mind?); others, like brush-stroke in painting, are left to look after themselves. Richard Hall believed that if you keep the front-of-the-mind busy with numbers and calculations, you leave the channels free for the transmission of images arising directly from 'behind' or the 'back'. Anton Ehrenzweig, the author of *The Psychoanalysis of Artistic Vision and Hearing* (1965), points out that artists do not imitate obviously striking foreground things, but prefer what would seem to be trivial matters, hardly noticed by others. Listen to composers' conversations.

When such different types of activity are going on at the same time in a composer's mind, contradictions will inevitably occur: pitch says this and rhythmic structure says that, and I can't bear the result. When this happens, as it inevitably must, I am stuck and in panic have to improvise a way over the difficult moment. Paradoxically these moments of failure sometimes seem to justify the whole piece, long after I've lost interest in the minutiae of the technical procedures, which at the time of composition seemed so important. Someone, perhaps it was Walter Benjamin, said that the work of art is only a record of an activity.

If all this is true, then that which a composer perceives in the works of another is already an artistic choice, the more significant if not a conscious one, and the version I make of a piece, with all its elisions and things wrongly remembered and distorted, is almost a synthesis-composition in itself. This might suggest that the use of models in composition should not even be separated from any other kind of compositional decision.

CW: *So what we said earlier may well hold the key to the 'composer and his idea of theory': composers theorise others 'in order not to imitate, but to distance them'? Where, though, does this leave the analysts, whose intentions are anything but to distance themselves from the works they are studying, and who indeed are often motivated by a belief that works of art do have some 'truth-content' which, with sensitivity and learning, may eventually stand revealed?*

AG: I am sure that musical analysis, and consequently theorising, is only likely to reveal something of value when it is based on a strong, subjective impression of a piece or a composer, and when the lineaments of that subjective impression determine the manner in which the analysis is conducted. For me, therefore, there is no correct or incorrect analytical method, but only the limitations imposed by the concern to proceed logically and to avoid overstating claims. Much contemporary analysis, which wears its learning heavily, falls down because it pretends to achieve and explicate more than the analytical activity can genuinely be expected to do. The great masterpieces, without exception (because it is the condition of their being masterpieces), are instantaneous and unique balances of conflicting forces. Any individual strand may be isolated and explicated, but the intention to portray the uniqueness of the whole naturally eludes theoreticians, because the only portrayal of the whole, in all its complexity, would be identical to the thing it portrayed. Theorisation can only be temporary, and also only partially satisfactory, if it holds our interest and inspires further work.

(1992)

Finding the key

On my father's piano lies a copy of Stravinsky's *Sérénade en La*. It is much too hard for me to play, but I have a go at it. My father finds me with the piece and says something to the effect that 'you can't possibly understand what that's about'. Thinking about this incident some fifty years later (I was no more than fifteen or sixteen at the time, already a clandestinely aspiring composer, if a bit 'off the beaten track' as far as conventional musical education was concerned), I suppose that what he was saying, or rather implying, was that Stravinsky's rather stiff and formal 'Hymne', which is the first movement of the *Sérénade*, stands in an oblique or critical relationship to his own past or the past, and that I, without the faintest 'glimmering' (one of my father's words) of that past, could not possibly hope to understand what the relationship consisted of and therefore could not understand the piece. The put-down, if that is in fact what it was, made a strong enough impression on me for me to recall it so long after. Before he had made his remark I had thought that I had 'got' (I won't now say 'understood') the piece: I'd appreciated its particular lilt, its harmonic and rhythmic form in comparison, say, with the 'Danseuses de Delphes' (the first of the Debussy *Préludes*), which I also liked very much at that time. Looking back I still believe that, possibly inadequately, I had for all that 'understood' the piece in its essentials. But, bowing to my father's great authority, I came to feel that there must be something more to 'understanding' music than I then realised, something that at that time he could or would not tell me. Locked out, as it were, and behind closed doors, I had to earn my initiation, find my own way. At each faltering step, as it seemed, the best he would say was, 'you may continue'. But he wasn't going to deliver up the key to the closed doors, past which, I too should understand, I had to find myself.

People like to say, when confronted with a piece of music that they know they are not going to enjoy, or haven't enjoyed in the past, 'I don't understand it'. This suggests that they commonly equate enjoyment and understanding. If you liked it, you understood it. In this sense, I had understood Stravinsky, but it was borne home to me by my father's admonition, that perhaps enjoyment and understanding were not equatable. In that case, understanding apart from enjoyment would mean, in the first instance, performing satisfactorily – as is said, 'with understanding' (of genre, harmony, phrase etc.) – and then parsing, describing to oneself in appropriate terminology, placing historically by relating the particular to the general and disentangling provenance and influences.

The composer too enjoys what he does: naively he enjoys thinking up tunes, harmonies and rhythms and putting them together using the traditional forms of rondo, sonata or Lied. He will require a bit of writing skill, but not much else. No more than for the listener is it necessary that he understand; he need not check up on his work or describe it to himself, nor place it historically or concern himself with his 'influences'. Certainly he should not try to identify his intentions apart from what he has actually imagined and written down. But once he becomes self-conscious and loses his child-like certainty (and there hardly exists a more effective way of ridding oneself of one's confidence than having a musician father), he will inevitably evaluate what he has done, become self-critical and try to improve. 'Good, but crude,' the father or the teacher says. 'You have not seen the implications of your musical ideas.' Then enjoyment, the first excitement of writing sounds down, is modified by evaluation and further development involving everything that is connected with understanding. Just as it is said that everybody has one novel in him, so too it might be said he has one piece of music. But then, anxiety hems in imagination and immediacy, and the strategy of acquiring and understanding becomes unavoidable. Some composers seem to manage to go on writing their first songs for ever – but they don't have musicians as fathers.

Everybody has to start somewhere. In the past, imitation normally constituted the point of departure for original work: composing one's own versions of the pieces one learned to play. For this reason, the aspiring composer is almost inevitably linked to a tradition of performing music, from which he draws his first understanding. My father said that for him and his schoolfriends the first models had been from Schumann's *Album for the Young* (and what good models they are!). For me it was these same Schumann pieces and also Bartók (*Mikrokosmos*) and Stravinsky (*Les cinq doigts*). But looking back now over the decades, I see another point of departure for myself as an aspiring composer – one that had nothing to do with the imitation of existing pieces and one that surely has nothing in common with the experience of earlier generations. From early on my games ('You must make your own toys,' said my mother) were made of number schemes and maps (real and imaginary) and their combinations operated by dice. Externally, their subject matter derived from *Boys' Own* material, from *Treasure Island* and boys' literature of that time concerned with war games, explorers and castaways: anything that involved elaborate maps or plans which could then be numbered and lettered (like city A–Z maps) and submitted to chance operations. The operation of these games was no more effective than the dice football and cricket board games that followed them, but they included the additional attraction of lists and rankings (Wisden). In fact, now I think of it, my father also liked such games, though for him the greatest pleasure consisted of working out complicated and implausible journeys around England with lots of changes, courtesy of Bradshaw.[1]

I cannot remember when I first tried to connect my game and number schemes to music. Certainly my father would not have approved of that! Nor indeed do I remember ever obtaining anything like a result from my experiments – no more with the musical ones than with the games. The attraction lay in carrying out the schemes (and writing them out beautifully) – then they just fizzled out. But what I suppose had an effect on me was that on the one hand I was experimenting with a kind of rudimentary composing by numbers which surely owes little to any tradition, while on the other I was writing the conventional imitative pieces. Furthermore, while composing by numbers might now be considered 'innovatory', raising Cage-like ideas of demolishing intentionality and opening the door to the unknown, then – in 1948 in the English home counties – it had no such portentous significance. The intention rather was to produce pieces of predetermined and conventional character, rather like Mozart's dice dances, which were certainly not known to me at that time. Maybe my inability to finish my conventional pieces led me to these games. But what is clear to me is that there was in such games a type of rudimentary experience, a line of thought extending from that time to the present, via both my teachers (Richard Hall and Olivier Messiaen) and the dabbling with row charts (Schoenberg, Webern and Boulez). To this day I remain fascinated with golden sections and any form of Pythagoreanism and at the same time a little wary of putting too much faith in forms.

The teachers I went to in my late teens, Henry Geehl (who, I believe, had worked for Elgar and was a director of the publishing firm Edwin Ashdown in London)⁷ or a bit later Herbert Linton (Lichtenthal) who was more of a proto-analyst of the Riemann school and had begun a conducting career in a German opera house before 1933, did not do a great deal for me, nor I for them. I was impatient; I wanted to compose, not to learn, and found it difficult to see any connection between the harmony and free counterpoint I was expected to do and the kind of pieces I did try to present to them, which they 'did not understand' and rejected out of hand. Doubtless masking diffidence under the posture of rebelliousness, I simply was not prepared to accept that academic techniques had anything much to do with learning to compose. But, as I remember it now, it was not, as my teachers surely believed, that I wanted freedom to express myself and champed at the bit when disciplined. On the contrary, and putting it now as I would today, I found the rules I was given perplexing in that they were insufficient to produce the required result. What I now know of course is that the 'rules' were only designed to keep a creative and musical beginner on the rails, to give him writing flexibility, and were never intended, as I then supposed, to have generative properties. I wanted 'rules' and the certainties they provided. I remember saying to an uncomprehending Henry Geehl that I understood the principles of beginnings and of cadences but that I could not see how to fill in the distances between the two. I did not realise then, and not till much later, that composition was in fact improvisation between fixed points; I was like a hurdler who doesn't understand that he has to run between the hurdles.

In Richard Hall I found a teacher who helped and inspired me.[3] Hall, who had been an organist and, as an Anglican priest, pre-centor of Leeds Parish Church, combined a real intellectual interest in Medieval and more recent music theory with 'occultist' thinking, Jungian psychoanalysis and comparative study of religions – Eastern and Western. But the two, the music-technical and the speculative, were not separate concerns; they came together in his own brand of number-determined cabbalism and resulted in the invention of specific compositional systems. At the same time (and where I was involved there always seems to have been an 'at the same time') in the late 1920s and 1930s, during the period of the general strike and mass unemployment, he had worked as an art and music teacher with groups of unemployed workers (inspired no doubt by the New Deal programmes in the United States), writing and teaching others to write and to perform on pipes and other instruments what they had written – very much in the manner of *Plöner Musiktag* (Hindemith's German *Gebrauchsmusik* work). But unlike Hindemith, he allowed his applied music to become a vehicle for numerically generated, constructivist experiments which spilled over into his more ambitious compositional projects when he lectured at teachers' training college level and later when he became professor of composition at the old Royal Manchester College. Later he moved to Dartington Hall but he ended his life as a minister once again, this time in the Unitarian Church.

At the time I met him Hall seemed to be deeply ambivalent

about his own compositions. He composed uninterruptedly, later in life extending his creative activity to the writing of poetry. But he never seemed to want to get his work performed and when there were possibilities he shied away. He certainly regarded creative work as a spiritual exercise and his constructivism was, I believe, always understood by him to represent something akin to prayer. His musical taste extended from Bach, Brahms and Hindemith to the English composers of the Delius–Holst–Vaughan Williams generation. He was deeply interested in the music of Scriabin, Busoni and Schoenberg, and later Webern, Berg and Messiaen. But, Scriabin apart, he had little taste for their 'expressionistic' excesses and regarded their music principally for its speculative and constructive intentions. It is certainly true that in the provinces at that time, with few resources available for performing new music, composers tended to be more interested in abstract constructional and experimental ideas for their own sakes, while externally cultivating and being limited by fairly conventional musical forces and forms. All that did not change until the 1950s, when resources became available for the cultivation of modern music.

I came to Richard Hall as a willing pupil, first privately and then at the College. What he did for me, first and foremost, was to help me separate real compositional concerns from a morass of preconceived ideas about what composition ought to be. However many ideas I had (and may still have) about music and its role in the world, however 'original' I may have believed my approach was and however interested I was in related topics, he gently taught me that I had to be concerned with the notes: only they make good music. It is the notes that the players communicate, and only when they do communicate do they become music.

It is hard and deflating for the aspiring and opinionated young composer to be told to stick to the notes. (One only learns that later.) But Hall made his lesson palatable by his quite unique ability to place even the simplest exercises he set into an intellectually stimulating context. I have always tried to imitate him when teaching myself. Finding a context, 'dressing up' a technical problem saves face and helps the pupil to forget the distance between his fantasies and his realities. Aspiring composers, now as then, cannot accept the need to acquire traditional skills just because an academic syllabus demands it of them. The old kind of authority has gone and do not let us waste time weeping for it. Without authority behind him, the successful teacher will be the one who finds the way (and it is a different way with every student) to lead his student to involve himself with compositional disciplines for their own sake and not merely to obtain, at the lowest level, a qualification and, a little higher on the scale, manual and intellectual dexterity (as, for instance, Boulez believes). How a student may be brought to realise that traditional compositional disciplines are intrinsically interesting might well be the subject matter of a new *Gradus ad Parnassum*. If he can find them, they contain hidden within them the real secrets of the art.

In the four years I spent with Hall I did not have to work particularly hard at anything I considered tedious. If I was bored by what I was expected to do, he was much more so, and easy to deflect from the matter in hand. Most lessons ended up with us looking at what he was writing. This was further facilitated by the fact that the College offered no diplomas for composition. I had to work hard to move him into an active state. Perhaps he was lazy; he was certainly quite happy to pass the time of day (especially the time assigned for my lesson) at the café next door to the College. Consequently I used to feel that I was doing most of the teaching: he sat and listened with a mysterious Buddha-like smile, occasionally commenting and deflating my speeches. But, as with all good teachers, one learned without knowing it and much of what has concerned me throughout the years since originated in what he somehow conveyed to me then.

All the music I composed as a schoolboy and as a student in Manchester has vanished without trace. In fact my first published piece, a piano sonata which I can date because it quoted the beginning of Prokofiev's Seventh Sonata, Prokofiev having died (in 1953) while I was writing it, already demonstrates a rudimentary synthesis of dodecaphony, 'modal' harmony and independent rhythmic construction, using the rhythmic cell technique learnt from Messiaen, whose music and theoretical treatise were both avidly studied in the Hall class. Immediately preceding the composition of this sonata I had experimented with Bartók-inspired mechanical canons and *Allegro barbaro*-type rhythmic studies, using numerically generated patterns of hand alternations with a rather limited harmonic practice which consisted of the repetition and variation of pairs of freely invented chords, sometimes with and sometimes without tonal references. It was my inability to get the harmony to move that led me to dodecaphony. The rotation of all twelve semitones does at least prevent one's getting stuck with the same harmony over and over again.

At the time, I lodged in a fairly grim part of Manchester with a landlady who allowed me to use her parlour piano for an hour after tea, in exchange for sing-along renderings of old favourites from *In a Persian Garden* and such like. I was seriously preoccupied with hearing what I wrote and liked to test any combinations I wrote down and learn them by heart, which I still do. For me, this practical testing constitutes the other side of the coin of experimental constructivism. If a composer utilises charts or other methods of generating unknown combinations, it becomes imperative to test them at each point. Or so I have always believed. But looked at in another way such a seemingly practical and common-sense procedure might well be regarded as contradictory. It could be argued that if a composer submits himself to a particular procedure, such as pitch-generating charts, that's it. He has made his choice. The rest is purely technical: making certain that the resultant notes fall appropriately for required instruments and so on. But where I have made use of charts or row tables and have memorised the harmonic and melodic material that has emerged from them, these memorised blocs begin to have a life of their own, in the sense that they determine their own continuations, and these continuations, which tend to be determined by such musical considerations as the need for repetition, sequence or contrast, do not necessarily fit in with the material derived from the chart. The resulting tension between the requirements of the actual invented music and those of the chart has to be resolved by compositional synthesis.

Maestoso

Ex. 40: Goehr, Sonata in One Movement

At that time in Manchester I worked mainly in the evenings and at night (because as a conscientious objector to military service I was still working as an orderly in a hospital and also had to fulfil my College obligations), so that with access to the piano limited to evenings I could not run up and down the stairs to test every chord I wrote down. I then got into the habit of memorising little blocs of music, believing that if they sounded well, they would continue to do so in whatever form or variant they might appear. So, for instance, my piano sonata was based on a slightly B minorish chordal structure, employing all twelve notes (see Ex. 40). Although the treatment had more in common with *bloc sonore* principles than with orthodox dodecaphony, by which I mean that the row cells were reordered, doubled and multiplied, the sonorities of the opening material were retained throughout the composition, really to ensure that I heard what I wrote. In some pieces, especially in the suppressed second movement of what is now my Fantasia Op. 4, I employed techniques similar to those used in the Sonata.

Subsequently I moved to another mode of composing, which must have emerged from ideas that were in the air, because it has something in common with Max Davies's pieces of the same period.[4] In my case, a slowly unfolding dodecaphonic structure, as for example a canonic arrangement of row forms of a Webern–

Dallapiccola type, was composed with durational and even dynamic series (in the imitation of the 'total serialism' of Boulez and Babbitt, whose work was known to me at that time). This then was overlaid by secondary diminutions derived from fragments of the original dodecaphonic structure, which now had to be understood as a *cantus firmus* or chorale. The difference between such procedures and Baroque imitation was, firstly, that the background *cantus* was itself a many-voiced structure and, secondly, that the diminutions, though sometimes conventionally imitated from appropriate models (such decorative arias as the slow movement of the Italian Concerto, the solo clarinet movement of the *Quatuor pour le fin de temps* or even folk music heard on the Third Programme in the extraordinary recordings of Alan Lomax and A. L. Lloyd), were also treated in a more modern way by taking a fragment of row as a *bloc sonore* and transforming it by permutation, expansion and multiplication. Although some of the results of such procedures might sound a bit rough today, the basic idea of synthesis seems to me to have been reasonable. Even then I seem to have wanted to combine really differing modes of musical expression and utilise connections between musics of varied provenances and times.[5] I have continued to do this all my life and it implies a belief that over and above all the styles, periods and genres of music history there exists a unity transcending all the variations and details. The unity is of music made and heard here and now. Although often mistaken for a 'Darmstadt composer', I never was one, any more than I was a follower of either Babbitt or Boulez, who seemed to me to be aspiring to a systematic integrity of structure which is completely foreign to my musical experience.

In those years, while I was a student in Manchester, my father continued to influence my thinking. On the one hand he was a severe, sometimes but not always constructive critic of my compositional essays, slaughtering and then improving by rewriting. For example, the slow ostinato middle part of my piano sonata was reworked by my father in proof to get rid of what he thought was a certain harmonic skimpiness resulting from poor counterpoint. Richard Hall hardly ever reworked pieces: probably he could not be bothered. I have always believed that active reworking is worth more than verbal criticism, but not every student will take it.

My father had formidable writing skills (which after he left Germany were exercised mainly in war documentaries, later in features, films and theatre) and an astonishing fluency which I could never hope to emulate. In fact my lack of it caused him to criticise me as a snob, believing that I would not do commercial music, such as films, because of some bogus 'arty' desire to stay pure. The truth was I did not have his abilities. When teaching, he could in a quite astonishing way infiltrate himself into a piece he was looking at, not only to correct and improve what was there, but to move off from a given point in a quite new direction which I could not have foreseen. Sometimes he got back to the original, sometimes he just left it when he got fed up with it. I believe this must have been a traditional way of working. Years later, the great conductor Antal Dorati, disliking the end of my violin concerto, simply composed a different (Hungarian) end to it between rehearsals. It was quite a problem of tact getting him to retain my original version. The ability spontaneously to reinterpret and extend constitutes the real stuff of composing and teaching, just so long as one remembers what the original idea was. Sometimes when looking at my pieces my father forgot what the idea was – and sometimes I do too – and then the piece would get lost. But I did learn the difference between sketching and working out detail here. One should write quite freely and crudely at the beginning; many composers get stuck because they over-elaborate their ideas at too early a stage, impatient to anticipate the final result. On the other hand change for its own sake can be no more than perverseness, especially when it comes to notation, and there is a lot to be said for Stravinsky's remark that one should always stick to the way one first wrote down an idea.

Possibly the most important aspect of my father's influence upon me, which continued long after his early death in 1960 and led to the feeling in the ensuing years of my never being quite certain where his ideas ended and mine began, came as a result of his activities as an explicator and analyst. He did music analysis as a

way of teaching conducting. This may have been the reason why
he did not much care for the Schoenberg-inspired preoccupation
with motivic structure that was much in the air at that time,
following the publication of the early *Style and Idea* (the Williams
and Norgate book[6]). His analytical methods were empirical,
veering towards Riemann's agogic and Schenker's voice leading.
He knew little of Schenker's work, as most of it was unavailable
– he had only the analysis of Beethoven's Fifth Symphony, the
handbook of the late Beethoven sonatas and the early book on
ornamentation.[7] But he certainly understood the principles and in
any case would not have been unduly bothered by the systematic
and methodological minutiae. His analyses of Bach cantatas and
the B minor Mass, as well as his earlier work on the Purcell
fantasias and Monteverdi (which had the important by-product of
compelling me to write out all fifteen of the Purcell Fantasias in
open score as well as a great part of the Vespers of 1610), his
sessions on Mozart symphonies, Beethoven and Schubert, Brahms's
Second Piano Concerto and the Schoenberg Chamber Symphony,
all designed for conductors and intended to demonstrate the
relationship between structure and performance, brought the repertoire to life in a way in which the dull lectures on form at College
never did. As a result, I could never regard classical and romantic
music as something to escape from, an attitude which was widespread in Darmstadt and elsewhere. For instance, Nono, with
whom I became very friendly, regarded escape from the past (but
not the remote medieval and renaissance past) almost as an ethical
imperative. I remember him emphatically agreeing, when someone
suggested that it was *a priori* better to imitate the clichés of new
music than those of old music. But for me exposure to analyses of
older music has always remained a direct inspiration and challenge.
There can be no knowing without the desire to emulate.

An example of my father's somewhat Socratic and slightly discursive manner is contained the work we did together on *Erwartung*
(see pp. 117ff.). He talked and showed; I wrote down. We only
had the vocal score and the Mitropoulos recording, though he
hired the full score from the publishers to check up on detail; most

of the work was done by ear and at the piano. But what was observed in the study was original at that time, as it did not at all concern itself with motivic structure (as, for instance, Schoenberg himself did in his talk about the Four Orchestral Songs), preferring to emphasise what it was, rather than how it was done. My father picked out tonal characteristics (which he thought were probably unconscious and not deliberately worked out), such as long-term 'leading notes' and the emphasis on certain pitch levels at the beginnings and ends of phrases.

Motivic composition as practised and taught by Schoenberg, Webern and Bartók, and in England particularly by Matyás Seiber and his pupil Hugh Wood, has much to be said for it. It is a rational approach to musical logic and contributes to sobriety and the avoidance of arbitrariness in composing. At its best, as for example in Dallapiccola, it produces a kind of Renaissance equilibrium. But it plays little part in my work. (My father said, 'One gets tired of intervals'.)

I have found that intervallic structure inhibits spontaneity when actually writing. Composing is a physical as well as an intellectual activity. Of course, a composer lays his plans, prepares himself inwardly and gets 'into training' like an athlete, to combat stiffness in writing, which kills the free play of fantasy and intuitive connection. Ideally when all the preparations have been laid out the composer should strike like the matador, lifting neither head nor hand from the manuscript paper till he has completed what he has to do. Only then can he hope to do what is necessary and no more. I have often felt in my own work and in that of students that narcissistic concern with calligraphic beauty, such as ruling lines, inhibits spontaneity; composers should write music as they write letters. See Bach.

More than likely it was the experience of music analysis which made me half-hearted about Darmstadt (where several of my works were first performed) and about the Messiaen class, although retrospectively I came to appreciate it far more than I did at the time (see pp. 42–57). For just in the area of analysis, which made up a substantial part of the syllabus, what was offered seemed banal and crude, when not enlivened by the sensitive observation of detail. The main exceptions were the analyses of Debussy and Ravel, of which I had no previous experience and which were stimulating and thought-provoking.

Conventional *Formenlehre* as practised at that time limited itself to the description of schemata, enlivened with observation of harmonic detail, orchestration and any other 'points of interest'. A student inevitably became bored by all this and generally dismissive, as it was not until the advent of more advanced analysis (and not always then) that music as the tension between formal scheme and what actually happened came into play. In fact, composers then did not seem to be much interested in what happened in the whole of a piece. It was a Darmstadt commonplace to focus on beginnings and special moments (such as the inevitable Bs of *Wozzeck*), hardly ever relating them to context. I remember being astonished when Nono, attempting to analyse a Webern instrumental song, copied as much of it as would go on a blackboard, and then proceeded to demonstrate intervallic symmetries and durational proportions as if what was written on the blackboard were a whole piece. Symmetry and proportion and other statistically observable phenomena in a piece were conceived at that time as constituting an ongoing process *per se*, not as contributing to the understanding of the whole.

As they were in any case ignorant and bored by past music, most Darmstadt composers were concerned with the re-invention of the wheel and subscribed to the apocalyptic notion of a new musical language. Scorn for the past, which has such disastrous results in all forms of human activity, brought about the trivial programme of attempting to categorise so-called 'progressive' elements in that music which was nevertheless still seen as somehow relevant (Stravinsky, Bartók, Debussy, Schoenberg etc.) and separating them from their residual and 'regrettable' backslidings into Romantic convention.

Most of what resulted creatively from these ideas seemed to me to be ugly and dull, of interest principally for its orchestration. The composers who stood out – of course Messiaen himself, Boulez and Berio and sometimes Nono and Maderna – were remarkable mainly for textures and colours. It was only years later that I began to appreciate the extraordinary gifts of Stockhausen. At that time he was simply too much for me. But I was hardly ever able to follow or even sense the existence of any compelling long-range development which, because of my experience of analysing classical music, seemed to me the *sine qua non* of all music. Of course it was then (and is now) improbable that all the talk of long-range structure was based on aural experience. ('Following the score rather than listening is a conspiracy against music,' said Messiaen.) For all that, because of the achievements of the past, it is perhaps an act of faith to believe that the particular intensity, the ebb and flow, the tensions of a piece and its timing all result from long-term compositional concerns, even if it is impossible to know how it works. Conversely the bitty, jump-start and stop piece that appeared in new music concerts then (and still does now) can generally be assumed to lack any overall determining conception of a meaningful kind. On a few hearings, it is surely impossible to know, without analysis of the score, how a piece works and why it excites enthusiasm. It is a two-way process: one chooses to study what pleases one aurally and the study of it deepens the effect of further hearings.

I have described elsewhere (in the letter to Boulez, pp. 15–17) how I felt when I returned to England in 1957, but I hardly conveyed the violence of my reactions against the avant-garde scene. Max Deutsch, a Schoenberg pupil in Paris, had refused to accept me as a pupil (because I was in the Messiaen class) and wrote a cutting letter, which came into my hands, suggesting that I was made for the Cologne Electronic Studios and a fine career following the false gods of Darmstadt. He, my father, Leibowitz (whose expulsion from Darmstadt I witnessed) and Hanns Eisler could not know how deeply the reservations they expressed about contemporary developments were affecting me.

My first encounter with Hanns Eisler, which took place in the year I was studying in Paris, was nothing short of a disaster and I vowed that day that I'd never talk to him again. The meeting took place in a luxurious hotel room where he was writing the score for Miller's *Sorcerers of Salem* (the film). First he slaughtered the score I had brought to show him, or rather the first page of it, which contained three successive chromatic notes for cellos. These he rejected. He got no further than the cellos and veered off into a general tirade against 'the new music' and the *Domaine musicale* in particular. 'Don't tell me; I knew Webern,' he shouted, pounding the poor upright with his fists in a not too accurate imitation of Webern's style. (He was in fact, as I later found out, a quite remarkable pianist with the backs of his hands.) 'There's nothing fundamentally new about Boulez that we haven't heard before.' But then it was also obvious that he had never heard any Boulez. Having successfully made my exit, I later had to return to deliver a score. This time, at a more mellow hour and with whisky, he leered at me and asked: 'Which Boulez scores should I look at and where can I get them?'

Although he could act it up in public (Villon was as much a part of him as Marx), I never met a more cultivated musician than Eisler. His conversation on any cultural topic sparkled and everything was trenchantly to the point. (The account of him in Thomas Mann's *Genesis of Dr Faustus*[8] draws a perfect thumbnail sketch.) He was very much a Schoenbergian, though respectfully amused by some of his teacher's famous quirks. (Politics, religion and literary taste were generally described as *peinlich* (embarrassing).) His musical taste was also much more catholic than that of his teacher. He was one of the first really to appreciate the importance of Janáček, and it was to him that I owe my own love of the Czech composer. What I learned particularly from Eisler was his unique way with words: I hardly ever choose a text without asking myself 'how would he have set it?' In this respect he ranks with Britten.

His own difficult life as much as any Marxist conviction had made him adaptable and unconventional as a composer. Eisler was remarkably fluent and could write anything he wanted at break-neck speed. In fact, he was deeply opposed to the over-specialised avant gardist and wanted artists to hang on to the middleground. But he did not want them merely to become lackeys courting popular success. He aimed to use popular material in personal and unconventional ways and to take his audience along with him. He probably failed in this impossibly high aim, but he showed a way. He was most unjustly attacked in the West (see, for example, Berio's comments in *Two Interviews*[9]); this was due partly to the enmity between Eisler and Dessau, who had many friends in the Western avant garde. In fact, official acceptance sat uneasily on his shoulders and he managed to be rejected by the musicians of the DDR because he was a Communist and by the Communists because he was a Schoenbergian. Hence his remark which I have quoted elsewhere: 'The only possible music is music that is unperformable in the East and in the West.' I do not know how I should update that sad but wise observation.

Although I described my reaction to the continental avant garde as violent, I nevertheless considered myself as part of it. Seen from a distance of thirty years, it is not at all clear that the work I was doing could not be considered as fairly typical of 'Darmstadt music', because of course there is a great variety available within what is loosely called a style, and even if one considers oneself to be writing from a viewpoint in opposition to that of one's contemporaries, one will nevertheless almost without thinking take on many of the hallmarks of a prevailing style.

My first compositional essay in the direction of combinatorial form (and coincidentally my first essay in modelling a composition on an earlier work) was a premature and over-ambitious attempt at fused fugal and sonata movement for the finale of my First String Quartet, based on the 'Jupiter' finale. (My dissertation for the *Prix* at the Conservatoire was a study of Sechter's analysis of this movement and for the record was awarded the *deuxième Prix d'étranger*.) The predetermined formal model determines the durations and functions of the sections and their relationship to the whole. But to live up to this one has to have a considerable control over the material and continuous inventiveness if one does not wish to fall into the trap of the mechanical filling out of pre-established functions. My plan was not well realised, nor was the invented material sufficiently contrasted to be and remain recognisable in the combinations; as a result the structure has disappeared 'into the mists of time' and even I cannot now follow it when I hear it. I tried to work out the same kind of idea in a more modest framework, a Capriccio for piano (inspired by a spirit of dialectical opposition to Stockhausen's *Klavierstück XI*), in which all the fragments appeared in all combinations but were tightly controlled by hexachords and their relationships. But only with *The Deluge*, a cantata for voices and instruments, did I feel that I had really found a way of dramatising formal ideas in a way that they would become immediately perceptible to the listener.

The Deluge remains to this day one of my favourites among my own pieces. Here, in each of its three parts, I managed to connect the musical ideas with the formal trajectories. The cantata was well received, and although it was considered a kind of latter-day expressionism (which with its da Vinci text it in part is), it was in fact my first successful essay in Baroque-inspired closed forms, in which the proportionally related and recurring durations of sections were determined by number and expressed by ritornello, concertante and tutti ideas. *The Deluge* was inspired in part by Werner Neumann's study of Bach's choral fugues,[10] which brought to my attention the idea of a musical bloc, identified by internal harmonic structure, texture of parts and dynamic character, which in combination with other analogous blocs (each of a fixed duration) could be permuted and combined to create the semblance of a fugue. This fertile concept (which considerably affected Tippett in his Concerto for Orchestra) is a more specifically art-music relative of Stockhausen's 'field', an idea which was much discussed at that time.

It may well appear idiosyncratic to some to describe a musical and creative development primarily in terms of what might be thought to be merely technical matters, when 'everybody knows' that the determinant factors of the creative urge lie quite elsewhere and that biography must have at least as much to do with the mystery of the artistic process as any amount of exegesis or technical explanation. In fact some great composers – Britten, for example – were known to dislike any prying into the how of what they achieved. (I certainly would prefer prying into the 'how' of my composing than into biographical detail, were I alive or dead.) But whether or not they regard their activities as autonomous (and there is no time in history when the drive towards artistic autonomy has been so stoutly defended and on so little basis), the connection between 'life', popularly regarded as the principal inspiration of musical creativity, may be less direct or less convincing than the belief that the real subject matter of music is to be found in its own processes and its own history, and even in the re-evaluation and reformation of its very language. I doubt whether there was ever a time when a student just learnt a technique and having done so became a composer. Or, put a different way, that is a perfect description of what second-rate composers do. It is precisely because the history of Western music shows a continuous inter-action between theoretical reflection and the transformation of its technical means of production that, inescapably, the tendency of music to feed upon itself is of greater significance (and serious interest) than the 'interesting' lives of composers.

The contemporary composer resembles the Renaissance alchemist, from whom the notion of 'finding the key' is borrowed. If alchemists were primarily concerned with experiments on sub-stances, from early on they were aware of the history of these experiments as occult knowledge. We find Faust, at the beginning of his adventures, reading old books. The knowledge obtained from such books was essential to their proto-scientific work, but from the way it was couched it would appear that it constituted a spiritual metaphor as much as a purely technical protocol. The composer, as much as any alchemist, is concerned with magic, the compulsion to fly and to transcend himself. The preoccupation with materials and the techniques of their transformation establish the conditions for his enterprise. Nor must he consider the finding of the key as a purely external activity (and if he does, he is as fated to fail as was the alchemist). Fascination with materials and techniques is the composer's metaphor for spiritual enlightenment. Even if he doesn't 'make gold', he can comfort himself with the thought that if alchemy is evaluated as merely a chronicle of failure

and fraud, its methodology is regarded as having been crucial to
the emergence of modern science.

The Little Symphony, which I wrote in 1961 in memory of my
father, borrowed its somewhat inappropriate title (it is thirty
minutes long) and the variation form of its principal (second)
movement from Hanns Eisler. The first movement is an imitation
of the chorale theme from the 'Catacombs' of Musorgsky's *Pictures
at an Exhibition* (see Ex. 41). Variation form imposes a more
or less regular division of real time: more, because traditionally
variations are dances and consequently each contains an equal

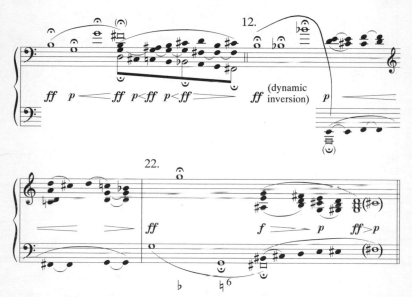

Ex. 41a: Musorgsky, *Pictures from an Exhibition*, 'Catacombs'

number of bars; less, because each may be performed at its own
appropriate tempo. It is also possible to retain the overall duration
of each variation while varying the tempo, thereby forcing an
alteration in the bar-count of each one. Furthermore, cadential
points can be emphasised, the more so by repeating each variation,
in that way stressing the dance-like periodicity of the continuity.

Alternatively groups of variations can be moulded together, avoiding the cadential points, and in that way creating the effect of through-composed forms. For the next twelve years I was pre-occupied in working out the implications of these different possibilities in a series of large-scale pieces called Symphonies and Concertos, as well as Variations.

Ex. 41b: Goehr, *Little Symphony*, 1st movement

The choice of 'Catacombs' as the theme for the Little Symphony variations was not coincidental, because it was the object of one of my father's most original analyses. He divided the brief compo-sition into three sections, each with a head-motif, related (though not literally) as original, inversion, summation. Each head motif 'cadences' modally on a pitch level which is retained as a pedal note, over or beneath which a quite unrelated chromatic sequence with a structure of fermatas and dynamic contrasts functions as a free consequent. My father considered that the forward-looking originality of 'Catacombs' and of other aspects of *Pictures* (looking forward particularly to Debussy's harmonic practice) could be explained as a semi-conscious harking back to a kind of real or imaginary modal practice which in Musorgsky's case had survived any academic training he received.

It was from this analysis that I later extrapolated a way of understanding Debussy's harmony, by combining the idea of pedal or note-in-common with Messiaen's more conventional vertical parsing of each individual chord without any concern for connections. By observing these 'pedals', or connections, I could throw light on the harmonic continuity of even some of the most baffling pieces, such as the *Etude par les sonorités opposées*. Debussy might well have applied some adaptation of an old commonly practised exercise, in which the students reharmonise a single pitch level (not pitch class!) or a small number of pitch levels, juxtaposing not only unrelated keys, but moving between tonal and pentatonic, modal or whole-tone derived chords.

At the same time, the method of what I then called active-pedal (active, because the pedal note determined the transposition of a sequence of chords derived from a series) was applied to pitch structure of combinatorial types. (This is explained in my 'Poetics' lecture, see p. 71ff.) This brought about far-reaching changes not only in compositional technique but in aesthetic attitudes, helping me achieve a greater fluency and resulting in a diminution of anxiety while composing. Anxiety may seem an odd term to apply to what is after all a self-selected activity. But in fact, serialism, while facilitating certain things, seemingly inhibits spontaneity. For example if one is content to follow Webern, in considering external form and texture as more or less identical with the compositional operations made, well and good. But if a gap emerges, if for instance one visualises a denser texture, a tutti in the orchestra or a more leisurely progress, one cannot achieve this by subsidiary extrapolation of material (as would be the case in tonal, but not modal, music) and one has to proceed by increasing the number of compositional operations. To do this requires the greatest and most concentrated effort and the writing tends to suffer by becoming stiff and stilted, leading in no time to a damming up of the natural flow of peripheral invention and the ability to perform 'musically' while composing. 'Perform' because the situation, fraught with anxiety, is exactly comparable to the muscular seizing up which affects pianists and string players who cultivate bad postures. The avoidance and elimination of such conditions has been a prime agent in my own technical development and a concern when teaching and advising others.

The use of variation form, composition as a sequence of bits of predetermined duration, can be meaningfully realised only in terms of cadential resolutions, though each individual variation requires a beginning gesture to establish metre, tempo and character. In historical terms this means Brahms, as opposed to Liszt, who with his beginning-oriented gestural moves prefigures the language of musical expressionism (cf. the discussion of this topic in the lectures on pp. 175ff. and 189ff.). It may be regarded, if not as a weakness, at least as a strong characteristic of Schoenberg's language, that he dealt with the cadential problem mainly by imitating gesturally its intended effect. In his music, at least after the decline of explicit tonality, this may be characterised by suddenness, even abruptness, and virtually never by a feeling of warmth in release and a relaxation of tension (a quality much in evidence, however, elsewhere in the music, to the extent that the analysis of his music in terms of warm and cold, soft and hard, would be a good way into it). My long pedal to some extent resolves the problem of cadence because, in the crudest sense, the longer a note is held or the more frequently it appears (and the frequent repetition of a pedal note is a standard way of creating internal polyphony in melodic structures), the more 'dominant' it will be. (This simple idea can be tested by looking back at the chorale theme of the Little Symphony, Ex. 41b.) Furthermore, it does not necessarily require a triadic language to make its effect (though one will make the function more immediately obvious). The expression of time divisions by cadences or harmonic caesuras is also a way of overcoming the fragmentary nature of much post-Webern music, which by the mid-1960s had deteriorated into fairly meaningless cliché and convention. The fragment, both small and large, has a long and glorious history (see Charles Rosen on Schumann in *The Romantic Generation*[11]), but it fulfils an expressive intention only when it is heard against an expectation of continuity. Fragmentation – the discontinuity or interruption of metre, tempo and gesture and the dislocation of smooth and congruent pitch progression – conveys a sense of strong expression or of special effect and ideally, as in Beethoven, should be understood as arising out of the conflicting implications of different materials pushed to their point of crisis, rather than merely as rhetoric device. Perhaps that is too puritanical. But whether it is or not, total and continuous fragmentation of texture and continuity rapidly leads to incomprehensibility. Rightly or wrongly I even tried to re-establish a sense of smooth background continuity rather than just accepting discontinuity as the external form of technical devices couched in terms of differentiation.

About this time I became very attracted by the idea of modelling. I was using variation technique as I had done in the Little Symphony, but by joining groups of variations together I was aspiring to the effect of through-composed forms. In these circumstances modelling implied choosing and carefully studying a movement – generally of a Classical or Romantic composer (in those years I variously used Mozart, Beethoven, Chopin, Schumann and Brahms as models) – and copying it rather as a painter might square off his canvas and deliberately reproduce an earlier painting. There is a great deal to be said for literally writing out (or making piano scores in the case of orchestral pieces), but that is not what I am suggesting I did. When modelling I was in my own terms and with my own means imitating the gestures of a musical idea, the nature of its continuation, the manner of its development and above all its exact proportions. This is not at all the same kind of thing as being influenced by remembered music, nor of course was the aim to create some kind of facsimile in modern dress. As I did it, following a model introduced an element of meditation on a previous work of art, and an interaction with it, into the act of composition. Although by doing this I became a student, compelling myself to complete a set task and keep going until the predetermined duration of a section had been filled out, it would have had no purpose had it not also provided an inspiration, setting off the invention of new material and new ways of doing things that I could not have conceived of in another way. As often as not the aim to re-create a model acted as no more than a point of departure, and after a little while the model was discarded. I imagine that modelling was an ideal way of combining the two parts of my life, teaching and composing; I can hardly ever give a lecture on a composition by a great master without wanting to do the same thing myself. As an attitude this may seem academic, but in fact I was brought up to believe that self-expression should not be cultivated for its own sake, that a composer should aspire to doing only what is necessary. If by chance one succeeds in doing something that is regarded by others as being original, so much the better, but one should not cultivate originality.

From the time when I was a student in the Messiaen class I was well aware of the basic objections felt by many musicians (including Messiaen), never mind the music-loving public, to the very idea of systematic, predetermined and what was called 'mathematical' composition implicit in Schoenbergian dodecaphony. There used to be a popular question (it is significant that it is asked no more) about the relationship of composer to predetermined material – a tone row, for instance. If you hear an E next and the row suggests an E♭, what do you do? Follow the row or your own instincts? The question, if asked at all, has considerable implications and they are more than can be categorised as a question of strictness vs freedom. If you follow the row when you don't want to, some doubt has to be thrown on the role of the free imagination; if on the other hand you decide to follow your own counsel, in a sense – perhaps a small sense – you will seem to yourself to be cheating, if not throwing a spanner into the works as you would be doing if, for instance, you decided to substitute a step of your own into the pattern of a formal dance involving others. There is some guidance to be obtained here from the past. Bach inevitably goes free when a contrapuntal combination such as a stretto involving fixed pitch levels doesn't work. But if the texture is that of canon, he has to stick with the notes or the basic idea will melt away. Such examples deal only with musical instants and an adjustment may even enrich the scheme by providing a temporarily new colouring, but that is not possible where larger formal issues are at stake, as they are in a twelve-note composition. Although no great damage is done when a composer transfers notes for the sake of euphony or some other passing consideration (and this is rarely observed by even the most astute listener), in practice such alterations throw up their own possible continuations out of the matrix-predicted structure. At such points the composer has to make an important existential decision; the more complex the predetermined conditions of a piece become, the less sense is there in preferring the E to the E♭ and the more tempted is he to put his faith in a probably mystic belief in the unity of the smallest part and the whole.

From time to time I had reverted to free composition to convince myself that though I spent most of my time composing, as it were, with a ruler, I could still draw freehand. I composed a suite entirely without rows for the Melos Ensemble to perform at Aldeburgh; from time to time I wrote songs and occasional pieces freely. Even the scherzo of the Little Symphony was freely invented and then coordinated into a serial structure which had to take note of the inevitable irregularities of pitch repetition that appear in spontaneous composition. The coordination of free ideas into serial structure can in fact be taken quite a lot further than has, as far as I am aware, been described elsewhere. It can be done by juxtaposing a freely invented fragment with inherent irregularities and a similar but regular hexachordal or other matrix structure. One then proceeds to treat the freely invented material *as if* it were the matrix structure or, putting it another way, the matrix structure 'carries' the free material through its own various transformations. In most of the pieces that I wrote between the Little Symphony and the Third String Quartet I tried, in a variety of differing ways, to bring the practice of free composition into some kind of dialectic relationship with more specifically constructivist methods. And for all these attempts to deal with what seemed to me a real limitation on expressivity I could not but feel that a particular way in which I composed would have to be discarded. I knew neither how this could be done nor what might replace it.

I had to write what I thought was to be an occasional piece – for the memorial service of a young woman. Her bereaved husband showed me a passage he had found in the writings of François de Sâles, where he speaks of a life as a full circle. If the life is, as it seems, prematurely cut off, it is to be regarded not as a part, but as a smaller but none the less complete circle. I must have been moved by this concept to visualise a circular composition, and taking the Gregorian funeral psalm (Psalm 4) I harmonised it modally and then step by step modulated it by transposing a short sequence within it, thereby introducing new pitch levels that did not appear in the original. For example, if the sequence D–E–F is transposed up a tone, it gives E–F♯–G. F becomes F♯, and when the two forms are combined, the result will be D–E–F♮–F♯–G. This is derived from a conventional late Renaissance modulatory technique discussed in E. Lowinsky's *Secret Chromatic Art in the Netherlands Motet*.[12] What I did that was new was to derive a melodic part from the transposition and combine it with the original, thereby moving from simple to complex, diatonic to chromatic and back to make a circular form. The composition for two solo voices (and/or two-part chorus), with organ for the harmonisations, and with the chant always repeated by a solo viola, was completed quickly. But having done it, I had a strong sensation that I had not finished with the material, or that the material had not finished with me, and I proceeded to write two further pieces with it: a *Fugue on the Notes of the Psalm* which was a complex permutational structure, and a *Romanza* for two solo violins and strings, which is in fact the psalm again but elaborately developed with proliferating ornament.

I realised now that there was no way back: the climate in which I worked had radically altered. At one stroke I had shed the technical paraphernalia of the last twenty years and, as I liked to say then, seemed to myself to stand entirely naked. The mood of that moment, with its evocation of greenness, is recalled in the last of the BBC talks on Modern Music and its Society, entitled 'Ripples in ever-spreading Circles' (see pp. 95–101).

The thought processes emerging from the Psalm 4 series perhaps differ substantially from what I did before only insofar as they are specifically based on what I would term common material. Much of my unease about my previous music – which I would sum up as consisting (in technical respects at least) of new means selected to produce new effects and relationships within a comparatively conventional musical paradigm in which melody, counterpoint, harmony and formal integration continue to exist – can be put down to the fact that too much was constructed that might formerly have been snatched from the air. I felt the need quite simply to make marks on the manuscript paper directly rather than to use only those that emerged from pre-ordered devices and were thus in the final analysis synthetic objects. For many years previously I had more or less satisfied myself with the observation that such synthetic, constructed themes, melodies and harmonies would, as often as not, invoke memories of other music in a way comparable to that described in Constable's remark (famously quoted by Francis Bacon), 'I never cease to wonder at the way paint on a canvas can come to resemble a horse.' By retaining and even emphasising these 'horses' I hoped to make my music multi-referential, to speak as it were through various voices. Incidentally this idea was specifically warned against, first by Schoenberg (albeit as a temporary prohibition), then by Boulez. The sudden emergence of, say, a conventional falling A minor arpeggio (I borrow the example from Stockhausen's early *Kontrapunkt*), reminding as it does of the 'Appassionata', will set up false expectations because they are then not realised in the continuation of the music. Turning this on its head, I would believe (and not only in serial music) that even if such an image as the opening of the 'Appassionata' is thrown up apparently accidentally (like Bacon's accidental drop of paint on the canvas[13]), it is not for nothing, and the composer must be humbly grateful for the sudden, unexpected image offered him by chance; he must not deny it – that way lies suicide – but retain it and allow it to have its proper place as a resonating and polyphonic element in his score, of course drawing appropriate inferences from it.

Yet in the end even such a many-voiced music would not mask

the fact that the original material of my music was not common. I say 'common', rather than 'natural' as did composers and theorists in the past, because 'natural' invokes a whole string of complicated and questionable ideas. A Dorian mode is no more 'natural' than a dodecaphonic series, but it does have a different genealogy. Whilst a dodecaphonic series results from a mental act, a Dorian mode is no more than a formalisation of continuous improvisational practice over a period of time and emerges rather than being thought up. All scales, modes (which are no more than collections of little conventional phrases) and even harmonic 'riffs' emerge from repetition, and it is these that I call common. While certain elements of late Romantic and atonal music have obtained similar status, especially in films and advertising, dodecaphony or serialism may, in ways I have described, invoke common material but never, as far as I can see, be it.

It might well have seemed to me, looking back at the experience of composing the Psalm 4 pieces and my feelings about the technical and spiritual climate preceding it, that I was doing no more than 'finding another key', devising yet another systematic solution in which (following the example for instance of Maxwell Davies) my earlier practice would be synthesised with common, not necessarily Gregorian, material. But in fact this did not happen.

After all that has been said before, it is tempting to draw a conclusion: a final return to old ways. But returning to the ways of the fathers, to key tonality – here now 'finding the key' in its usual musical meaning – is a deeply suspicious conception. I do not believe that any return is possible or desirable. The task of a composer was always and is now to make images, techniques and conventions his own. If this means either, as it did for Alban Berg, using the sound world of late Romantic tonal practice within a dodecaphonic practice or, as I am now doing, integrating short-term serial relationships into a figured-bass type structure, of themselves such practices are neither a return to anything nor an automatic innovation. They constitute no more nor less than the exercising of any composer's right to choose the means required for the realisation of his intention.

In 1975 I embarked on the study of figured bass using C. P. E. Bach's *Versuch* and shortly after the completion of the Psalm 4 pieces began experimenting with the old way of composing short two-voiced structures in a dissonant relationship to each other, establishing and resolving tension by traditional means. Such a structure of two voices could then be 'figured' in varied ways, producing different harmonisations and colours. The actual notes or phrases that formed my point of departure were not much different in style from those that I would have invented for a serial composition; what was new for me was the immediate imagining of musical ideas in two voices. More significant still was the new relationship of the first idea to its continuation. It might be possible to consider a serial matrix structure as already embodying the delineaments of a whole composition; but that would be a some-what contrived, theoretical notion. In practice I would proceed by adding phrase to phrase to build up a musical paragraph. But from the outset, my figured-bass model is a whole piece, with a beginning, embryo middle and close. It cannot be added to; it is only possible to lengthen its duration by prolonging the distance between its original notes. Such a procedure brings great advantages. First and foremost it means that, like a painter or a writer, a composer is able to realise a first conception of a piece on the spot, thereby retaining its urgency and its particular flavour and mood. Furthermore the removal of the need to continue a structure again reduces a composer's anxiety. I work with greater freedom and imagination when I already know what the end will be. Compositional elaboration, which obviously is the larger part of the writing of any piece in any way, is not to be understood as a way of delaying the arrival of that end, but the fact that it is always there helps considerably in retaining a composition's sense of its own urgency.

That is as far as I intend to go here. Using the first person singular to avoid any impression of generalisation, I have tried to illuminate two related facts of compositional belief and experience. The first, which is embodied in the title of this study and of the whole collection, might almost be considered to be a modern myth:

it is the belief that an artistic life can be viewed as a progress towards a goal – a kind of search for the key that will open the door ... The door to what? The door to everlasting life, eternal youth, the creation of unremitting beauty? This is of course a myth in as much as it can never be realised. The creation of beauty relies on a happy and spontaneous coming together of many things at any time and in any circumstances. There will always be another shift of thought, a new insight or a new mood or emphasis; the concept of a key remains elusive or even illusory. Secondly, the reality of music, whether music as it is made, music as it is performed or music as it is perceived, lies in its external form, in the sensuality of sound. In no way can a descriptive or analytical account of the processes of composing of itself convey the nature and quality of actual music when unyoked from a sensuous perception of it. But conversely no sensuous perception of it can be reliably complete when unaccompanied by an understanding of the way it is made. Perhaps this flies in the face of everyday musical experience and may also be judged to be some sort of justificatory myth. But if the way music is made is not of itself music, neither is music merely the sum of its sounds. The complete grasp of music's nature is neither more nor less than the perception of the unity of internal processes and external form.

(1997)

1. Bradshaw was a timetable of all trains running in the British Isles. Like most of the trains it described, it has disappeared.

2. [Henry Ernest Geehl, b. London, 28 September 1881; d. Beaconsfield, 14 January 1961; English composer, conductor and pianist. Taught at Trinity College of Music, London, from 1918, and was a music editor for Ashdown and Enoch.]

3. [See AG's descriptions of Hall on pp. 28ff.]

4. For example, his *Alma Redemptoris mater* (1957).

5. (Boulez, looking at and criticising one of my early pieces, said: 'You can't have *this* harmony and *this* orchestration in the same piece as you have just had *that* one!')

6. Schoenberg, *Style and Idea*, ed. L. Stein, trans. Leo Black (London: Williams and Norgate, 1975).

7. Heinrich Schenker, *Ein Beitrag zur Ornamentik als Einführung zu Ph. E. Bachs Klavierwerke* (Vienna, 1904, rev. 1908; repr. 1954). [Translated into English in *Music Forum* IV (1976), pp. 1–140.]

8. *Die Entstehung des Doktor Faustus* (Amsterdam: Bermann-Fischer, 1949), trans. as *The Story of a Novel: The Genesis of* Doctor Faustus, by Richard and Clara Winston (New York: Alfred A. Knopf, 1961), pp. 103–4 (in the translation).

9. Luciano Berio, *Two Interviews*, trans. David Osmond Smith (New York and London: Boyars, 1985).

10. *Bachs Chorfuge, ein Betrag zur Kompositionstechnik Bachs* (Leipzig: Breitkopf und Härtel, 1950).

11. Charles Rosen, *The Romantic Generation* (London: HarperCollins, 1996), pp. 48–115.

12. Edward Lowinsky, *Secret Chromatic Art in the Netherlands Motet*, Columbia University Studies in Musicology 6 (New York: Columbia University Press, 1946; repr. 1967).

13. [See the discussion of the importance of accidents in painting in David Sylvester, *Interviews with Francis Bacon: 1962–1979* (London: Thames and Hudson, 1980), pp. 16–18.]

Appendix

The Times, Saturday, 28 October 1961

A Dying Tradition?

The English choral tradition, still firmly ensconced and active, forming the tastes of a very large number of English music lovers, has always been unique. Massive choirs startled and moved Haydn in the London of the 1790s, and the Continental giants of the nineteenth century whose music found favour with the English public – Mendelssohn, Dvořák and Gounod – found them not only inescapable but valuable. In many respects, and for music of a certain kind, the enormous English-style choir is a magnificent instrument. Furthermore, it is composed of amateurs whose devotion to their art is often the source of the only musical activity in their part of the country; it is the choir upon which musical ambitions in many areas are centred.

For this reason the effect of *Sutter's Gold*, Mr Alexander Goehr's new cantata for the recent Leeds Festival, is somewhat disturbing. Not only, the critics have informed us, was the choir so ill at ease with a work far from radical by contemporary European standards as to present the audience with a feeling of their struggle with an unfamiliar idiom, but the critics, aware of the direction in which music is moving, have been prompted to question the validity in our present circumstances of a splendid Leeds tradition. For a Leeds Triennial Festival a large-scale choral and orchestral work is commissioned. Thirty years ago *Belshazzar's Feast* appeared with a violence that disturbed conservatives who could hardly hear, beneath its earthquake sonorities, the controlling power of the long tradition in which Sir William Walton was nurtured. In

1958 Mr Peter Racine Fricker's *A Vision of Judgment* came from a composer whom we knew only as a radical composer of orchestral and chamber works. To produce a work by Mr Goehr, a composer of intricate works in the contemporary idiom whose earlier and impressive choral work, *The Deluge*, is on a chamber-music scale, keeps the commission in step with precedents.

Have we reached the end of this tradition? Is it no longer possible, through the evolution of style and compositional technique, for a young, forward-looking composer to write for a large amateur choir in a style that expands the singers' technique and broadens their musical outlook while following his own style and musical preoccupations? Such pessimistic ideas have risen from the gap between *Sutter's Gold* and its performers. Even a splendidly liberal custom may reach the end of its utility. But the prospect of such events as future Leeds festivals devoting themselves exclusively to the music of the past or to new works which are consciously 'traditional' or conservative in style is disheartening, and we shall await the next commission with some anxiety. The gulf between the progressive composer and adventurous amateur performers must be regarded as a challenge.

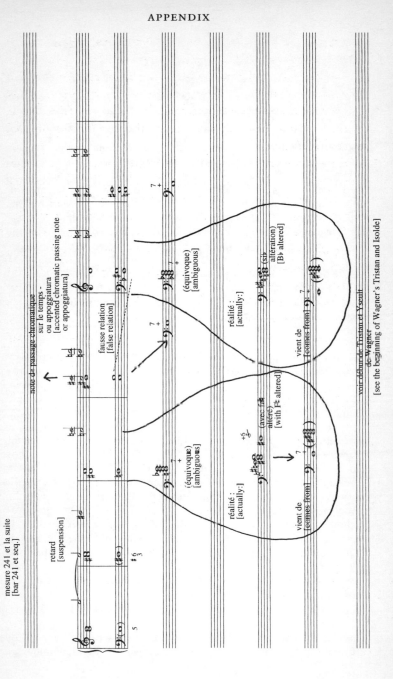

Transcription of Fig. 1, Messiaen's analysis of Mozart Symphony No 41 K551 (translation added by AG)

307

Sources

'A Letter to Pierre Boulez': lecture given on the South Bank, London, as part of the concert series 'Brave New Worlds', 1987

'Is There Only One Way?': *The Score*, No. 26 (January 1960), pp. 63–5

'Manchester Years': unpublished typescript given as a lecture on the occasion of the awarding of an honorary doctorate at Manchester University, 1990

'The Messiaen Class': lecture given at Cambridge, 1988

'Poetics of my Music': an Inaugural Lecture delivered at the University of Leeds on 9 October 1972 [AG was appointed to the Chair of Music there in 1971]; first printed in the *University of Leeds Review*, Vol. 16, No. 2 (1973), pp. 170–85

'Modern Music and its Society': four talks, BBC Radio 3 (December 1979) [editing here has been kept to a minimum, in order to preserve the flavour of the original]

'Arnold Schoenberg's Development towards the Twelve-Tone System': in *European Composers of the Twentieth Century*, ed. Howard Hartog (Harmondsworth: Penguin, 1957), pp. 88–106

'Schoenberg and Karl Kraus: The Idea behind the Music': given first as a lecture at the University of Southampton in 1983, and subsequently published in *Music Analysis*, Vol. 4, Nos 1–2 (March–July 1985), pp. 59–71

'Musical Ideas and Ideas about Music': lecture given in celebration of Birkbeck College's 153rd anniversary, 1976, and subsequently published in *Foundation Orations* (London: Birkbeck College, 1978)

'Traditional Art and Modern Music': a paper delivered first at the University of Hong Kong in 1985 and later at the Cambridge University Music Analysis Conference in 1986

'Brahms's *Aktualität*': a revised version of 'A Sense of Proportion', given first in Cambridge in 1983, and subsequently published in *The Third Dimension: Voices from Radio 3*, ed. Philip French (London: Stourton Press, 1983), pp. 25–31 (a shorter version of the latter was published as 'Brahms the Progressive?', *The Listener*, 7 July 1983, pp. 32–3)

'Franz Liszt': given at Cambridge in 1984

'Some Thoughts about Stravinsky': *Stravinsky Festival*, Part II Brochure (London, 1981)

'Music as Communication': a lecture in the fourth series of Darwin College [Cambridge] Lectures, given in 1989 under the title 'Communication'

and first published in *Ways of Communicating*, ed. D. H. Mellor (Cambridge: CUP, 1990), pp. 125–42
'The Composer and his Idea of Theory: A Dialogue': first published in *Music Analysis*, Vol. 11, Nos 2–3 (July–October 1992), pp. 143–75

Index

Note: Works are indexed under the name of their composer/creator.
AG = Alexander Goehr.

Abdy Williams, C. F., 114
acciaccatura technique, 40n.7
Adorno, Theodor, 110, 175, 212
  Philosophy of New Music, 212
affect(s), musical, 216–20
African music, 147, 161, 221–2
Albeniz, Isaac, 32
  Iberia, 40n.7
Aldeburgh, 297
Altenberg, Peter, 131, 138
Amy, Gilbert, 45
Antheil, George, 87
Aprahamian, Felix, 42
Arab music, 25n.14
architecture, 98
Aristotle, 221
Arnold, Malcolm, 32
Arom, Simha, 161
Attwood, Thomas, 158
avant-garde music, 3–6, 8, 9, 17–20,
    143, 286, 288
  and communication, 231–4
  in Manchester, 38, 39

Babbitt, Milton, 12, 76n.7, 240, 250,
    263, 281
Bach, C. P. E., 103, 301
  *Treatise on the True Art of Playing
    the Clavier*, 145
Bach, David, 135
Bach, J. S., 18, 32, 111, 187, 283, 296
  AG and, 7, 265, 269–70, 281, 289
  works
    Art of Fugue, 22
    Chaconne, 187
    Goldberg Variations, 37–8

Hammerklavier Sonata, 111
Italian Concerto, 281
Mass in B minor, 170, 283
  The Musical Offering, 37, 111
  St John Passion, 230, 231
  The Well-Tempered Clavier, 22
Bachelard, Gaston, 51
background music, 145
  Muzak, 151–2, 153
Bacon, Francis, 74, 299
Baines, William, 40n.5
Balmont, Constantin, 87
Bangkok, 158
Baroque music, 144
Barrault-Renaud Company, 2
Bartók, Béla, 4, 86, 265, 274, 284
  Mikrokosmos, 274
  Suite Op. 14, 265
Baudelaire, Charles Pierre, 219
Bauhaus, 17
Bax, Arnold, 32
BBC, 42, 150, 281
Beaubourg, 80
Beethoven, Ludwig van, 63, 107, 110,
    264, 269–70, 283, 295
  Appassionata Sonata, 299
  Missa solemnis, 171, 176
  Piano Sonata Op. 31, 264
  Piano Sonata Op. 90, 257
  Piano Sonata Op. 111, 197–8, 224
  String Quartet Op. 59
    ('Razumovsky'), 227–8
  String Quartet Op. 135, 111
  Symphony No. 3 (*Eroica*), 170, 226
  Symphony No. 4, 204
  Symphony No. 5, 47–8

Benjamin, Walter, 131, 154, 260, 270
Berg, Alban, 10, 21, 53, 86, 114, 300
    and Kraus, 131, 132
    and Puccini, 254
    works
        Clarinet Pieces Op. 5, 36, 116
        early songs, 209
        Lulu, 209
        Violin Concerto, 55
        Wozzeck, 209, 285
Berio, Luciano, 154, 286, 288
    Sinfonia, 154
Berkeley, Lennox, 28, 32
Berlin, Isaiah, 259, 260, 265
    The Crooked Timber of Humanity,
        265
    'The Naïveté of Verdi', 259
Berlioz, Hector, 180
biography (of composers), 289–90
Birtwistle, Harrison, 31, 35–6, 37, 38,
        94, 261, 268
    Entr'actes and Sappho Fragments,
        261
    The World is Discovered, 261
Blacher, Boris, 34
Bliss, Arthur, 32
bloc sonore, 10–15, 70–1, 280, 281
Blok, Alexander, 87
Blue Rider almanac, 79, 86
Boehmer, Konrad, 153
Boulanger, Nadia, 31
Boulez, Pierre, 91, 92, 93–4, 299
    and AG, 1, 2, 3, 24n.9, 262, 263,
        264, 281, 285–6, 302n.5
    and *bloc sonore*, 10–15, 70–1
    and Debussy, 17
    and Eisler, 28/
    and IRCAM, 6, 24n.9
    Marigny concerts, 2, 3, 49
    and Messiaen, 49, 53, 54
    on 'pauvre Berg', 254
    and pitch distortion, 72–3
    and serialism, 6, 23
    works
        Doubles, 11–12
        Improvisations sur Mallarmé, 23

Livre pour quatuor, 1
Le Marteau sans maître, 2, 7,
    11–12, 23, 25n.15, 62, 93–4
Piano Sonata No. 1, 11
Piano Sonata No. 2, 11, 25n.14,
    37, 44, 93–4
Piano Sonata No. 3, 11, 14
Pli selon pli, 11–12, 14, 93–4
Répons, 233
Structures I, 11–12, 22
Structures II, 11–12
Bradshaw, 274
Brahms, Johannes, 102, 103–4, 110,
        114, 170, 175–87, 268
    AG and, 269–70, 295
    early works of, 209
    Liszt and, 179–80, 190–1, 194,
        202–3, 294
    modern sensibility of, 186–7
    operatic projects of, 181
    relevance of, 175–6, 187
    Schoenberg and, 107, 178, 181–5
    Schumann and, 186, 187, 190–1
    Wagner and, 180–1
    works
        Double Concerto, 62–3
        Four Serious Songs, 183–5, 203
        Handel Variations, 180
        'Meerfahrt', 182
        Piano Concerto No. 2, 283
        Symphony No. 4, 181
        'Verrat', 183
Brecht, Bertolt, 9, 131
Brelet, Gisèle, 212
Brendel, Alfred, 189
British Music Society, 40n.5
Britten, Benjamin, 7, 8, 15, 25n.14, 32,
        153
    and AG, 266, 287
    and biography, 289–90
    'effects' of, 254
    as naive and sentimental artist, 259
    works
        *Serenade for Tenor, Horn and
            Strings*, 40n.1
        Spring Symphony, 16

Brown, Earle, 33
Busoni, Ferruccio, 30, 194–5
Bussler, 114
Byrd, William, 39, 170

Cage, John, 54, 87, 88–9, 149, 233,
    266–7
Calderón de la Barca: *The Noisy Secret*,
    181
Canetti, Elias, 131, 132
    Die Fackel im Ohr, 131
Cardew, Cornelius, 17, 269
Carewe, John, 2, 17, 48
Carpenter, Patricia, 129
Carter, Elliott, 33–4, 94
Catholic Church, 143–4
Catullus, 258
Cendrars, Blaise: *L'or*, 3
Cézanne, Paul, 211
China, 25n.14
Chopin, Fryderyk, 180, 187, 269–70,
    295
    Liszt and, 179, 194, 195
Classical music, 18, 61, 117
    escape from, 283, 285
    masterpieces of, 170–3
    popularity of, 143, 155
closure, 240, 242, 252–4
collage, 154–5
communication, 214–35
    and communion, 215, 220–3
    with listener, 225–30
concert(s), 143, 144
    pop, 152–3
Cone, Edward T., 208
Conservatoire, Paris, 1
    Messiaen class, 1, 2–3, 42, 44–56
Constable, John, 74, 299
contemporary music, 77–8
Cooke, Deryck: *The Language of
    Music*, 146
Copland, Aaron, 153, 208
Corelli, Arcangelo, 240, 242
Council of Trent, 143–4
counterpoint, 109–12, 121, 128
Couperin, François, 40n.7

Cowell, Henry, 88–9
Craft, Robert, 208
    *Stravinsky in Pictures and
    Documents*, 210
Crumpsall General Hospital, 28, 280

Dada, 8
Daily Mail, 38
Dallapiccola, Luigi, 10, 12, 208,
    260–1, 284
    Five Sappho Fragments, 261
    6 Songs of Alcaeus, 261
Darmstadt Summer School, 2, 4–5, 7,
    39, 45, 76n.7, 281, 283, 284,
    285–6
Dartington Hall, 276
Debussy, Claude, 18, 21, 103, 106–7,
    157
    AG and, 242, 262, 263–4, 269–70,
    285, 293
    Liszt and, 194–5
    Messiaen and, 11, 40n.7, 48–9, 51,
    56n.5
    works
        Etude par les sonorités opposées,
        293
        Jeux, 17, 51
        La mer, 56n.5, 62
        Pelléas et Mélisande, 48–9, 51
        Prélude l'après-midi d'un faune,
        48, 51
        Préludes, 272
Dehmel, Richard, 126
Delius, Frederick, 32
Dent, Edward, 77
Desprès, Josquin, 5, 170
Dessau, Paul, 288
Deutsch, Max, 2–3, 258, 286
de Wet, Louis, 8
Dieren, Bernard van, 30
d'Indy, Vincent, 103
dodecaphony *see* twelve-tone technique
Dorati, Antal, 282
Dow, John, 37, 38
Dukas, Paul, 55, 103
Dupré, Marcel: *Traité d'orgue*, 55

Ehrenzweig, Anton, 62, 270
The Psychoanalysis of Artistic Vision and Hearing, 270
Eimert, Herbert, 4, 20
Eisenstein, Sergei, 9
Battleship Potemkin, 19
Eisler, Hanns, 8, 9, 15, 20, 153–4, 258, 286–8, 291
electronic music, 72–3, 84, 149
collage, 154–5
pop music, 152–3
Elgar, Edward, 275
Elinson, Iso, 28
Eliot, T. S., 160, 207, 258
Ellis, David, 31
Emmanuel, Maurice, 55
Engel, Carl, 127
enjoyment of music, 273
Epstein, David, 129
eroticism, 137–8
excellence, 159–61, 164–5, 168, 169–74
Expressionism, 115, 135, 137–8, 139

Fackel, Die, 63–4, 131, 132
Falla, Manuel de, 208
Faust, 290
film music, 282, 287
Finzi, Gerald, 32
First World War, 78, 89–90, 138
Kraus and, 131, 132, 133–4, 138
Flaubert, Gustave: and models, 237–8
fragmentation, 294–5
Freud, Sigmund, 115, 131
Fricker, Peter Racine: *Vision of Judgment*, 16
Futurism, 25n.15, 87–8
Fux, Johann Joseph, 102

Gagaku, 147, 221
Geehl, Henry, 275–6
genius *see* mastery
George, Stefan, 87, 132, 138
Buch der hängenden Gärten, 137
German music, 102–4
counterpoint in, 110

mastery in, 171, 193
modern composers, 154
Neudeutsche Schule, 178, 179–80
rhythm in, 112–13
Schoenberg and, 104–5
see also individual composers
Gershwin, George, 33
Gervais, Françoise, 51
Gestalten, 128, 130
Ghyka, Matila C., 52
Essai sur le rythme, 113
Glock, William, 38
Goehr, Alexander
in Bangkok, 158
childhood and early life, 258, 266, 272–6
and closure, 240, 242, 252–4
at Darmstadt, 2, 4–5, 7, 45, 284, 285–6
early compositions, 258, 278–81
first teachers, 275–6
in Manchester, 10, 27–40, 42, 276–81
in Messiaen class, 2–3, 42, 44–56, 284–6, 296
and models, 262–5, 269–70, 274, 295–6
and number schemes, 274–5
Oxford scholarship, 28, 30
in Paris, 1, 2–3, 8, 9, 286–7, 288
political views, 27–9, 33, 280
and recomposition, 255–8
and synthesis, 238–48, 281
at Tanglewood, 152
and theory, 236–71
in Tokyo, 221
and twelve-tone technique, 245–50, 278–9, 280–1, 296–7, 300
working methods, 265–7, 279–80, 282, 284, 301
works
Arden Must Die, 261
Behold the Sun, 244, 261
Capriccio for piano, 289
Cello Sonata, 261

The Death of Moses, 238, 241,
243, 244, 252, 254–5, 261
The Deluge, 3, 15, 261, 289
Eve Dreams in Paradise, 261
Fantasia Op. 4, 2, 280
Fantasias for Clarinet and Piano
Op. 3, 38
Fugue on Psalm IV, 298–9, 300
Little Symphony, 3, 291–2, 294,
297
Metamorphosis/Dance, 261
Piano Sonata Op. 2, 2, 38, 265,
278–9, 280, 281
Piano Trio Op. 20, 245–51
Psalm IV, 261, 298–9, 300
Romanza on Psalm IV, 298–9,
300
Sing Ariel, 266
Sonata for Cello and Piano Op.
45, 238
Songs of Babel, 38
String Quartet No. 1, 1, 3, 288–9
String Quartet No. 2, 69
String Quartet No. 3, 256, 257
Suite Op. 11, 3, 266
Sutter's Gold, 3, 15–16
Violin Concerto, 69, 282
Goehr, Walter, 3, 25n.14, 28, 42, 48,
258, 266, 272–3, 274, 286
influence on AG of, 281–4
models for, 274
music analysis by, 102–23, 282–4,
292–3
Goethe, Johann Wolfgang von: 'Wer
nie sein Brot mit Tränen ass', 201
Goldsmith's College, London, 236
Gombrich, Ernst, 62
Gounod, Charles, 44
Gozzi, *King Stag*, 181
'great men' *see* mastery
Greek music, 46, 53
Gregorian chant, 7, 46, 113, 163–5,
168, 269–70, 298, 300
Grundgestalt, 128, 129–30

Hába, Alois, 33, 56n.6

Hall, Richard, 25n.118, 28–30, 31, 32,
33, 34, 35, 42, 247, 270, 276–8,
279, 281–2
and British Music Society, 40n.5
compositions of, 32–3, 38, 276–7
Hallé Orchestra, 32, 37
Handel, George Frideric, 187
harmony
AG and, 242, 252
Debussy and, 293
electronic music and, 149
interpersonal, 223
Schoenberg and, 105–9, 112, 115,
121, 122, 135–6
Stravinsky and, 209–12
twelve-tone technique and, 70
Hauer, Josef Matthias, 10, 35, 70, 135
Haydn, Franz Joseph, 113–14, 187
The Creation, 147
Nelson Mass, 171
The Seasons, 147
string quartets, 170
Heaton-Smith, Roy, 31–2
Hebbel, 'Blume und Duft', 200
Heine, Heinrich: 'Meerfahrt', 182
Heinichen, Johann David, 254
Henry Watson Library, 30
Herwegh, Georg: 'Ich möchte hingehn',
202–3
Hindemith, Paul, 4, 32–3, 56n.5, 109
A Composer's World (book), 32
Plöner Musiktag, 276
String Quartet No. 3, 33
String Quartet No. 4, 33
Hindu music, 46, 53
Hollander, John, 238
Holloway, Robin, 268
Honegger, Arthur: *Pacific*, 231, 49
Hopkins, Gerard Manley, 185
Howarth, Gary (Elgar), 37, 38
Huddersfield College of Music, 40n.5
Hull, Arthur Eaglefield, 40n.5

ideology, 14, 94–5, 97–8
International Society for

Contemporary Music (ISCM), 77–8, 79
IRCAM, 6, 24n.9, 80
Isaac, Heinrich, 5
Isaacs, Leonard, 42
Israel, 27
Ives, Charles, 86, 87, 88–9

Janáček, Leos, 20, 267, 287
Jankélévitch, Vladimir, 51
Japan, 147, 221
Jeanne Bretey Composition Scholarship, 30
Joachim, Joseph, 180, 186–7
Jolivet, André, 47
Jones, Daniel, 41n.12
Josquin Des Près, 5, 170
Joyce, James, 18, 113
    Finnegans Wake, 120
    Ulysses, 9

Kafka, Franz, 157, 221, 260
    Notebooks, 221
Kandinsky, Wassily, 18, 79, 138, 196
Kant, Immanuel, 191–2, 193
    The Critique of Judgment, 191–2
Kaper, Bronislaw, 255
Keller, Hans, 230, 238–40, 258–9, 264
Kerman, Joseph: Musicology, 237
Kermode, Frank, 266
Kierkegaard, Soren, 139
King's College, London, 236
Klammer, Armin, 24n.12
Klee, Paul, 18
    Pedagogical Sketchbooks, 99
Klein, Yves, 91
Kokoschka, Oskar, 131, 137
Kolisch, Rudolf, 132
Kraus, Karl, 63–4, 131–5, 136–7, 139, 160, 177, 219
    and Expressionism, 137–8
    and Schoenberg, 131, 134, 135–40, 200
    works
        Die letzten Tage der Menschheit, 131

'Rückkehr in die Zeit', 140
    Sprüche und Widersprüche, 132–3
Krenek, Ernst, 10, 35, 70, 247
    and Kraus, 134, 135

Labour Party, 8–9
language, 130, 133–5
    music and, 215, 216
Le Corbusier, 98, 207
Leeds Festival Chorus, 26n.23
Leeds Parish Church, 276
Leeds Triennial Festival, 15–16
Leibnitz, Gottfried Wilhelm, 147
Leibowitz, René, 3, 7, 12, 286
Lemcke, Karl: 'Verrat', 183
Liegler, Leopold, 133
Ligeti, György, 94
Linton (Lichtenthal), Herbert, 275
listeners/listening, 217–20
    avant-garde music and, 231–4
    communication with, 225–30
    understanding and, 272–3
Liszt, Franz, 160, 178–80, 189–205, 294
    Brahms and, 179–80
    charges of incompetence against, 189–91, 194–5, 201, 204
    Chopin and, 179, 194, 195
    Schoenberg and, 178, 194–5, 199–200, 201
    Schumann and, 180, 190, 194, 202
    works
        Apparitions, 190
        'Blume und Duft', 200–1
        Christus, 180
        Dante Sonata, 180
        Funérailles, 81–2, 196–7, 203
        'Ich möchte hingehn', 202–3
        Sonata in B minor, 180, 190, 197
        Trauergondel, 204–5
        'Wer nie sein Brot mit Tränen ass', 201
Liverpool Philharmonic Orchestra, 26n.23
Lloyd, A. L., 281
Lochheimer Liederbuch, 113

Logue, Christopher, 3
Lomax, Alan, 281
London Symphony Orchestra, 42
Loos, Adolf, 131, 138
Loriod, Yvonne, 42, 44
Lowell, Robert, 219
Lowinsky, E.: *Secret Chromatic Art in the Netherlands Motet*, 298
Luther, Martin, 113
Lutyens, Elizabeth, 38

Machaut, Guillaume de, 5, 17
  Hoquetus David, 166, 167–8
Maderna, Bruno, 286
Mahler, Gustav, 82, 86, 103, 106, 110, 112, 115, 176
  AG and, 262, 263–4, 265
  works
    Symphony No. 7, 106
    Symphony No. 8, 176
    Symphony No. 9, 106, 112
    Symphony No. 10, 112
Maine, Sir Basil, 235n.1
Malevitch, Kasimir, 22
Mallarmé, Stéphane, 13–14, 18, 19, 92
Manchester, 10
  AG in, 10, 27–40, 42, 276–81
Manchester Spanish, 32
Mann, Thomas, 177
  The Genesis of Dr Faustus, 287
Manzoni, Alessandro, 179
Marc, Franz, 79
Marigny Theatre, 49
Martenot, Maurice, 42
Marxism, 8, 14, 27–8, 153, 287
mastery, 159–61, 167, 169–74, 192–4, 195–6
  child-prodigies and, 208
  masterpieces, 159–60, 170–3, 192
Mattheson, Johann, 254
  Der vollkommene Capellmeister, 237, 265
Maxwell Davies, Peter, 30–1, 36–7, 38, 39, 261, 268, 280, 300
  trumpet sonata, 37, 38
Medieval music, 5, 10, 39, 113, 170

melody, 7–8, 61–4, 66
  Schoenberg and, 66, 114–15
  Stravinsky and, 210–12
Melos Ensemble, 297
Mendelssohn, Felix, 110
Messiaen, Olivier, 3, 18, 35, 40n.7, 72, 88–9, 278, 279
  and clapping game, 42, 44, 220–1
  Conservatoire class, 1, 2–3, 42, 44–56, 284–6, 296
  and Debussy, 40n.7, 48–9, 51, 56n.5, 262, 264
  and duration, 52–3
  on listening, 286
  and nature, 49–51
  and *resonance*, 11
  and rhythm, 112
  and Stravinsky, 208, 224
  Technique de mon langage musicale, 42
  and Varèse, 88
  works
    Ascension, 42
    Catalogue d'oiseaux, 40n.7
    Chronochromie, 51, 53
    Harawi, 25n.15
    Livre d'orgue, 49, 53
    Mode de valeurs et des intensités, 53
    Oiseaux exotiques, 2, 49–50
    Préludes, 42
    Quatre études de rythme, 44, 49
    Quatuor pour le fin du temps, 281
    Turangalîla-Symphonie, 42, 49, 220
    Vingt regards, 40n.7, 42
    Visions de l'Amen, 42
Meyer, Leonard B., 230
microstructures, 5
Milhaud, Darius, 4
Miller, Glenn, 33
Miller, Henry: *The Air-Conditioned Nightmare*, 88
Mitropoulos, Dimitri, 283
models, 262–5, 269–70, 274, 295–6
modern music, 77–101

public response to, 78, 96–7, 144, 232
social context of, 78–80, 89–91, 94–101
state funding of, 80, 96–7
terminology of, 77–8
see also avant-garde music
Moeran, E. J., 32
Mondrian, Piet, 18, 22
Monteverdi, Claudio, 7, 170, 189, 195, 269–70, 283
Orfeo, 165, 167, 168
Vespers, 25n.14, 40n.1, 283
moral welfare, 176–7
Morley College, 40n.1
Morris, William, 8–9
Morton, Lawrence, 208
Mossolov, Alexander: *The Iron Foundry*, 87
Mozart, Wolfgang Amadeus, 105, 113–14, 208, 283, 295
Attwood and, 158
Wagner and, 178, 205n.13
works
Jupiter Symphony, 46, 170, 288
Symphony in G minor, 69, 226
'Music While You Work', 150
musical affect(s), 216–20
musical idea(s), 59–76, 142, 144, 145–50, 160
ethical imperative and, 134, 139, 160
genius and, 196
Muzak and, 152
Schoenberg and, 64, 65–6, 70, 124–30, 131, 135–6, 138–40, 148–9, 160, 179
Musorgsky, Modest, 49, 189, 195, 267
Pictures at an Exhibition, 291, 292–3
Muzak, 151–2, 153

naive and sentimental artists, 258–61
Nancarrow, Conlon, 33
Nestroy, Johann Nepomuck, 132
Neudeutsche Schule, 178, 179–80

Neumann, Werner, 289
New Music Manchester, 38
Nietzsche, Friedrich Wilhelm, 216, 258, 260
Noh, 251
Nono, Luigi, 2, 9, 91–2, 208, 283, 285, 286
Northern School of Music, 35
notations, 161–3
Nottebohm, Gustav, 187
Novalis, 134

Ockeghem, Johannes, 5, 17
Offenbach, Jacques, 132
Ogdon, John, 30–1, 37, 38
oriental music, 39, 147, 158
Oxford University, 28, 30

Palestrina, Giovanni Pierluigi da, 102, 144
Papua New Guinea, 44
Paris, 1, 2–3, 8, 9
Conservatoire, 1, 2–3, 42, 44–56
1889 World Exhibition, 103, 157
patronage, 143–4, 150
Pease, James, 26n.23
pentatonic music, 29–30, 46
performance, 5–6
difficulty of, 223–5
Perle, George, 10, 71
Petri, Egon, 30
Picasso, Pablo, 157, 207
Pierce, Lucy, 37–8
Pisk, Paul A., 132
Pitfield, Thomas, 31
Planned Music Ltd, 151
Plato, 221
pop music, 152–3, 154
art music and, 154–5
popularity: of music, 142–5, 152–5
Pousseur, Henri, 7
Prinzhorn, Edgar, 127
Pritchard, John, 26n.23
Proctor-Gregg, Humphrey, 32, 37, 39
Prokofiev, Sergey, 173
Le pas d'acier, 87

Piano Sonata No. 7, 278
Puccini, Giacomo, 254
Purcell, Henry, 7, 25n.14
  Fantasias, 283
Pye, James, 32

Rameau, Jean-Philippe, 103, 230
Ravel, Maurice, 11, 40n.7, 285
  Gaspard de la nuit, 52
  Ma mère l'oye, 209–10
  Valses Nobles et Sentimentales, 80,
    81
Rawsthorne, Alan, 32
recompositions, 255–8
Reger, Max, 103, 106, 110, 192
religious music, 176
Renaissance music, 5, 10
repertoire, 169
reproduction of music, 142–3, 144–5
  Muzak, 151–2, 153
  pop music, 152–3
rhetoric, 253–4
rhythm
  German music and, 112–13
  Schoenberg and, 109, 112–14,
    121–2
rhythmic cell, concept of, 53
Riehe, Die, 4
ritornello, 61
Romantic art, 137–8
Romantic music, 5, 18, 66, 110, 265,
  283, 285
  popularity of, 144, 155
Rosen, Charles, 189
  The Romantic Generation, 294
Rossini, Gioachino Antonio, 148
Rousseau, Jean-Jacques, 230
Royal Festival Hall, 42, 144
Royal Manchester College of Music,
  28, 30, 31, 35–6, 37–9, 276–81
Ruggles, Carl, 86, 88–9
Russell, Bertrand, 146
Russian Revolution, 87, 211
Russolo, Luigi, 87–8
Ryle, Gilbert, 162–3

Sabaniev, L., 86
Sâles, François de, 298
Scarlatti, Domenico, 40n.7, 187
Schenker, Heinrich, 102–3, 171–3,
  180, 192–4, 204, 240, 242, 252,
  283
  Der freie Satz, 172
  Das Meisterwerk in der Musik, 171
Scherchen, Hermann, 41n.12, 78
Schiller, Johann Christoph Friedrich
  von, 180, 258–61
Schillinger, Joseph, 33–4, 108
  Strata Harmony, 33–4
Schillinger Method of Musical
  Composition, 33
Schlegel, Friedrich, 134
Schoenberg, Arnold, 15, 18, 20, 21–2,
  78, 79, 86, 88–9, 104–23, 170,
  207, 294, 299
  AG and, 8, 9, 10, 31, 34–5, 60, 262,
    263, 265
  and Brahms, 178, 181–5
  Conservatoire class, 3
  and counterpoint, 109–12, 121, 128
  difficulty of music, 115–16, 122, 135
  Eisler and, 287
  and the ethical imperative, 134, 139,
    160
  and German music, 104–5
  and harmony, 105–9, 112, 115, 121,
    122, 135–6
  in Japan, 251
  and Kraus, 131, 134, 135–40,
    177–8, 200
  and Liszt, 178, 194–5, 199, 201–2
  and melody, 66, 114–15
  and the musical idea, 64, 65–6, 70,
    124–30, 131, 135–6, 138–40,
    148–9, 160, 179
  musical writings
    Fundamentals of Musical
      Composition, 240, 255
    Gedanke manuscript, 126–30, 251
    Harmonielehre, 105, 131, 262
    'New Music, Outmoded Music,
      Style and Idea', 148–9

'Problems in Teaching Art', 135
Structural Functions of Harmony,
  34, 105, 130
Style and Idea, 34, 105, 127, 283
'The Relationship to the Text', 142
and polyphony, 12
religious beliefs, 125
and rhythm, 109, 112–14, 121–2
and Stravinsky, 208
twelve-tone technique, 65–6, 70,
  110, 114, 116, 120–1, 127, 128,
  135, 139
unfinished projects, 126, 130
and Webern, 5, 6–7
works
  Das Buch der hängenden Gärten,
    104–5, 137
  Cello Sonata, 252
  Chamber Symphony No. 1, 64,
    106, 107, 112, 115, 265, 283
  Chamber Symphony No. 2, 122
  Erwartung, 8, 47, 108, 114,
    117–20, 138, 283–4
  Five Orchestral Pieces, 108, 111,
    116
  Four Orchestral Songs, 114, 284
  Die glückliche Hand, 111, 114
  Herzgewächse, 138
  Die Jakobsleiter, 88, 126, 138–9,
    263
  Kleine klavierstücke Op. 19, 81,
    116
  Moses und Aron, 121, 122, 124–5,
    126, 130, 134, 138, 139, 241,
    243, 244, 252, 254–5
  Ode to Napoleon, 121
  Pelleas und Melisande, 109
  Piano Suite, 114
  Pierrot lunaire, 25n.13, 111, 114,
    138
  Serenade, 109
  Six Little Piano Pieces Op. 19, 81,
    116
  String Quartet No. 2, 108
  String Quartet No. 3, 114
  String Quartet No. 4, 84, 114

  Suite Op. 25, 136
  A Survivor from Warsaw, 121
  Three Piano Pieces, 108–9
  Variations for Orchestra, 121
  Verklärte Nacht, 106, 138
Schoenberg, Gertrud, 263
Scholem, Gershom, 260
Schopenhauer, Arthur, 142, 147–8,
  260
Schubert, Franz, 105, 114–15, 187,
  269–70, 283
Schumacher, Ernst Friedrich, 98
Schumann, Clara, 190
Schumann, Robert, 110, 115, 258,
  269–70, 295
  Album for the Young, 274
  Brahms and, 186, 187, 190–1
  Liszt and, 180, 190, 194, 202
Schütz, Heinrich, 170
Scriabin, Alexander, 30, 64, 79, 86–7,
  88–9
  Prometheus, 86, 196
Sechter, Simon, 46, 105–6
  *Die richtige Folge der
    Grundharmonien*, 105–6
Second World War, 79, 89–90, 97, 150
Seiber, Matyás, 284
sentimental and naive artists, 258–61
serialism, 2, 6–8, 22, 300
Sessions, Roger, 12
Shakespeare, William, 131, 132,
  188n.12
Shostakovich, Dmitri, 33, 153, 208
social considerations, 16, 32, 161,
  215–16
socialism, 8–9, 14, 18 19, 27–8
Socialist Realism, 18–19
Society for Private Musical
  Performances, 78
Sonnenschein, Professor, 113
Sorabji, Kaikhosru Shapurji, 30
  Opus clavicembalisticum, 30–1
Sorcerers of Salem (film), 287
Soulage, 91
Spitta, Philipp, 187
Stanford, Charles, 264

Musical Composition: A Short Treatise for Students, 269
state control, 145
state funding, 80, 96–7, 155
Stein, Leonard, 130
Steuermann, Eduard, 131, 132
Stevenson, Ronald, 30
Stockhausen, Karlheinz, 7, 49, 91, 92–3, 94, 154, 253–4, 286
    Gruppen, 94, 233
    Hymnen, 154
    Klavierstücke I–IV, 47
    Klavierstücke XI, 289
    Kontra-Punkte, 299
    Kreuzspiel, 254
Strang, Gerald, 130
Strauss, Richard, 103, 106, 253
    Elektra, 106
    Salome, 106
    Symphonia domestica, 49
Stravinsky, Igor, 4, 10, 18, 20, 21, 87, 170, 207–12, 272, 274
    attitudes toward, 207–8
    on composing, 62, 282
    and conclusions, 253
    and dualities, 260–1
    and harmony, 209–12
    and melody, 210–12
    on musical expression, 216
    and rhythm, 112
    and Varèse, 88, 208
    works
        Abraham and Isaac, 208
        Berceuses du chat, 208
        Cantata, 261
        Les cinq doigts, 274
        In Memoriam Dylan Thomas, 208
        Mass, 207
        Monteverdi homages, 261
        Les noces, 207, 208, 209, 211, 212
        Oedipus Rex, 181
        Persephone, 207
        Petrushka, 208, 211
        Pribaoutki, 208
        Pulcinella, 207, 212

The Rake's Progress, 207
The Rite of Spring, 53, 78, 88, 144, 207, 209, 210, 211, 224
Sérénade in A for piano, 264, 272
The Soldier's Tale, 207
Symphony of Psalms, 207
3 Shakespeare Songs, 261
Threni, 208
Violin Concerto, 207
Stravinsky, Vera, and Robert Craft: *Stravinsky in Pictures and Documents*, 210
Strindberg, August, 131
Strobel, Heinrich, 79
Surrealism, 8
synthesis, 238–48, 281

Tanglewood, 152
Tchaikovsky, Pyotr, 62–3, 144
technological progress, 98
Théatre Marigny, 2, 3
theory, 236–40
    AG and, 236–71
Third Programme, 281
Tiomkin, Dmitri, 255
Tippett, Michael, 7, 8, 25n.14, 32
    AG and, 258, 264–5
    works
        A Child of Our Time, 40n.1, 265
        Concerto for Orchestra, 289
        The Midsummer Marriage, 264–5
        Piano Sonata, 264–5
        String Quartet No. 1, 264–5
        String Quartet No. 2, 264–5
        Symphony No. 1, 264–5
Tokyo, 221
Tovey, Donald, 34, 252
traditional music, 157–9, 170, 173–4
Trakl, 265
Tremblay, Gilles, 45, 54
Turner, J. M. W., 209
twelve-tone technique, 4, 8, 10, 30, 34–5, 65–70, 296–7
    AG and, 245–50, 278–9, 280–1, 296–7, 300
    bloc sonore, 10–15, 70–1, 280, 281

pitch distortion and, 73–4
Schoenberg and, 65–6, 70, 110, 114,
116, 120–1, 127, 128, 135, 139
Tyrrell, John, 267

understanding music, 217-20, 272–3

Van Dieren, Bernard, 30
Varèse, Edgard, 4, 18, 83–4, 88, 89,
91, 93
Offrandes, 25n.15
Varèse, Louise, 88
Vaughan Williams, Ralph, 32
Symphonia Antartica, 32
Vittoria (Victoria), Tomás Luis de, 170

Wagner, Richard, 48, 102, 103, 106,
110, 114, 115, 122, 170, 266
and bourgeois culture, 177
Brahms and, 180–1
and closure, 252–3
controversy surrounding, 176, 177
early works of, 209
influence of, 189
Liszt and, 194–5
on Mozart, 178, 205n.13
relevance of, 175
works
Die Meistersinger von Nürnberg,
180
Parsifal, 176
Der Ring des Nibelungen, 63, 115
Tannhäuser, 190
Tristan und Isolde, 38, 64, 106,
115, 148
Walton, William: Second Symphony,
32

Weber, Carl Maria, 110
Webern, Anton, 4–5, 6–8, 9, 10, 18,
21–2, 60, 86, 88–9, 116, 263,
284
influence of, 91, 92
Kraus and, 131
and the musical idea, 63–4
and twelve-tone technique, 66–7, 70
works
Cantata No. 2, 6, 70
Concerto for 9 instruments Op.
24, 136, 266
5 canons Op. 16, 168–9
Orchesterstücke Op. 6, 83
Piano Variations Op. 27, 224–5
Symphony, 263
Wedekind, Frank, 131
Weill, Kurt, 154
Mahagonny, 181
Weininger, Otto, 131, 137
White, Eric Walter, 208
Widman, Joseph, 181
Wintle, Christopher, 236–8
dialogue with AG, 238–71
Wittgenstein, Ludwig, 131, 138,
146–7, 188n.12
Wolf, Hugo, 103, 115
Wolf-Ferrari, Ermanno: A School for
Fathers, 37
Wolpe, Stefan, 88–9
Wood, Hugh, 268, 284

Xenakis, Iannis, 94

Yasser, Joseph, 33

Zhdanov, Andrei, 8
Zionism, 27–8